Zoroastrians in Early Islamic History

Edinburgh Studies in Classical Islamic History and Culture
Series Editor: Carole Hillenbrand

A particular feature of medieval Islamic civilisation was its wide horizons. The Muslims fell heir not only to the Graeco-Roman world of the Mediterranean, but also to that of the ancient Near East, to the empires of Assyria, Babylon and the Persians; and beyond that, they were in frequent contact with India and China to the east and with black Africa to the south. This intellectual openness can be sensed in many inter-related fields of Muslim thought, and it impacted powerfully on trade and on the networks that made it possible. Books in this series reflect this openness and cover a wide range of topics, periods and geographical areas.

Titles in the series include:

The Body in Arabic Love Poetry: The 'Udhri Tradition Jokha Alharthi
Arabian Drugs in Early Medieval Mediterranean Medicine Zohar Amar and Efraim Lev
Towards a History of Libraries in Yemen Hassan Ansari and Sabine Schmidtke
The Abbasid Caliphate of Cairo, 1261–1517: Out of the Shadows Mustafa Banister
The Medieval Western Maghrib: Cities, Patronage and Power Amira K. Bennison
Christian Monastic Life in Early Islam Bradley Bowman
Keeping the Peace in Premodern Islam: Diplomacy under the Mamluk Sultanate, 1250–1517 Malika Dekkiche
Queens, Concubines and Eunuchs in Medieval Islam Taef El-Azhari
Islamic Political Thought in the Mamluk Period Mohamad El Merheb
The Kharijites in Early Islamic Historical Tradition: Heroes and Villains Hannah-Lena Hagemann
Classical Islam: Collected Essays Carole Hillenbrand
Islam and the Crusades: Collected Essays Carole Hillenbrand
The Medieval Turks: Collected Essays Carole Hillenbrand
The Books of Burhān al-Dīn: Literacy and Book Ownership in Mamluk Jerusalem Said Aljoumani and Konrad Hirschler
Medieval Damascus: Plurality and Diversity in an Arabic Library – The Ashrafiya Library Catalogue Konrad Hirschler
A Monument to Medieval Syrian Book Culture: The Library of Ibn ʿAbd al-Hādī Konrad Hirschler
The Popularisation of Sufism in Ayyubid and Mamluk Egypt: State and Society, 1173–1325 Nathan Hofer
Defining Anthropomorphism: The Challenge of Islamic Traditionalism Livnat Holtzman
Making Mongol History: Rashid al-Din and the Jamiʿ al-Tawarikh Stefan Kamola
Lyrics of Life: Saʿdi on Love, Cosmopolitanism and Care of the Self Fatemeh Keshavarz
Art, Allegory and The Rise of Shiism In Iran, 1487-1565 Chad Kia
The Administration of Justice in Medieval Egypt: From the 7th to the 12th Century Yaacov Lev
Zoroastrians in Early Islamic History: Accommodation and Memory Andrew D. Magnusson
A History of Herat: From Chingiz Khan to Tamerlane Shivan Mahendrarajah
The Queen of Sheba's Gift: A History of the True Balsam of Matarea Marcus Milwright
Ruling from a Red Canopy: Political Authority in the Medieval Islamic World, From Anatolia to South Asia Colin P. Mitchell
Islam, Christianity and the Realms of the Miraculous: A Comparative Exploration Ian Richard Netton
The Poetics of Spiritual Instruction: Farid al-Din 'Attar and Persian Sufi Didacticism Austin O'Malley
Sacred Place and Sacred Time in the Medieval Islamic Middle East: An Historical Perspective Daniella Talmon-Heller
Conquered Populations in Early Islam: Non-Arabs, Slaves and the Sons of Slave Mothers Elizabeth Urban

edinburghuniversitypress.com/series/escihc

Zoroastrians in Early Islamic History

Accommodation and Memory

Andrew D. Magnusson

EDINBURGH
University Press

Edinburgh University Press is one of the leading university presses in the UK. We publish academic books and journals in our selected subject areas across the humanities and social sciences, combining cutting-edge scholarship with high editorial and production values to produce academic works of lasting importance. For more information visit our website: edinburghuniversitypress.com

Edinburgh University Press Ltd
The Tun – Holyrood Road
12 (2f) Jackson's Entry
Edinburgh EH8 8PJ

First published in hardback by Edinburgh University Press 2023

Typeset in 11/15 Adobe Garamond by
Cheshire Typesetting Ltd, Cuddington, Cheshire

A CIP record for this book is available from the British Library

ISBN 978 1 4744 8952 2 (hardback)
ISBN 978 1 4744 8953 9 (paperback)
ISBN 978 1 4744 8955 3 (webready PDF)
ISBN 978 1 4744 8954 6 (epub)

Contents

Acknowledgements vi
A Note on Transliteration and Abbreviation viii

Introduction: Zoroastrianism, Islam and Accommodation 1

1 Myth and Countermyth in Zoroastrian Historiography 19

2 Umar's Dilemma: The Taxation of People Without a Book 33

3 Marriage, Meat and the Limits of Accommodation 55

4 Salman's Charter as a Site of Memory 78

5 Fire Temple Desecration and Triumphal Tales of Violence 112

6 Rhetorical Zoroastrians in Early Islamic Discourse 136

Conclusion: An Ambivalent Accommodation 159

Appendix A Translation of an Iranian Recension of Salman's Charter 167
Appendix B Translation of an Indian Recension of Salman's Charter 169
Bibliography 172
Index 195

Acknowledgements

After working on this book for more than a decade, I am thrilled to see it published at last. I have incurred many debts in writing it. First, I am grateful to Nicola Ramsey, Rachel Bridgewater and the editorial staff at Edinburgh University Press. Thanks also to Richard Payne and the anonymous reviewers who contributed immeasurably to the strength of this work. Chris Petty graciously read several chapters. Jen Sanchez edited an earlier version of the manuscript with her discerning eye. Ashlan Johnson prepared the Index.

Much of Chapter Five appeared previously in A. C. S. Peacock (ed.), *Islamisation: Critical Perspectives from History* (Edinburgh University Press, 2017), pp. 102–17. I treated some of the issues from Chapter Four, in a substantially different form, in an article entitled 'On the Origins of the Prophet Muhammad's Charter to Salman al-Farisi', published in *ARAM Periodical* 26, no. 1 (2014): 189–98. I was honoured to present portions of my research at Oxford University, Columbia University and St Andrews University.

This book began as a dissertation at the University of California in Santa Barbara (UCSB), where I benefited from the guidance of Debra Blumenthal, Juan Campo and Nancy Gallagher. Touraj Daryaee of the University of California at Irvine was kind enough to serve as an outside reader. Dwight Reynolds offered me many opportunities for professional development as a graduate student. R. Stephen Humphreys was the ideal advisor. I am thankful for his kindness, guidance and support over the years.

At UCSB I received financial assistance from the Middle East Studies Center, the Abdul Aziz ibn Al Saud Chair of Islamic Studies, History Associates and the Interdisciplinary Humanities Center. The State Department's CLS

Program funded a summer of language study in Morocco. The generosity of the Santa Barbara Scholarship Foundation made my graduate education possible. I must also express gratitude to the faculty in Middle Eastern Studies/ Arabic at Brigham Young University for sparking my interest in Islamic Studies as an undergraduate. They include Glen Cooper, Arnold Green, William Hamblin, Connie Lamb and Dilworth Parkinson. James Toronto, in particular, was a strong mentor. He taught me by example to be a critical thinker and a more compassionate person.

I consider myself fortunate to have supportive colleagues at the University of Central Oklahoma (UCO). Patti Loughlin and Ryan Kiggins asked for regular updates on this project, which encouraged me to persist when I despaired of ever finishing it. Justin Quinn Olmstead has been a wonderful collaborator on many ventures. A New Faculty Grant from UCO allowed me to purchase primary sources in Arabic and Persian.

Thanks are due to the many friends who guided me along the way and made the journey more enjoyable: Hanan Awad, Elliott Bazzano, Donna Lee Bowen, Thomas Carlson, Shauna Huffaker, Cameron Jones, Sara Kamali, Pedram Khosronejad, Gershon Lewental, Kelly Morse-Johnson, Eric Massie, Husam Mohamad, Munther al-Sabbagh, James Tallon, and others.

My family has been incredibly patient as I laboured on this project. More than once they caught me deep in thought about Zoroastrians when I should have been engaging with them. I truly am an absent-minded professor. My father taught me to love history and my mother gave me the discipline to study. Thank you. I am grateful to my parents-in-law who provided childcare at crucial stages in the writing process. Michelle sustained me emotionally from beginning to end. Our two children were born before I could finish this book, which motivated me to work faster. It is dedicated to them with love.

A Note on Transliteration and Abbreviation

This book follows the system of transliteration used by the *International Journal of Middle East Studies* for Arabic and Persian. To avoid confusion with single quotation marks and apostrophes, the letters *hamza* and *ayn* are indicated only in the middle of words in the body of the work. Persian *izafe* is rendered –i or –yi.

Translation of material into English generally precedes its transliteration, which follows in parenthesis. I have fully transliterated names and terms using dots and macrons when directly quoting sources but have otherwise left off diacritical marks for general readability and to make the prose more accessible to the non-specialist.

A few abbreviations appear in the text and footnotes. Words or phrases transliterated from Arabic are prefaced with Ar.; New Persian words with N.P. In the footnotes, references to the *Encyclopaedia of Islam*, 2nd edition, are abbreviated EI2. I occasionally cite the third edition of that work as well (EI3). *Encyclopedia Iranica* has been abbreviated EIr. Foreign terms are usually italicised, with the exception of some that are frequently used, such as jizya and hadith.

Dates of birth and death are given in parenthesis after the first mention of a person's name. A slash separates years reckoned according to the Islamic or hijri calendar (AH) and years of the Common Era (CE).

To Neve and Seth

Introduction
Zoroastrianism, Islam and Accommodation

In the seventh century, when Zoroastrians first met Muslims, the end of the world seemed nigh. According to later Zoroastrian sources, demons of wrath pillaged Iran and dishevelled devils ruled in wickedness. Arabs destroyed ancient customs, imposed evil laws and consumed polluted matter. Zoroastrians awaited the arrival of the legendary heroes who would deliver them and the saviour who would ultimately purify the earth. In other words, Zoroastrians imagined their first encounter with Muslims apocalyptically.[1] Muslim narrators remembered it differently. When the caliph Umar ibn al-Khattab (ruled 13–23 AH/634–644 CE) first heard about Zoroastrians he was perplexed. Umar reportedly exclaimed, 'I do not know how to treat Zoroastrians!'[2] It was an exasperated acknowledgement that they did not fit neatly into his religious paradigm. Umar's confusion about Zoroastrians, the struggle to accommodate them in the early caliphates and the ambivalence felt by subsequent generations of Muslims is the subject of this book.

Zoroastrianism in Late Antiquity

In order to appreciate the significance of this interreligious encounter, it is important to understand the nature of Late Antique Zoroastrianism. Under the Sasanian dynasty (224–651 CE) of Persia, Zoroastrianism became an imperial religion. The faith of individual emperors in the Achaemenid (550–330 BCE) and the Arsacid or Parthian (247 BCE–224 CE) periods, Zoroastrianism gained official status in the third century when Ardashir I, the founder of the Sasanian dynasty, sought an ideology to legitimise his rule.[3] Scholars have recently questioned how exclusive the empire's relationship was with Zoroastrianism, especially early in its history.[4] Sasanian subjects practiced a variety of faiths, from Judaism and Christianity to Manichaeism, and their communal leaders were often present at court. Yet the Zoroastrian priestly sources from the period, while certainly not disinterested, suggest that Sasanian monarchs had more than a personal interest in Zoroastrianism. That religion enjoyed a privileged status in the empire.[5]

Most Zoroastrians recognised Ahura Mazda, the Wise Lord, as the creator of order, light and purity. Ahura Mazda, also known as Ohrmazd in Pahlavi sources, was engaged in a cosmic struggle against Ahriman (or *Angra Mainyu*, 'the Evil Spirit' in the Avestan language), the sower of chaos, darkness and pollution. Zoroastrians believe that Ahura Mazda will eventually triumph and a defiled earth will be restored to its paradisiacal state. Zoroastrian cosmology also includes *Amesha Spentas* – seven immortal beings created to assist in the struggle against Ahriman. Some Zoroastrian sources even identified Ahura Mazda as *Spenta Mainyu* (the Beneficent Spirit), one of these divine helpers.[6]

Ahura Mazda created the earth as the battleground between the forces of good and evil. He forged a perfect world and celebrated with a *yasna* (religious ceremony), but Ahriman attacked his creation. The Evil Spirit spoiled fresh water with salt, fire with smoke and plains with mountains.[7] Ahura Mazda created humans to assist in the fight against Ahriman and the demons. Humanity's pious acts, especially ritual reenactment of the Yasna ceremony, would slowly purify the world and lead to the ultimate triumph over evil.[8]

Late Antique Zoroastrians debated the role of Zurvan in their cosmogony. Could Zurvan, the embodiment of undifferentiated Time, have existed before creation and thus be independent of Ahura Mazda? Some Zoroastrians supposed Zurvan to be the father of both Ahura Mazda and Ahriman. According to legend, Zurvan performed the Yasna ceremony for 1,000 years before Ahriman was conceived in a moment of doubt about its efficacy. Ahura Mazda was born simultaneously from the merit accrued by performing the ritual. These twin gods then created the world and everything in it. While this story is obviously related to the Zoroastrian cosmogony, the precise relationship between Zurvanism and Zoroastrianism has vexed scholars for decades. Once dismissed as a heresy, scholars now recognise it as a variation of the Zoroastrian myth of creation.[9]

Zurvanism featured prominently in Zoroastrians' interactions with other religions. Manichaeans may have elevated Time to divine status in order to demonstrate its existence prior to, and thereby its superiority over, Ahura Mazda. Richard Payne has noted the role that Zurvanism played in Christian polemics against Sasanian Zoroastrians. Christians pressed them to explain, for example, whether Zurvan or Ahura Mazda's creation was ritually re-enacted in the Yasna.[10] These impossible questions were designed to vindicate Christianity and to cast doubt on the efficacy of the sacred ritual. Zoroastrians continued to grapple with Zurvanism into the early Islamic period, as noted by the Muslim scholar of religion Muhammad ibn Abd al-Karim al-Shahrastani (d. 548/1153).[11]

Zoroastrians also recognised other beings as worthy of worship (N.P., *yazata*). Subordinate to Ahura Mazda, they were the personification of abstract values such as Life and Order. Among the most prominent of these Worshipful Ones were Anahita and Mithra. Anahita, or Anahid, was the female steward of water and fertility, whose cult was prominent in the Sasanian period.[12] Mithra was the guardian of truth and the enforcer of contracts. He had devotees in the Roman and Persian Empires. Zoroastrians celebrated feasts and recited hymns in honour of these powerful beings who acted as intercessors with Ahura Mazda.[13] Zoroastrian eschatology also recognises a saviour, Saoshyant, who will come at the end of time to inaugurate the resurrection of humankind and renovate the earth.[14]

Sasanian Zoroastrians venerated fire as a symbol of the light and purity of Ahura Mazda, and emperors patronised the construction of temples to house the sacred flame. These temples were generally square structures, with an arched opening in each wall, topped by a dome (N.P., *chahār-i tāq*).[15] The fire altar stood on a pedestal in the middle. In Late Antiquity there was a hierarchy of village, provincial and imperial fires. An imperial fire burned perpetually for each of the classes of the Sasanian Empire: the temple at Kariyan in Fars housed the Farnbag fire of the priests, the Gushnasp fire burned at Shiz in Azerbaijan for the soldiers and the Burzen-Mihr fire near Nishapur in Khurasan represented the agriculturalists.[16]

The Zoroastrian priesthood helped believers to reach or remain in a state of ritual purity.[17] In addition to the Yasna ceremony, they recited the sacred collection of hymns and texts known collectively as the Avesta, and performed ablutions.[18] There appear to have been two major classes of priests in Late Antiquity. *Herbads* were teacher-priests, responsible for inducting candidates into the priesthood and leading the faithful in devotion. Herbads were occasionally dispatched to rural areas to establish or regulate the imperial cult. *Mobeds* attended to the sacred fire. In the waning days of the Sasanian Empire their responsibilities included judicial and administrative matters as well. In the Islamic sources, herbads are sometimes described as custodians of the fire. 'Herbad' was also a generic term for priest, so it could be that Muslim authors confused the titles. Or perhaps herbads' duties had also shifted. The scantiness of the record makes it difficult to know for sure.[19]

Terminology

Zoroastrianism is an Indo-Iranian religion that developed over millennia in Central, West and South Asia. Because of its diversity, Jenny Rose prefers to speak of Zoroastrianisms or 'Zoroastrian beliefs and practices' to avoid the implication that there is one monolithic religion.[20] Zoroastrian beliefs and practices varied in Late Antiquity. There was the institutionalised Zoroastrianism of the Sasanian Empire in southwestern Iran, and what Richard Frye called 'the religion of the Magi' in Central Asia.[21] There also existed a set of distinct, indigenous practices and beliefs – wife sharing, nonviolence, reincarnation – in the Zagros Mountains. Muslim authors called these beliefs, which coexisted with Zoroastrianism, *Khurramdiniyya*.[22] This work, for the most part, focuses on the institutional and imperial religion associated with southwestern Iran.

In an effort to make the prose accessible to non-specialists, this book employs the English terms *Zoroastrians* and *Zoroastrianism*. The most common Arabic term to describe Zoroastrians is *majūs*, meaning Magi or priests. Muslims applied this plural word indiscriminately to all Zoroastrians, priesthood and laity alike. *Mazdeans* would perhaps be a more accurate translation as the Wise Lord is the object of worship rather than his priests, but it is likely unfamiliar to lay readers. The New Persian term *maghān* is used in local histories such as *Tarikh-i Bukhara* to describe the adherents of the Central Asian fire cult. As already noted, there was a difference between the priestly, hierarchical, institutionalised religion of the Sasanians and the simpler, heterodox, iconographic forms of Avestan religion that persisted outside of their realm.[23] Therefore, *Maghān* will be translated as *Magians* to differentiate it from *majūs*. Early Muslim authors did not always make such careful distinctions, so this work refers generically to followers of Late Antique sacredotal cults of fire as *Zoroastrians*.

Zoroastrianism is known in Old Persian as *Mazdayasna* (worship of Ahura Mazda) or *Daena Vanguhi* (the Good Religion) – a phrase that appears in the Gathas, the oldest portion of the Avesta. Contemporary Zoroastrians call their faith *the Good Religion* (*Behdīn*) in New Persian. As these terms may not be recognisable outside of the community Jenny Rose prefers to use the word 'Zoroastrianism'.[24] Zoroaster is the Greek form of the Persian name Zarathushtra. Practitioners of the Good Religion recognise Zoroaster as the first human to perform the Yasna.[25] Therefore, later Arabic sources sometimes use the word *Zardushtiyya* – literally, 'Zoroastrianism' – to describe Mazda worshippers. That designation may overemphasise Zoroaster's importance in Late Antiquity. Described in the Avesta as a model believer, he does not feature in any surviving Sasanian inscription.[26] Zoroaster appears to have attained prominence later, in dialogue with Islam and Christianity. However, his name is now synonymous with the faith, so *Zoroastrianism* has become the accepted term among scholars to describe the Good Religion and a variety of affiliated beliefs.[27]

Iran

The geographical nomenclature used by scholars to describe regions where Zoroastrianism prevailed is fraught. Sarah Bowen Savant prefers *Iran* instead of *Persia* when speaking of the early Islamic period. In Arab-Muslim parlance 'Persia' (Ar., *Fārs*) referred to both the southwestern province of the plateau and the entire Sasanian Empire. People associated with either locale were *Persians*.[28] Sasanian rulers, by contrast, conceived of their realm as encompassing *Ērān* and *Anērān*. This Middle Persian terminology, which appears in an inscription of Shapur I (ruled 240–272), is potentially polyvalent. The words literally mean 'Iranians' and 'non-Iranians', although precisely how those oppositional identities were defined is unclear. As noted by Shaul Shaked, in religious sources they often signify 'Zoroastrians' and 'non-Zoroastrians'.[29]

This Late Antique terminology surfaced again in the modern period. Under the influence of secular nationalism, Reza Shah renamed his country 'Iran' (N.P., *īrān*) in 1935 to emphasise the nation's mythical Aryan roots.[30] After the revolution of 1979 the state became the Islamic Republic of Iran. Khodadad Rezakhani uses the name *Iran* cautiously, even to describe Persia in Late Antiquity, lest it be conflated with the current regime.[31] As *Iran* is both historically attested and familiar to twenty-first-century readers, it is used throughout this book to describe the plateau, the empires it hosted and the diverse peoples living there. The term does not intend to make any particular ethnic, religious or nationalist statement in this context.

Tolerance and its Discontents

Scholars of early Islamic history have struggled for decades to produce a sophisticated way of theorising the relationship between Muslims and adherents of other religions who lived under caliphal rule after the seventh century. Stale and unproductive assertions about the inherent tolerance or intolerance of Islam are still too common. Tolerance is the idea that a society should allow unpopular beliefs or minority religions to compete in the marketplace of ideas, even if they are abhorrent to the majority, because government ought not to coerce belief. It is a virtue that emerged out of the Enlightenment in the eighteenth century. For example, Enlightenment thinkers such as John Locke and Thomas Jefferson used the idea of tolerance to argue that Muslims could be citizens of Great Britain or the United States, even if they did not necessarily think that would happen.[32] Many modern North Atlantic societies were built on Enlightenment values, but these ideas did not exist before the eighteenth century. Therefore, tolerance is not a useful barometer for gauging the relationship between governments and religious communities in earlier ages. Nor is it helpful for understanding societies founded on ideals other than those derived from the Enlightenment. Nevertheless, tolerance continues to inspire serious scholarship on intercommunal history in the pre-modern Middle East.[33]

In addition to being a liberal value, tolerance is a tool of governance. It is inextricable from secularism, the Enlightenment idea that people's beliefs do not have public significance and therefore should be kept private. According to Wendy Brown, the tendency of secular governments to legislate majoritarian norms – often derived from culture, which includes religion – and their reluctance to make structural changes to achieve substantive equality has led elected officials in the twenty-first century to shift the responsibility for tolerance to individual citizens, civil society or the private sphere. Hence governments call for tolerance without legislating it. By identifying certain groups as in need of tolerance, the state marks them as different, which increases suspicion of and resentment toward them. The government then regulates religion in the name of protecting these marginalised groups.[34]

Brown's is a trenchant critique of the work that the idea of tolerance does within liberal societies.[35] It is complimented by Saba Mahmood's recent study of secularism in Egypt, which argues that the government's ostensible neutrality in matters of faith contrasts with its frequent intervention in supposedly private affairs, creating new frontiers for the regulation of religion and the contestation thereof, and more calls for secularism as the antidote. The increased power of the state is the inevitable result of this cycle.[36] Brown notes that the discourse of tolerance also permeates foreign relations, where secular governments project power against societies that are deemed intolerant, including several in the Middle East.[37]

Eschewing tolerance as a paradigm for interpreting intercommunal histories, Richard Payne has made the case that Late Antique Zoroastrians, once accused of persecuting Christians, in fact practiced a 'differentiated, hierarchical inclusion of religious others rooted in Zoroastrian cosmological thought'.[38] The suggestion is not that cross-confessional strife was absent in the Sasanian Empire. Imperial authorities punished Christians for challenging the supremacy of Zoroastrianism, attacking fire temples, proselytising, and ignoring the ruler's demands. Violence was rare but formed part of the imperial response when necessary. However, its intent and effect were ultimately inclusive.[39] David Nirenberg made similar arguments in the 1990s: writing about Jews in the medieval Kingdom of Aragon, he provocatively argued for the fundamental interdependence of domination and coexistence in the Middle Ages. There is no reason why, he suggested, *convivencia* need designate only harmonious interaction. Violence and aggression are also meaningful, as opposed to meaningless, forms of association.[40]

Anver Emon has argued that Islamic law fostered a religiously differentiated hierarchy in the early caliphates. Muslim rulers struggled to balance the inherent tension between Islamic universalism and imperial governance. Islamic universalism stipulated that Islam, as the last divine revelation, was a universal religion for all people and therefore should be dominant in society. However, caliphs presided over religiously diverse populations from North Africa to Central Asia. Therefore, non-Muslims enjoyed religious autonomy provided that they did not deny Islamic universalism by publicly asserting the superiority of their religions.[41]

Perhaps the tension between the demands of Islamic universalism and imperial governance ought not to be surprising. It is possible that Muslims, although politically dominant, remained a minority in the Middle East for centuries after the Islamic conquests. Thomas Carlson has suggested that 'the achievement of demographic majority by Muslims even within the Middle East was much closer to 1500 than to 600'.[42] Previous scholarship assumed that Islamisation proceeded apace after the seventh century, at least partially due to Richard Bulliet's innovative and influential study of conversion on the basis of naming conventions in biographical dictionaries.[43] It was a brilliant heuristic exercise, but one that privileged evidence from cities and educated elites. Jack Tannous now estimates that non-Muslims constituted a majority of the total population from Nile to Oxus until at least the eleventh century.[44] Similarly, Jamsheed Choksy believes that Islam did not exert significant influence in rural Iran before 1000 CE.[45] Although reasonable, these suppositions remain to be proven.

If the number of Muslims in the Middle East during Late Antiquity was relatively small, the language that scholars employ to describe the peoples and cultures of the region should reflect that fact. In the *Venture of Islam*, Marshall G. S. Hodgson proposed the adjective 'Islamicate' rather than 'Islamic' to describe societies from the Nile to Oxus Rivers (another neologism, to replace the problematic term 'Middle East') as a way of acknowledging the presence and contributions of non-Muslims (as well as historical influences that have little to do with religion) after the seventh century.[46] This terminology has since transformed related fields, notably Persianate Studies, which includes under its purview populations within Iran that do not identify with Persian culture and societies outside of Iran that do.

Another point to bear in mind is that communal boundaries were porous in Late Antiquity. Scholars have documented extensive interaction between

Muslims and non-Muslims in the early caliphates. They shared food, dressed alike and married each other. Most people were probably simple believers without deep theological literacy.[47] Hence they practiced similar forms of asceticism, reverenced one another's sacred emblems and sought out the same healers.[48] It was a 'messy world', according to Thomas Sizgorich.[49] While anecdotes illustrate what was possible in the realm of social interaction, it is more difficult to say how frequent or widespread such contact was. Considering the nature of historical writing, which tends to note the exceptional, even documented examples may not be representative. Certain types of cross-confessional contact were probably reserved for non-Muslim elites with sufficient social capital.[50] Certainly not everyone was comfortable with social mixing. Some Muslim jurists sought to outwardly differentiate if not humiliate non-Muslims, and some voluntary martyrs died to assert the distinction between communities.[51] Therefore, simplistic notions about the harmonious nature of interfaith relations in early Islamicate society warrant scepticism. Non-Muslims by and large remained subordinate in the early caliphates even if, like Zoroastrians in Sasanian Iran, early Muslims practiced a differentiated, hierarchical form of inclusion.

Defining Accommodation

Muslim jurists writing in Arabic often collectively classified non-Muslims as Protected People (*ahl al-dhimma*). These Protected People, or *dhimmis*, were not to be attacked by Muslim armies within the early caliphates if they submitted to taxation. In practice, Jews, Christians, Buddhists, Hindus, Sabi'ans and Zoroastrians were included in this category. Among these groups, followers of the biblical tradition enjoyed a prototypical or normative status as People of the Book (*ahl al-kitāb*). The Qur'an expresses some affinity for, as well as criticism of, Jews and Christians on the basis of their shared reverence for Abrahamic prophets and scripture. While historians have focused most of their attention on the People of the Book, Hindus and Buddhists have received some scholarly attention.[52] More research on non-normative *dhimmis* is needed, as their experience offers potentially valuable insights into the logic, mechanisms and limits of imperial accommodation in the early caliphates.

Shelagh Day and Gwen Brodsky define accommodation as 'the adjustment of a rule, practice, condition or requirement to take into account the specific needs of an individual or group'.[53] The Supreme Court of Canada recognised the principle of accommodation in a 2006 ruling. The court decided in favour of a Sikh boy who sought to wear a ceremonial dagger at school. The *Multani* decision affirmed that accommodation was a means to protect religious beliefs in a diverse society and to respect minorities.[54] Beverley McLachlin, one of the justices who adjudicated the *Multani* case, had previously suggested that it is in the best interest of governments to accommodate.

> Diverse societies face two choices. They can choose the route of no accommodation where those with power set the agenda and the majority rules prevail. The result is the exclusion of some people from useful endeavours on irrelevant, stereotypical grounds and the denial of individual dignity and worth . . . The other route is the route of reasonable accommodation. It starts from the premise of each individual's worth and dignity and entitlement to equal treatment and benefit. It operates by requiring that the powerful and the majority adapt their own rules and practices, within the limits of reason and short of undue hardship, to permit realisation of these ends.[55]

One goal of accommodation, couched here in the logic of liberalism, is to further the state's interest in the productivity ('useful endeavours') of its citizens.

This goal is not unique to modern, liberal democracies. Empires are, by definition, regimes of domination motivated at least in part by the extraction of resources from subjected populations.[56] In the pre-modern world, the most useful endeavour that an imperial subject could be engaged in – at least in the eyes of the government – was the production of taxable surplus through agriculture or trade.[57] In the early caliphates, rulers cared a great deal about the collection of jizya, the conscription of corvée labour and the political loyalty (or at least acquiescence) of non-Muslims. Liberal values like individual dignity and tolerance were not a concern. The goal was the productive employment of the population. Accommodation was, in other words, the means to an end.

Some scholars of the modern, liberal state have criticised the idea of accommodation because it is a conservative principle of inclusion that does not require dramatic, structural change in society. It allows for individual exceptions but maintains the normative standards that are a product of differential power between groups. Therefore, accommodation perpetuates systems of inequality by limiting the amount of difference that powerful groups in society must absorb.[58] As Lori Beaman states, 'In both the law and public discourse, the claimant or person requesting accommodation cannot be and is not imagined as an equal. When we "accommodate" someone, we grant an exception to the rule, rather than questioning the inclusiveness of the rule itself.'[59] For critics of accommodation, the fact that majorities must choose to accommodate minorities makes it an unsuitable doctrine for liberal societies that profess the fundamental equality of all citizens.

While the idea of accommodation is arguably unbecoming of modern democracies, it is applicable to pre-modern societies, where differential power and religious inequality were enshrined in imperial hierarchies. The caliphates endorsed the legal superiority of Muslims. Therefore, as Stephen Humphreys has noted, 'In the study of Islamic societies, it is not enough to know whether a person is a Muslim or not, but that is the first thing which we must know.'[60] Accommodation involves adjusting normative standards in order to fit seemingly extraordinary people into existing systems.[61] If Jews and Christians, by virtue of their status as People of the Book, were presumed to set the standard for Muslim engagement with non-Muslims in medieval Islamdom, then Zoroastrians and other *dhimmis* were exceptional. As People without a Book, they could be accommodated.

That does not imply that accommodation was ever universal or absolute. Arabian polytheists, for example, seemingly did not qualify, and there were limits to the concessions that People without a Book received. As Anver Emon notes:

> One important question of governance – one that arguably transcends the premodern and modern periods – concerns the fact that where diversity exists, governing enterprises will often attempt some form of regulation and accommodation of minorities. This question does not concern whether a state will accommodate, but rather how it will do so and in light of what circumstances.[62]

Because accommodation is variable and limited, it is also contested. Early Muslims disagreed about which groups were acceptable and which concessions they warranted. Therefore, accommodation can be ambivalent or even disputed.

Previous studies have applied the term *accommodation* to disparate phenomena in the pre-modern Middle East without properly defining it.[63] In this book, to accommodate means *to extend a special dispensation to a non-normative group in order for society to benefit from its useful endeavours.* While the idea of accommodation has not previously been used to analyse encounters between Muslims and non-Muslims in medieval Islamdom, it is well suited to the task.

Outline of Chapters

This book will demonstrate that Muslims chose to accommodate Zoroastrians after the prophetic period, a decision that subsequent generations remembered with ambivalence. Chapter One describes the historiography of Muslim-Zoroastrian relations and the tendency of scholarship to fluctuate between myths of inveterate hostility and countermyths of harmonious bliss. It suggests that some of the challenges that Zoroastrians face in the twenty-first century influence dour conceptions of the community's past.

Chapter Two demonstrates that early Muslims taxed Zoroastrians without recognising them as People of the Book. Although Muslim exegetes did not attribute a divinely revealed scripture to Zoroastrians, hadith transmitters affirmed that Muhammad collected jizya from them. That controversial practice was defended by the Banu Tamim, an Arabian tribe closely allied with the Sasanians and keenly interested in the welfare of Zoroastrians. Later attempts by Muslim jurists to stifle inquiry into the issue reveal the ambivalence that some Muslims felt about the exceptional status of Zoroastrians. This chapter demonstrates the contested nature of accommodation.

Theories of memory come to bear in Chapter Three, which argues that early hadith collections function as a sort of judicial archive where Muslim jurists registered their discomfort with further concessions to Zoroastrians. Legal experts attempted to limit cross-confessional contact by suggesting that Muslims should neither marry Zoroastrians nor eat meat slaughtered by them. Although this prohibition was likely a later opinion, it was attributed to the Prophet Muhammad. At least one jurist challenged the ban on the basis of a prophetic report circulated by Ali's family that urged Muslims to treat Zoroastrians like People of the Book. The effort was unsuccessful, and most schools of law affirmed the inferiority of the Good Religion in the social hierarchy. Whether their boundary marking was effective is debatable, but it demonstrates the limits of accommodation.

Chapter Four analyses the *ahd-nama*, a charter of religious freedom that the Prophet Muhammad supposedly granted to the descendants of Salman al-Farisi. Although certainly a later forgery, this document was an attempt to claim privileges for Salman's Zoroastrian relatives. It freed them from the most onerous impositions of Islamic law, declared the inviolability of their temples and guaranteed them a stipend from the local treasury. Salman's charter was a site of memory where Muslims remembered the Prophet's pious example. It bears a strong resemblance to other charters forged on behalf of Jews and Christians, demonstrating that Zoroastrians were subject to the same laws of differentiation as other non-Muslims. Persian historians faithfully transmitted this document for centuries until it arrived in South Asia, where it has become a site of memory for modern Parsis to lament the trials that their progenitors faced under medieval Muslim rule.

Chapter Five contrasts earlier examples of accommodation with a triumphal narrative of Islamic supersession that developed later. Local Persian histories, written centuries after the events they purport to describe, celebrated the conquest of Iran as the triumph of Islam over Zoroastrianism. Muslims symbolically represented their supposed superiority by inventing tales of temple desecration. The goal was to make Muslims seem dominant from the seventh century. Careful analysis of competing accounts and their proper contextualisation reveals the rhetorical character of these narratives. Their authors chose to forget the history of accommodation.

Chapter Six examines the ways that Muslims outside of Iran remembered Zoroastrians. From Iberia to India, early Islamic discourse is replete with references to so-called 'Zoroastrians'. These were not actual followers of the Good Religion but pagans, heretics and deviants. The term *majus*, it seems, could be applied to other liminal groups. The fact Muslims made such unflattering comparisons suggests a lingering ambivalence about the accommodation of Zoroastrians. It also demonstrates that the Good Religion provided a template for understanding and potentially integrating other non-normative groups into early Islamicate societies.

The Conclusion emphasises the contemporary relevance of the ideas treated in this book based on a heart-wrenching example from the modern Middle East. In 2014, fighters for the Islamic State of Iraq and Syria (ISIS) massacred and enslaved Yazidis at Sinjar. More than 100 experts in Islamic law called on the leader of ISIS to account for the violence. In an open letter published online, they argued that Yazidis are comparable to Zoroastrians and therefore ought to be protected under Islamic law. Citing some of the same historical sources and legal precedents as this book, they noted that their pious predecessors had accommodated Zoroastrians. That decision, made centuries ago with some ambivalence, continues to resonate. It remains a valuable lesson in the present.

Notes

1. Touraj Daryaee, 'Apocalypse Now: Zoroastrian Reflections on the Early Islamic Centuries', *Medieval Encounters* 4, no. 3 (1998): 192; Robert G. Hoyland, *Seeing Islam as Others Saw It: A Survey and Evaluation of Christian, Jewish and Zoroastrian Writings on Early Islam*, Studies in Late Antiquity and Early Islam 13 (Princeton, NJ: Darwin Press, 1997), 321–27.
2. Aḥmad ibn Yaḥyá al-Balādhurī, *Kitāb futūḥ al-buldān*, Salah al-Din Munajjid (ed.) (Cairo: Maktabat al-Nahdah al-Misriyah, 1956), 2:327; Aḥmad ibn Yaḥyá al-Balādhurī, *The Origins of the Islamic State*, trans. Philip Hitti (Beirut: Khayats, 1966), 1:424.
3. Dietrich Huff, 'Formation and Ideology of the Sasanian State in the Context of Archaeological Evidence', in Vesta Sarkhosh Curtis and Sarah Stewart (eds), *The Sasanian Era*, vol. 3, The Idea of Iran (London: I. B. Tauris, 2008), 35.
4. Philip G. Kreyenbroek, 'How Pious Was Shapur? Religion, Church, and Propaganda under the Early Sasanians', in *The Sasanian Era*, vol. 3, The Idea of Iran (London: I. B. Tauris, 2008), 7–16; Shaul Shaked, 'Religion in the Late Sasanian Period: Eran, Aneran, and Other Religious Designations', in *The Sasanian Era*, vol. 3, The Idea of Iran (London: I. B. Tauris, 2008), 105.
5. Richard E. Payne, *A State of Mixture: Christians, Zoroastrians, and Iranian Political Culture in Late Antiquity*, Transformation of the Classical Heritage 56 (Oakland, California: University of California Press, 2015), 165.

6. Philip Kreyenbroek, 'Millennialism and Eschatology in the Zoroastrian Tradition', in Abbas Amanat and Magnus T. Bernhardsson (eds), *Imagining the End: Visions of Apocalypse from the Ancient Middle East to Modern America* (London: I. B. Tauris, 2001), 34–35.
7. Kreyenbroek, 35.
8. Payne, *State of Mixture*, 83.
9. Shaked, 'Religion in the Late Sasanian Period: Eran, Aneran, and Other Religious Designations', 111.
10. Payne, *State of Mixture*, 80–82.
11. Shaul Shaked, 'Some Islamic Reports Concerning Zoroastrianism', *Jerusalem Studies in Arabic and Islam* 17 (1994): 43–84.
12. Payne, *State of Mixture*, 79.
13. John R. Hinnells, *Persian Mythology* (London: Hamlyn, 1973), 53.
14. Kreyenbroek, 'Millennialism and Eschatology in the Zoroastrian Tradition', 36–39.
15. Jamsheed K. Choksy, 'Reassessing the Material Contexts of Ritual Fires in Ancient Iran', *Iranica Antiqua* 42 (2007): 229–69; Mary Boyce, 'On the Zoroastrian Temple Cult of Fire', *Journal of the American Oriental Society* 95, no. 3 (1975): 454–65.
16. Michael Morony, *Iraq after the Muslim Conquest* (Princeton, NJ: Princeton University Press, 1984), 283.
17. On Zoroastrian conceptions of purity and pollution, see Jamsheed K. Choksy, *Purity and Pollution in Zoroastrianism: Triumph over Evil* (Austin: University of Texas Press, 1989).
18. Payne, *State of Mixture*, 8, 21.
19. M.-L. Chaumont, 'Recherches sur le clerge zoroastrien: le herbad (deuxieme article)', *Revue de l'histoire des religions* 158, no. 2 (1960): 166.
20. Jenny Rose, *Zoroastrianism: An Introduction* (London: I. B. Tauris, 2011), xviii.
21. Richard N. Frye, *The Golden Age of Persia: The Arabs in the East* (London: Weidenfeld and Nicolson, 1975), 100.
22. Patricia Crone, *The Nativist Prophets of Early Islamic Iran: Rural Revolt and Local Zoroastrianism* (Cambridge: Cambridge University Press, 2012).
23. Richard N. Frye, 'The Fate of Zoroastrians in Eastern Iran', in Rika Gyselen (ed.), *Au carrefour des religions: mélanges offerts à Philippe Gignoux* (Leuven, Belgique: Peeters, 1995), 70.
24. Rose, *Zoroastrianism: An Introduction*, xix.
25. Payne, *State of Mixture*, 88.

26. Rose, *Zoroastrianism: An Introduction*, 102.
27. Crone, *Nativist Prophets of Early Islamic Iran*, 319.
28. Sarah Bowen Savant, *New Muslims of Post-Conquest Iran* (Cambridge: Cambridge University Press, 2013), 8–12.
29. Shaked, 'Religion in the Late Sasanian Period: Eran, Aneran, and Other Religious Designations', 106–9.
30. On the cogency of such claims in early twentieth-century Iran, see Afshin Marashi, *Exile and the Nation: The Parsi Community of India and the Making of Modern Iran* (Austin: University of Texas Press, 2020).
31. See Khodadad Rezakhani, *ReOrienting the Sasanians: East Iran in Late Antiquity* (Edinburgh: Edinburgh University Press, 2017), 11–12.
32. Nabil Matar, 'Islam in Britain, 1689–1750', *Journal of British Studies* 47, no. 2 (2008): 284–300; Denise A. Spellberg, *Thomas Jefferson's Qur'an: Islam and the Founders* (New York: Alfred A. Knopf, 2013).
33. Christopher MacEvitt, *The Crusades and the Christian World of the East: Rough Tolerance*, The Middle Ages Series (Philadelphia: University of Pennsylvania Press, 2008); Yohanan Friedmann, *Tolerance and Coercion in Islam: Interfaith Relations in the Muslim Tradition* (New York: Cambridge University Press, 2003).
34. Wendy Brown, *Regulating Aversion: Tolerance in the Age of Identity and Empire* (Princeton, NJ: Princeton University Press, 2006), especially Chapter 4.
35. For a critique of Brown's work, see Slavoj Žižek, 'Tolerance as an Ideological Category', *Critical Inquiry* 34, no. 4 (2008): 660–82.
36. Saba Mahmood, *Religious Difference in a Secular Age: A Minority Report* (Princeton, NJ: Princeton University Press, 2016).
37. Brown, *Regulating Aversion*, 145–79; Mahmood, *Religious Difference in a Secular Age*, 42, 91–97.
38. Payne, *State of Mixture*, 26.
39. Ibid., 38.
40. David Nirenberg, *Communities of Violence: Persecution of Minorities in the Middle Ages* (Princeton, NJ: Princeton University Press, 1996), 7–8.
41. Anver M. Emon, *Religious Pluralism and Islamic Law: 'Dhimmis' and Others in the Empire of Law* (Oxford: Oxford University Press, 2012), 60–66.
42. Thomas A. Carlson, 'When Did the Middle East Become Muslim? Trends in the Study of Islam's "Age of Conversions"', *History Compass* 16 (2018): 7.
43. Richard W. Bulliet, *Conversion to Islam in the Medieval Period: An Essay in Quantitative History* (Cambridge, MA: Harvard University Press, 1979).

44. Jack Tannous, *The Making of the Medieval Middle East: Religion, Society, and Simple Believers* (Princeton, NJ: Princeton University Press, 2020), Part IV.
45. Jamsheed K. Choksy, *Conflict and Cooperation: Zoroastrian Subalterns and Muslim Elites in Medieval Iranian Society* (New York: Columbia University Press, 1997), 87, 143.
46. Marshall G. S. Hodgson, *Venture of Islam* (Chicago: University of Chicago Press, 1974), 56–67.
47. Tannous, *The Making of the Medieval Middle East.*
48. Michael Philip Penn, *Envisioning Islam: Syriac Christians and the Early Muslim World* (Philadelphia: University of Pennsylvania Press, 2015), Chapter 4.
49. Thomas Sizgorich, *Violence and Belief in Late Antiquity: Militant Devotion in Christianity and Islam*, Divinations (Philadelphia: University of Pennsylvania Press, 2009), Chapter 8; these examples were drawn from Sizgorich's work as well as Tannous, *The Making of the Medieval Middle East*; Penn, *Envisioning Islam: Syriac Christians and the Early Muslim World*; Christian Sahner, *Christian Martyrs under Islam: Religious Violence and the Making of the Muslim World* (Princeton, NJ: Princeton University Press, 2018); Uriel Simonsohn, *A Common Justice: The Legal Allegiances of Christians and Jews under Early Islam* (Philadelphia: University of Pennsylvania Press, 2011); and David Freidenreich, *Foreigners and Their Food: Constructing Otherness in Jewish, Christian, and Islamic Law* (Berkeley: University of California Press, 2011).
50. Sizgorich, *Violence and Belief in Late Antiquity*, 268.
51. Milka Levy-Rubin, *Non-Muslims in the Early Islamic Empire: From Surrender to Coexistence* (New York: Cambridge University Press, 2011), Chapter 5; Sahner, *Christian Martyrs under Islam: Religious Violence and the Making of the Muslim World*, Chapter 4; Levy-Rubin, *Non-Muslims in the Early Islamic Empire*, Chapter 5.
52. See, for example, Finbarr Barry Flood, *Objects of Translation: Material Culture and Medieval Hindu-Muslim Encounter* (Princeton, NJ: Princeton University Press, 2009); Johan Elverskog, *Buddhism and Islam on the Silk Road*, Encounters with Asia (Philadelphia: University of Pennsylvania Press, 2010).
53. Shelagh Day and Gwen Brodsky, 'The Duty to Accommodate: Who Will Benefit?', *Canadian Bar Review* 75 (1996): 435.
54. Lori G. Beaman, *Reasonable Accommodation: Managing Religious Diversity* (Vancouver: University of British Columbia Press, 2010), 2.
55. Day and Brodsky, 'The Duty to Accommodate: Who Will Benefit?', 434.

56. John Mackenzie, 'Empires in World History: Characteristics, Concepts, and Consequences', in John Mackenzie (ed.), *Encyclopedia of Empire* (Malden, MA: Wiley, 2016).
57. On the structure and logic of empire in this period, see Patricia Crone, *Pre-Industrial Societies: Anatomy of the Pre-Modern World* (London: Oneworld, 2015).
58. Day and Brodsky, 'The Duty to Accommodate: Who Will Benefit?', 435.
59. Beaman, *Reasonable Accommodation*, 208.
60. R. Stephen Humphreys, *Islamic History: A Framework for Inquiry*, revised edition (Princeton, NJ: Princeton University Press, 1991), 256.
61. Day and Brodsky, 'The Duty to Accommodate: Who Will Benefit?', 462.
62. Emon, *Religious Pluralism and Islamic Law*, 23.
63. Peter Jackson, 'World Conquest and Local Accommodation: Threat and Blandishment in Mongol Diplomacy', in Judith Pfeiffer and Sholeh Quinn (eds), *History and Historiography of Post-Mongol Central Asia and the Middle East: Studies in Honor of John E. Woods* (Wiesbaden, Germany: Harrassowitz, 2008), 3–22; Jonathan Berkey, 'Circumcision Circumscribed: Female Excision and Cultural Accommodation in the Medieval Near East', *International Journal of Middle East Studies* 28 (1996): 19–38; Norman Calder, 'Legitimacy and Accommodation in Safavid Iran: The Linguistic Theory of Muhammad Baqir al-Sabzavari (1090/1679)', *Iran* 25 (1987): 91–105.

1

Myth and Countermyth in Zoroastrian Historiography

Scholars who write about interreligious encounters in the pre-modern Middle East are sometimes tempted to compose apologetic accounts of pluralistic harmony or polemical narratives of cross-confessional strife. The interpretive pendulum easily swings between myth and countermyth as Mark Cohen has documented with regard to Jewish historiography.[1] For example, historian Salo Baron used the disparaging term 'lachrymose' in 1928 to describe a school of interpretation that viewed the experience of medieval European Jews through a veil of tears.[2] Proponents of this dismal perspective described Jewish history as if it lurched from crisis to crisis. The lachrymose narrative was based in part on eschatological beliefs about the coming of the Messiah and Jewish redemption. Its counterpart was the Jerusalem school of historiography, which David Nirenberg describes as 'a post-Holocaust, secularised version' of the lachrymose school. Though its messianism was more muted, the Jerusalem school shared with the lachrymose school a teleological view of history, in which each pogrom foreshadowed greater persecutions to come.[3] Both schools painted a fairly bleak picture of Jewish–Christian relations in medieval Europe. According to Cohen, they developed in response to the nineteenth-century myth of a Jewish Golden Age in Islamicate Spain. That rosy narrative, which contrasted so sharply with the anti-Semitism of Christendom in the Middle Ages, was intended to prod modern Europeans to achieve the promise of liberalism by extending political and social equality to Jewish citizens.[4]

Similar tendencies toward mythmaking exist in the study of Zoroastrian history. The period from the Islamic conquest of Persia to the end of the so-called Iranian *intermezzo* – that is, from the seventh to the eleventh centuries – was supposedly an unmitigated disaster for adherents of the Good Religion. According to Zoroastrian tradition, Muslims forced them to convert to Islam by the sword.[5] Zoroastrians who continued to practice their religion struggled under the weight of the jizya, or capitation tax, a form of economic *jihad*.[6] Most of the Avesta was lost or shamelessly burned by Muslims.[7] Parsis fled to India to escape the contemptuous and intolerable treatment of the Umayyads.[8] Abbasid caliphs inaugurated a general persecution of Zoroastrians, who lost their protected status in Islamic law.[9] By the ninth century, 'the Zoroastrian population was left with the options of apostasy, migration, martyrdom or marginalisation'.[10] Such ideas encourage a grim conception of Muslim–Zoroastrian relations in Late Antiquity.

Some elements of this sad narrative warrant reconsideration. Richard Payne and Michael Penn have critically examined Late Antique myths about the persecution of Christians in the Sasanian and Byzantine Empires.[11] The goal of critical inquiry is not to minimise the trauma of tumultuous events on the affected populations. It is an effort at dispassionate analysis of primary sources to ensure that, insofar as is possible, interpretation of events accords with the best available evidence in order to prevent the perpetuation of tropes.

The conquest of Iran was undoubtedly troubling for Zoroastrians, although historians lack contemporary documentation of their reactions. The Introduction noted the eschatological significance with which it was imbued by later priests.[12] Yet the fall of the Persian Empire was not a foregone conclusion. The last Sasanian emperor, Yazdagerd III, fought Umar's less numerous forces for years. The contours of the invasion are relatively well documented in the early Islamic sources.[13] The Sasanian military engaged in several major battles with caliphal armies in the 630s before the emperor fled eastward. Local resistance continued as Arab-Muslim forces made their way across the Iranian plateau in pursuit. Some cities had to be subdued more than once. Yazdagerd was finally assassinated in 651 at Merv, and attempts to revive the dynasty thereafter faltered.[14]

The few extant Zoroastrian sources from the period suggest that the priesthood struggled to maintain itself without imperial support. In the wake of the conquest, agents appointed by the caliphs reportedly confiscated Sasanian royal properties, including fire temples, in Iraq.[15] By the ninth century, the sacerdotal hierarchy began to break down. The functional distinction between different types of priests blurred as there were too few to perform the necessary rites. Also, Zoroastrian sources aver, priests were insufficiently trained and impoverished worshippers could not afford their services.[16] Scholars of Islam have reasonably suggested that these factors may have encouraged conversion but, again, there is not strong evidence.[17]

After the conquest, Muslims taxed non-Muslims at a differential rate on the basis of religion, as Sasanian Zoroastrians had done with non-Zoroastrians before them.[18] The notion that Muslims burned the Avesta resembles tropes about the destructive nature of Alexander's invasion of Achaemenian Persia in the fourth century BCE.[19] Philip Kreyenbroek has noted that medieval Zoroastrians recycled apocalyptic prophecies about Macedonians and applied them to Arabs.[20] A group of Persian Zoroastrians, now known as Parsis, migrated from Iran to India, arriving as early as the eighth century. Alan Williams has questioned the historical value of the scant literary evidence that suggests they were driven by oppression. Instead, André Wink proposes that Arab competition for trade in the Persian Gulf may have led to 'a readjustment of commercial patterns' and perhaps the opening of new economic opportunities built on existing contacts with India.[21] The idea warrants further exploration.

A sense of historical persecution is an important component of modern Zoroastrian identity.[22] This communal conception seems to have permeated scholarship. It is evident, for example, in the works of Mary Boyce (1920–2006), formerly Professor of Iranian Studies at the School of Oriental and African Studies at the University of London. Boyce was a leading voice in the field of Zoroastrian Studies in the latter half of the twentieth century.[23] In the preface to *A Persian Stronghold of Zoroastrianism* she laments, 'It is a cause of keen regret to me that it is impossible to write about the Zoroastrians of Yazd without casting the Moslems [*sic*] in the role of villains, just as it is impossible to write an account of Jews in Europe without showing Christians in a hateful light.'[24] Boyce's conviction that Zoroastrians suffered immeasurably at the hands of medieval Muslims persists in her later writings.[25]

Some scholars have tried to temper morose conceptions of medieval Zoroastrian history. Jamsheed Choksy notes, for instance, that Boyce's portrayal of life under Muslim rule as constant misery does not match the evidence.[26] Choksy argues that patterns of conflict and cooperation, established in the conquest era, varied across Iran and set the tone for future interaction between communities. His own relatively nuanced account of Muslim–Zoroastrian relations to 1300 CE concludes that followers of the Good Religion were 'a subordinate, subjugated, or inferior class, that is, a subaltern community experiencing crisis, displacement, and marginalization not only during that time but also later'.[27] This assessment rests largely, although not exclusively, on information preserved in Islamicate sources. While Choksy valuably incorporates other evidence, particularly from Zoroastrian sources, the Islamicate sources warrant further interrogation and contextualisation. As an example, *Tarikh-i Bukhara* hints at the tenuous nature of Umayyad control of Bukhara after Qutayba ibn Muslim conquered that city in the early eighth century. While it might seem obvious, and even true to the source, to characterise tension in Transoxiana as religious in nature, Michael Haug has questioned the value of framing violence in communal or ethnic terms, especially in a frontier province where the political situation was constantly in flux, military control by any party was tenuous, and group identities – let alone individual motivations – are difficult to isolate.[28] Critical analysis, sensitive to the vicissitudes of the political situation and the rhetorical construction of religious identities, is essential.

Other scholars have stressed the precarious legal position of Zoroastrians in the early caliphates. According to Aptin Khanbaghi, 'Zoroastrianism did not enjoy the same level of tolerance granted to the Jews and Christians within the realm of Islam'.[29] Zoroastrians were supposedly excluded from the caliphal administration after the failure of Zoroastrian revolts in the ninth century. Followers of the Good Religion subsequently lost their protected legal status and converted to Islam en masse.[30] It is true that most early Muslim jurists did not regard Zoroastrians as People of the Book and prohibited or regulated certain forms of interaction with them. However, mass conversion of Zoroastrians is not well documented in the early Abbasid era, and any role that Islamic law might have played in driving such a trend remains to be proven. Patricia Crone has convincingly argued for the nativist character of the so-called Zoroastrian revolts in Iran during the early Abbasid era.[31] Only one revolutionary, Bihafaridh, appears to have sought the revitalisation of the Good Religion, and there is no evidence for a purge of Zoroastrians from the bureaucracy in response. Rather, Luke Yarbrough traces the origins of Muslim opposition to the employment of non-Muslims to hadith emanating from Kufa, where Arab elites competed for lucrative government posts in the mid-eighth century.[32] While it is evident that Zoroastrians were at a disadvantage relative to Jews and Christians in the legal hierarchy of medieval Islamdom, it is less clear what practical effect that might have had.

Contemporary Zoroastrian Struggles

Present concerns often influence conceptions of the past, and contemporary Zoroastrians face a number of difficulties that colour perceptions of Muslim–Zoroastrian relations in earlier periods. As Mark Cohen has demonstrated, twentieth-century tensions between the State of Israel and its neighbours led to a neo-lachrymose narrative of Jewish history that exaggerated the persecution of Jews living under medieval Muslim rule.[33]

It is a fact that Zoroastrians endure discrimination in the Islamic Republic of Iran. They are a recognised religious minority in the country's post-revolutionary Constitution, which guarantees them a representative in the parliament (N.P., *majles*), as well as freedom to worship and conduct their personal affairs according to the tenets of their faith. Yet Zoroastrians are at a disadvantage relative to Muslims in matters of education, military service and employment as Imami Shiʿism has, since 1979, defined the parameters of a citizen's participation in society. For instance, university admission exams test Zoroastrians' knowledge of Islamic theology even though they are legally exempted from such coursework in secondary school.[34] The ownership of communal lands around the Zoroastrian cemetery in Tehran is disputed by the Revolutionary Guards, meaning that military exercises routinely obstruct access to the site and disrupt Zoroastrian funerary customs.[35] While Zoroastrians experience prejudice in Iran, especially in terms of professional advancement, they also enjoy some social freedoms that Muslims generally do not, such as access to alcohol and mixed-gender gatherings. Young Zoroastrians confront the same challenges as all Iranian youths: a lack of affordable housing, unfavourable economic prospects and the desire to emigrate.[36] The Hebrew Immigrant Aid Society (HIAS) helps many Zoroastrians to leave Iran for Austria, where they stay temporarily at an HIAS centre in Vienna funded by the US government. HIAS assists them with applying for refugee status and resettling in the United States. They flee the country in droves.[37]

This current state of affairs affects the way that Zoroastrians perceive their medieval history. According to Jamsheed Choksy, it has revived dismal conceptions of the past. 'Iran's reversal in 1979 to a political system where Islam predominated . . . once more deeply shook the foundational psyche of the Zoroastrian community, bringing back communal memories of harsh times from centuries past and triggering survival responses.'[38] Many Zoroastrians chose to emigrate after the Islamic Revolution rather than accept what they perceived as 'a modern version of *dhimmi* status'.[39] Parsis confront different but nonetheless palpable challenges in twenty-first-century India. They profited immensely from their collaboration with the British in the nineteenth and early twentieth centuries, but their collective wealth, influence and prestige have waned in the post-colonial era. The size of the community continues to dwindle.[40]

Demography

Demographic trends in the Zoroastrian community seem to bolster gloomy conceptions of its history. The Zoroastrian population of Iran is steadily decreasing. It has declined 25–30 per cent since the establishment of the Islamic Republic, primarily due to emigration and birthrates below replacement levels. There are now less than 20,000 Zoroastrians in Iran by one estimate.[41] The Parsis of India face similar demographic challenges. In the 1980s, anthropologist Paul Axelrod surveyed Parsi attitudes toward marriage and family in Mumbai. Controlling for variables such as urbanisation and income level, Axelrod linked their relatively low rates of marriage and fertility to the lifestyles and economic expectations that they developed under British rule.[42] On average, Parsi women are better educated than other Indian women, so they marry later or not at all and have fewer children. Many Parsi men and women prefer unarranged marriages, which allows them to seek partners outside of the community. Parsis generally do not consider the children of exogamous unions to be Parsis, nor do they accept converts.[43] Those who marry within the faith are accustomed to and expect a high standard of living. Some Parsis emigrate in pursuit of careers to provide that standard of living and thereby isolate themselves from potential partners within the community. As a result, the death rate among Parsis exceeds the birthrate. Approximately 70,000 Parsis live in India at present.[44]

As the Zoroastrian population plummets in Iran and India, the priesthood struggles to perpetuate itself. For decades, the community in Iran has not been able to train enough priests to meet its liturgical needs. For example, a priest told Mary Boyce in 1963–1964 that he would soon exhaust his supply of consecrated bull's urine, which is used for purification rituals, because there were no longer sufficient priests at Yazd to perform the rite of consecration.[45] Traditionally, the priesthood was limited to males of paternal priestly lineage. Initiates undertook years of study and training to master liturgical languages and ceremonies. Zoroastrians are now reconsidering these standards as families have fewer children and young men pursue more lucrative or prestigious careers outside of the priesthood.[46] In Iran, assistant priests can now be appointed from previously ineligible families.[47] The community's contemporary struggles shape the way that scholars interpret Zoroastrian history.

Countermyths

Several attempts in the early twentieth century to improve Muslim–Zoroastrian relations produced apologetic countermyths. In 1925, responding to an encounter with Parsis in Bombay, Khwaja Kamal-ud-Din (1870–1932) wrote a treatise on Zoroastrianism. Kamal-ud-Din was an Ahmadi Muslim missionary, prolific author, and imam of the Woking mosque in England.[48] He argued that Zoroaster was a prophet but insisted that Parsis practice a corrupt form of his teachings, including fire worship and dualism. Kamal-ud-Din does not cite any sources, and his conviction that Islam is the culminating faith for humanity means that Zoroastrianism comes up short by comparison. The book's proselytising intent is clear. The Afterword all but invites Parsis to abandon their faith for Islam. At the same time, Kamal-ud-Din also defies the reader to produce one example of Muhammad or the first caliphs forcing Zoroastrians to convert by the sword.[49]

Kamal-ud-Din's idiosyncratic attempt to reinterpret the history of interreligious encounter was undoubtedly in part a reaction to Orientalist conceits about the fall of the Sasanian Empire. In the early twentieth century scholars such as Edward Browne and Josef Markwart argued that Arabs had destroyed the imperial might, cultural refinement and tolerant religion of Iran in the seventh century.[50] The uncouth invaders forcibly imposed Islam instead. According to Reza Zia-Ebrahimi, some secular Iranian nationalists adopted such racialised thinking. They disdained Arab influences in Persian culture, alleging that Iranians were Aryans whose inherent faith was Zoroastrianism.[51] Zia-Ebrahimi may underestimate the pre-modern and indigenous roots of this ethnic chauvinism, which to some extent has been a part of anti-Arab rhetoric among Iranian Muslims and Zoroastrians since the early Islamic era.[52] Yet he is correct that this ideology remains potent in Iran.

The early twentieth century witnessed increased contact between Persians and Parsis. To nuture these burgeoning connections, the Parsi Orientalist G. K. Nariman published a series of articles arguing that Muslims had been unjustly blamed for the decline of Zoroastrianism after the conquest of Iran. Nariman admitted that there had been racial tension between Persians and Arabs in the past, and conceded that overzealous converts to Islam were guilty of abuse toward their former co-religionists in the caliphal era. Yet he insisted that these excesses do not detract from the overall spirit of tolerance in early Islamicate history. He argued that an ossified priesthood was largely responsible for the decay of fire temples and the failure of Zoroastrians to transmit knowledge of the Good Religion to the next generation.[53] These arguments reflected the views of late nineteenth-century Parsi reformists who, based on contact with Protestant missionaries, criticised their priesthood as benighted and backward.[54]

Nariman was a member of the Iran League, a Parsi organisation in Bombay that sought improved relations with the Pahlavi dynasty and the broader Muslim population of Iran. He was a passionate supporter of the secular nationalism of Reza Shah and editor of the *Iran League Quarterly*. Nevertheless, the Parsi community of Bombay ostracised Nariman for challenging the narrative of historical persecution at the hands of Muslims. He ultimately lost his editorship.[55] Nariman's Muslim counterpart was Taher Rezwi. In 1928, Rezwi published *Parsis: A People of the Book*, which highlights positive episodes in the history of Muslim–Zoroastrian relations.[56] Nariman wrote the book's preface. Rezwi asserted that Muhammad and the first caliphs treated Zoroastrians like People of the Book. He challenged the notion that Zoroastrians are dualists who worship fire, and sought to prove that they never condoned consanguineous marriage. Rezwi cited numerous primary sources from the early Islamic period to substantiate his claims, but denied passages that portrayed Zoroastrians in a negative light. For example, Rezwi rejected the idea that the Prophet Muhammad had prohibited Muslims from marrying Zoroastrians, reassuring the reader that the prohibition was meant for polytheists like Manichaeans and Mazdakites. Rezwi admitted that his work was apologetic but claimed that it was not 'conceived in the spirit of a propagandist'.[57]

This rosy interpretation of medieval Muslim–Zoroastrian relations did not gain wide acceptance, but a favourable conception of ancient Persia and Zoroastrianism became part of Iranian nationalist discourse in the Pahlavi era (1925–1979). When Reza Shah seized power, he used civilisational rhetoric to pursue secularising reforms that would weaken the power of Muslim clergy and supposedly allow Iranians to reclaim their former glory. His celebration of the nation's pre-Islamic past was part of a broader cultural movement of neoclassicism in the interwar period that sought to disassociate Iran from Islam.[58] It accelerated under Reza Shah's son and successor, Mohammad Reza Shah, who elevated Zoroastrianism to the status of a 'civic religion' according to Michael Stausberg.[59] That might overstate the case, but the Pahlavi era is certainly perceived as a golden age for the Good Religion in Iran. Mohammad Reza Shah continued to curb the influence of the Islamic religious establishment, which inter alia triggered the revolution of 1978–9 that ultimately toppled him. Critics of the Islamic Republic, both inside and outside of the country, sometimes still invoke Persia's pre-Islamic past to delegitimise the current government. Zoroastrians, meanwhile, are caught in a 'discursive oscillation' between recognising Imami Shi'ism as an Iranicised religion and criticising Islam as Arab in origin and thus antithetical to Persian culture.[60]

Conclusion

The present work strives to chart a course between myth and countermyth in the history of interreligious encounter in early Islamicate Iran. It does so without presuppositions about Zoroastrian decline or Muslim perfidy. Subsequent chapters employ the concepts of accommodation and memory to demonstrate that imperial administrators integrated Zoroastrians into the caliphal order largely on their own terms and for their own benefit. They determined to tax Zoroastrians without recognising them as People of the Book. This study also acknowledges the limits of accommodation. Muslim jurists advocated against marrying adherents of the Good Religion and against eating meat slaughtered by them. Theories of memory allow the reader to consider the ways that early Muslims chose to remember Zoroastrians. Persian historians faithfully preserved a writ from Muhammad that supposedly exempted Salman al-Farisi's family from the impositions of Islamic law. At the same time, authors of local histories invented tales of fire temple desecration to assert the triumph of Islam. Muslims outside of Iran denigrated Zoroastrians rhetorically by associating them with pagans, heretics and deviants. In other words, Muslims remembered the accommodation of Zoroastrians ambivalently. This ambivalence is a defining feature of early Islamic discourse on the Good Religion.

Notes

1. Mark R. Cohen, *Under Crescent and Cross: The Jews in the Middle Ages* (Princeton, NJ: Princeton University Press, 1994), 3–14.
2. Ibid., xv.
3. Nirenberg, *Communities of Violence*, 9.
4. Cohen, *Under Crescent and Cross*, 4.
5. Janet Kestenberg Amighi, *The Zoroastrians of Iran: Conversion, Assimilation, or Persistence* (New York: AMS Press, 1990), 59.
6. Debabrata Das, *Essays on Islam and Zoroastrianism* (Kolkata: Sanskrit Pustak Bhandar, 2007), 43.
7. Michael Stausberg, 'The Invention of a Canon: The Case of Zoroastrianism', in A. van der Kooij and K. van der Toorn (eds), *Canonization and Decanonization: Papers Presented to the International Conference of the Leiden Institute for the Study of Religions* (Leiden: Brill, 1998), 265, 270 notes the tendency of scholars to attribute the loss of the Avesta 'rather vaguely to the Islamization of Iran'.
8. 'Abd al-Husayn Zarrinkub, 'The Arab Conquest of Iran and Its Aftermath', in *Cambridge History of Iran*, vol. 4: From the Arab Invasion to the Saljuqs (Cambridge: Cambridge University Press, 1975), 32.
9. Marietta Stepaniants, 'The Encounter of Zoroastrianism with Islam', *Philosophy East and West* 52, no. 2 (2002): 166.

10. Aptin Khanbaghi, *The Fire, the Star and the Cross: Minority Religions in Medieval and Early Modern Iran* (London: I. B. Tauris, 2006), 159.
11. Payne, *State of Mixture*, Chapter 1; Penn, *Envisioning Islam: Syriac Christians and the Early Muslim World*, Chapter 1.
12. See, for example, Bamanaji Dhabhara (ed.), *The Persian Rivayats of Hormazyar Framarz and Others: Their Version with Introduction and Notes*, reprint of the 1932 edition (Bombay: K. R. Cama Oriental Institute, 1999), 484; Daryaee, 'Apocalypse Now: Zoroastrian Reflections on the Early Islamic Centuries', 192; Hoyland, *Seeing Islam as Others Saw It*, 321–27.
13. The most recent study of these events is Robert G. Hoyland, *In God's Path: The Arab Conquests and the Creation of an Islamic Empire* (New York: Oxford University Press, 2015); for a more speculative treatment see Parvaneh Pourshariati, *Decline and Fall of the Sasanian Empire: The Sasanian-Parthian Confederacy and the Arab Conquest of Iran* (London: I. B. Tauris, 2008).
14. Rezakhani, *ReOrienting the Sasanians: East Iran in Late Antiquity*, Chapter 9.
15. Morony, *Iraq after the Muslim Conquest*, 283–84, 300.
16. Philip G. Kreyenbroek, 'The Zoroastrian Priesthood after the Fall of the Sasanian Empire', in *Transition Periods in Iranian History: Actes Du Symposium de Fribourg-En-Brisgau (22–24 Mai 1985)* (Leuven, Belgium: Peeters, 1987), 151–66.
17. Robert G. Hoyland, *Muslims and Others in Early Islamic Society* (Burlington, VT: Ashgate, 2004), xxvi; Bernard Lewis, 'Islam and Other Religions', in *The Jews of Islam* (Princeton, NJ: Princeton University Press, 1984), 17.
18. Choksy, *Conflict and Cooperation*, Chapter 4.
19. Stausberg, 'Invention of a Canon', 267–70; J. Christoph Bürgel, 'Zoroastrians as Viewed in Medieval Islamic Sources', in Jacques Waardenburg (ed.), *Muslim Perceptions of Other Religions: A Historical Survey* (New York: Oxford University Press, 1999), 206.
20. Kreyenbroek, 'Millennialism and Eschatology in the Zoroastrian Tradition', 52.
21. Alan Williams, *The Zoroastrian Myth of Migration from Iran and Settlement in the Indian Diaspora: Text, Translation and Analysis of the 16th century Qeṣṣe-ye Sanjān/The Story of Sanjan* (Leiden: Brill, 2009); André Wink, *Al-Hind: The Making of the Indo-Islamic World*, vol. 1, Early Medieval India and the Expansion of Islam, 7th–11th Centuries (Leiden: Brill, 1990), 105.
22. John R. Hinnells, *Zoroastrians in Britain: The Ratanbai Katrak Lectures, University of Oxford, 1985* (Oxford: Clarendon Press, 1996), 303; Michael Stausberg, 'From Power to Powerlessness: Zoroastrianism in Iranian History', in Anh Nga Longva and Anne Sofie Roald (eds), *Religious Minorities in the Middle*

East: Domination, Self-Empowerment, Accommodation, Social, Economic, and Political Studies of the Middle East and Asia, vol. 108 (Leiden: Brill, 2012), 177.

23. Ehsan Yarshater (ed.), *Encyclopaedia Iranica* (London: Routledge, 1982), s.v. 'Mary Boyce' (John Hinnells).
24. Mary Boyce, *A Persian Stronghold of Zoroastrianism* (Oxford: Clarendon Press, 1977), viii.
25. Mary Boyce, *Zoroastrians, Their Religious Beliefs and Practices* (London: Routledge & Kegan Paul, 1979), Chapter 10; *Zoroastrianism: Its Antiquity and Constant Vigour* (Costa Mesa, CA: Mazda Publishers, 1992); 'Zoroastrianism in Iran after the Arab Conquest', in Pheroza Godrej and Firoza Mistree (eds), *A Zoroastrian Tapestry: Art, Religion & Culture* (Usmanpura: Mapin, 2002).
26. Choksy, *Conflict and Cooperation*, 154.
27. Choksy, 11.
28. For the specific example of violence at Bukhara after Qutayba ibn Muslim's conquest, see Robert Haug, *The Eastern Frontier: Limits of Empire in Late Antique and Early Medieval Central Asia* (London: I. B. Tauris, 2019), Chapter 5; compare Choksy, *Conflict and Cooperation*, 43.
29. Khanbaghi, *The Fire, the Star and the Cross*, 159.
30. Khanbaghi, 20–27.
31. Crone, *Nativist Prophets of Early Islamic Iran*, Chapter 8.
32. Luke Yarbrough, 'Upholding God's Rule: Early Muslim Juristic Opposition to the State Employment of Non-Muslims', *Islamic Law & Society* 19, no. 1/2 (2012): 11–85.
33. Cohen, *Under Crescent and Cross*, Chapter 1; see also Joel Beinin, *The Dispersion of Egyptian Jewry: Culture, Politics, and the Formation of the Modern Diaspora*, Contraversions 11 (Berkeley: University of California Press, 1998), Introduction.
34. Eliz Sanasarian, *Religious Minorities in Iran* (Cambridge: Cambridge University Press, 2000), 83–84.
35. Sarah Stewart, 'The Politics of Zoroastrian Philanthropy and the Case of Qasr-e Firuzeh', *Iranian Studies* 45, no. 1 (2012): 59–80; Jamsheed K. Choksy, 'How Iran Persecutes Its Oldest Religion', *CNN*, accessed April 26, 2014, http://www.cnn.com/2011/11/14/opinion/choksy-iran-zoroastrian/index.html?iref=allsearch.
36. Navid Fozi, *Reclaiming the Faravahar: Zoroastrian Survival in Contemporary Iran* (Leiden: Leiden University Press, 2014), Chapter 6.
37. Richard Foltz, 'Zoroastrians in Iran: What Future in the Homeland?', *Middle East Journal* 65, no. 1 (2011): 79, 82.

38. Jamsheed K. Choksy, 'Despite Shāhs and Mollās: Minority Sociopolitics in Premodern and Modern Iran', *Journal of Asian History* 40, no. 2 (2006): 179.
39. Rose, *Zoroastrianism: An Introduction*, 186.
40. Shaun Walker, 'The Last of the Zoroastrians', *The Guardian*, August 6, 2020, http://www.theguardian.com/world/2020/aug/06/last-of-the-zoroastrians-parsis-mumbai-india-ancient-religion; see also Tanya Luhrmann, *The Good Parsi: The Fate of a Colonial Elite in a Postcolonial Society* (Cambridge, MA: Harvard University Press, 1996).
41. Stausberg, 'From Power to Powerlessness', 188.
42. Paul Axelrod, 'Cultural and Historical Factors in the Population Decline of the Parsis of India', *Population Studies* 44, no. 3 (1990): 401–19.
43. Choksy, 'Despite Shāhs and Mollās', 172.
44. Rose, *Zoroastrianism: An Introduction*, 216.
45. Boyce, *A Persian Stronghold of Zoroastrianism*, 93.
46. Shahin Bekhradnia, 'The Decline of the Zoroastrian Priesthood and Its Effect on the Iranian Zoroastrian Community in the Twentieth Century', *Journal of the Anthropological Society of Oxford* 23, no. 1 (1992): 37–47; Dastur Firoze M. Kotwal, 'A Brief History of the Parsi Priesthood', *Indo-Iranian Journal* 33, no. 3 (1990): 165–75.
47. Foltz, 'Zoroastrians in Iran: What Future in the Homeland?', 80.
48. Khizar Humayun Ansari, 'Kamal-Ud-Din, Khwaja (1870–1932), Islamic Scholar and Missionary', in *Oxford Dictionary of National Biography* (Oxford University Press, 2013), https://www.oxforddnb.com/view/10.1093/ref:odnb/9780198614128.001.0001/odnb-9780198614128-e-94519.
49. Khwajah Kamal-ud-Din, *Islam and Zoroastrianism* (Woking, England: Basheer Muslim Library, 1925).
50. Reza Zia-Ebrahimi, '"Arab Invasion" and Decline, or the Import of European Racial Thought by Iranian Nationalists', *Ethnic and Racial Studies*, no. 3 (2012): 14; Marashi, *Exile and the Nation*, Chapter 4.
51. For a sustained treatment of this topic, see Reza Zia-Ebrahimi, *The Emergence of Iranian Nationalism: Race and the Politics of Dislocation* (New York: Columbia University Press, 2016).
52. Zia-Ebrahimi, '"Arab Invasion" and Decline', 4–5; compare Stausberg, 'From Power to Powerlessness', 182.
53. G. K. Nariman, *Persia & Parsis* (Bombay: Iran League, 1925); G. K. Nariman, *The Ahad Nameh* (Bombay: Iran League, 1925); G. K. Nariman, 'Islam and Parsis', *Islamic Culture* 1 (1927): 632–39; G. K. Nariman, 'Was It Religious

Persecution Which Compelled the Parsis to Migrate from Persia to India?', *Islamic Culture* 7 (1933): 277–80.

54. Monica Ringer, *Pious Citizens: Reforming Zoroastrianism in India and Iran* (Syracuse, NY: Syracuse University Press, 2011).
55. Marashi, *Exile and the Nation*, 69, 253; Dinyar Patel, 'Gustaspshah Kaikhusroo Nariman: Improving Ties between Zoroastrianism and Islam', *FEZANA: The Federation of Zoroastrian Associations of North America* 15 (2009): 44.
56. S. M. Taher Rezwi, *Parsis, A People of the Book: Being a Brief Survey of Zoroastrian Religion in the Light of Biblical & Quranic Teachings* (Calcutta: D.B. Taraporewala & Sons, 1928).
57. Ibid., 14.
58. Marashi, *Exile and the Nation*, Introduction.
59. Stausberg, 'From Power to Powerlessness', 184.
60. Fozi, *Reclaiming the Fravahar*, 13.

2

Umar's Dilemma: The Taxation of People Without a Book

In 120/737–738, a landed notable (N.P., *dihqān*) of Herat addressed an aristocratic assembly at Balkh during the feast of Mihrijan, a Persian celebration of the autumnal equinox once closely associated with Zoroastrianism. His speech heaped praise on the visiting Umayyad governor of Khurasan, Asad ibn Abd Allah al-Qasri, by comparing al-Qasri's noble leadership to that of the pre-Islamic Sasanians. 'We are a group of non-Arabs (Ar., *'ajam*). We ruled the world for 400 years. We ruled it with forbearance, reason, and dignity [even though] we did not have a divinely inspired scripture (*kitāb nāṭiq*) nor a divinely commissioned prophet (*nabī mursal*).'[1] The themes around which this notable constructed his backhanded compliment of the emperors of Persia seem to imply that he was a Muslim.[2] The dihqan, like most Muslims before the tenth century, believed that Zoroastrians lacked a recognised prophet and book of scripture, at least as defined in Islamic terms.

Even among Zoroastrians, the relative importance of Zoroaster and the Avesta seems to have increased over the centuries. Although Zoroaster's name has become synonymous with the faith, particularly for outsiders, Jenny Rose notes that he did not always enjoy the distinctive status that he currently holds in the Good Religion.[3] Michael Stausberg has argued that Zoroastrians identified and promoted the Avesta as their scripture in the centuries after the Islamic conquest of Iran.[4] Contact with Muslims undoubtedly influenced these developments to some extent, yet scholars have paid insufficient attention to it.[5] This is despite the fact that Arabic sources preserve a wealth of information about the Good Religion as Muslim bureaucrats, collectors of hadith and jurists discussed Zoroastrians' status relative to People of the Book.

The term 'People of the Book' (Ar., *ahl al-kitāb*) is a Qur'anic designation for religious communities that possessed a divinely revealed book of scripture before the advent of Islam. The Qur'an mentions two such books (3: 3): the Torah (*tawrāt*) given to Moses and the Gospel (*injīl*) given to Jesus. As a result, Muslims considered Jews and Christians to be People of the Book. The Qur'an placed Jews and Christians – and a mysterious third group, the Sabi'ans – on equal footing with Muslims regarding the possibility of salvation (2: 62, 5: 69). Although the Qur'an posits a certain theological continuity with the People of the Book based on the notion that their scriptures carry a common message, it also presumes that the People of the Book corrupted that message over time. As Islam began to expand throughout the Arabian Peninsula, the Qur'an instructed Muslims to fight the People of the Book until they submitted to a capitation tax called jizya (9: 29). The People of the Book evolved from a religious distinction to a legal category as Islamic law began to develop in the first and second/seventh and eighth centuries.

The claim that medieval Muslims regarded Zoroastrians as People of the Book appears frequently in the secondary literature. Jamsheed Choksy states, 'Coexistence and interaction between Muslims and Zoroastrians were informed by the Muslim belief that Zoroastrians were people with a revealed scripture (*ahl al-kitāb*).'[6] Georges Vajda asserts that 'use of this term [People of the Book] was later extended . . . to Zoroastrians'.[7] Claude Cahen claims that Zoroastrians became People of the Book by transcribing the orally transmitted Avesta.[8] According to Michael Stausberg, 'Only as a "people" or "religion of the book" (*ahl al-kitāb*) were the Zoroastrians entitled to pay the jizya and gain a certain legal status and "protection" by the authorities similar but at the same time inferior to that of the Jews and the Christians.'[9] There is little evidence from early Islamic history to substantiate these arguments, which appear to be assumptions based on the fact that Muslims taxed Zoroastrians after the conquest of Iran, or that many contemporary Zoroastrians consider themselves to be People of the Book.

This chapter will demonstrate that early Muslims generally did not regard Zoroastrians as People of the Book. Nevertheless, caliphal administrators collected tax from adherents of the Good Religion. They attributed that decision to the Prophet Muhammad and circulated statements attributed to him (individually called hadith in Arabic) to justify the practice. Some Muslims struggled to reconcile those statements with the Qur'anic notion that it is only permissible to tax People of the Book. Tax collectors harmonised reports in order to establish a clear precedent, while Muslim jurists encouraged conformity. As a result, collections of hadith contain layers of debate about the status of the Good Religion in early Islamicate society. They reveal that Muslims ultimately chose to accommodate Zoroastrians in an effort to affirm the existing order despite the fact that followers of the Good Religion lacked an acceptable book.

Zoroastrians in Qur'anic Exegesis

The Qur'an does not describe Zoroastrians as People of the Book. It mentions them once, in Surat al-Hajj (22: 17), amidst a list of those whom God will judge at the Last Day. That list includes both believers and polytheists.

> Verily, those who believe and those who practice Judaism and the Sabi'ans and the Christians and the Zoroastrians and those who practice polytheism, verily God will distinguish between them on the Day of Resurrection. Verily God is a witness of all things (*Inna lladhīna āmanū wa-lladhīna hādū wa-l-ṣābi'īn wa-l-naṣārā wa-l-majūs wa-lladhīna ashrakū inna allāha yafṣilu baynahum yawm al-qiyāma inna allāha 'alā kull shay'in shahīd*).

Modern scholars cannot agree on the proper interpretation of this verse. Some believe that it implicitly classifies Zoroastrians as People of the Book. The Orientalist Ignaz Goldziher (1850–1921) stated that 'the Qur'an groups the Zoroastrians with [Jews and Christians], rather than with the pagans'.[10] Aptin Khanbaghi shares Goldziher's opinion.[11] Likewise, Jacques Waardenburg and Guy Monnot cite 22: 17 as evidence that Zoroastrians were People of the Book.[12] Other scholars favour a neutral reading of this verse that does not imply anything about their theological standing.[13] On the opposite end of the interpretive spectrum, the Egyptian scholar Hamid Abd al-Qadir (d. 1966) insisted that the Qur'an places Zoroastrians on the same level as polytheists.[14]

Christoph Bürgel interprets the grammatical structure of this verse to imply that Zoroastrians were People of the Book. He contends that the key to interpreting it is

> the second relative pronoun before *ashrakū*; there is a clear caesura between 'they that believe' with the following specification and 'they that commit idolatry.' According to this verse, the Madjus [Zoroastrians] clearly belong to the believers, as do the Christians, the Jews, and the Sabaeans."[15]

Bürgel's reading of the text is plausible but not definitive. In the Qur'an 'believers' is often a synonym for 'muslims' (meaning people who practiced uncorrupted religion and accepted Muhammad's leadership), especially in a verse like this one, which differentiates belief from other types of religion.[16] Most Jews and Christians were not 'believers' in that sense, and the verse does not state that God will favourably judge them or any other group associated with the second relative pronoun. What an implied caesura, if it exists, might mean for Zoroastrians is a matter of conjecture.

Early Muslim exegetes certainly did not interpret Q 22: 17 to suggest that Zoroastrians were People of the Book. In fact, they had little to say about the verse. Abu Abd Allah Muhammad ibn Ahmad al-Qurtubi (d. 671/1272) briefly identified each of the groups listed in the verse but did not interpret its meaning at all.[17] Abu Muhammad al-Husayn ibn Mas'ud al-Baghawi (d. 516/1122) specified that 'those who practice polytheism' means idol worshippers, and the phrase 'God will distinguish between them' means that He will judge between them – not particularly insightful comments.[18] Most exegetes were content to reproduce the verse's ambiguity about the eternal fate of non-Muslims. The author of *Tanwir al-Miqbas min Tafsir Ibn Abbas* simply said that God 'is aware of their differences and works'.[19] While God distinguishes between the believers and unbelievers, Abu l-Qasim Mahmud ibn Umar al-Zamakhshari (467–538/1144–1075) insisted that He has more than one type of reward.[20] Abd Allah ibn Umar al-Baydawi (d. 685/1286) asserted that God 'rewards each of them what is proper for each, and admits him into the place prepared for him'.[21] According to Imad al-Din Isma'il ibn Umar ibn Kathir (d. 774/1373), 'The Most High knows all about the people of these various religions, whether believers or the equivalent among the Jews, and Sabi'ans . . . and the Christians, and the Zoroastrians, and those who are polytheists . . . Verily, it is the Most High who "distinguishes between them on Resurrection Day".'[22] Most exegetes, like Ibn Kathir, simply reserved judgement for God.

A few commentators, however, hazarded opinions about which groups would be found wanting on Judgement Day. Abu Ja'far Muhammad ibn Jarir al-Tabari (d. 310/923) gave what is perhaps the most optimistic opinion of Q 22: 17 for the adherents of other faiths. He implied that God distinguishes between hypocrites and true believers without regard for religion. Yet he also reproduced the harsh interpretation of Qatada ibn Di'ama (d. 117/735), a Successor to the Companions of the Prophet: 'There are six religions [Islam, Christianity, Judaism, Sabi'anism, Zoroastrianism, polytheism]. Five belong to Satan; one belongs to God.'[23] Centuries later, Abu l-Fadl Abd al-Rahman ibn Abi Bakr al-Suyuti (849–911/1445–1505) similarly explained that the verse condemns all but the believers to hellfire.[24] Only Fakhr al-Din Razi (544–606/1149–1210) endeavoured to differentiate the groups mentioned in this verse: 'It is certain that of all the religions, God mentioned the six in this verse on account of their differences regarding the prophets, peace be upon them.'[25] He clarified that Muslims, Jews, Christians and Sabi'ans follow true prophets while Zoroastrians follow would-be prophets (Ar., *ittibā' al-mutanabbi'*) and polytheists do not follow prophets at all. Suffice it to say, none of these exegetes identified Zoroastrians as People of the Book, and this verse did not figure prominently in early Islamic debates about their status in society.

The Transcription of the Avesta

Early Muslims did not consider Zoroastrians to be People of the Book even though the Avesta may have existed in written form by the seventh century. Its precise date of transcription is uncertain. Priests orally transmitted the sacred liturgy for centuries, but there is not conclusive evidence for a written Avesta in the Sasanian era.[26] Nevertheless, research by Alberto Cantera indicates that the Pahlavi script used to write the Avesta predates the Islamic conquest of Iran. He estimates its invention between the fifth and seventh centuries.[27] Philip Huyse proposes the sixth century, especially during the reign of Khusrau I Anushirvan (531–579).[28] Xavier Tremblay cautions that there may have been partial transcriptions of the Avesta at various times, meaning scholars might expect more than a single archetype.[29] Based on the philological and paleographic evidence, it seems likely that the Avesta was at least partially written by the late Sasanian period.

Other Zoroastrian texts were composed in the caliphal era. Zoroastrians committed *The Book of a Thousand Judgements* (*Mātikān i hazār dātistān*), a primary source of Sasanian law, to writing in the early Islamic era.[30] The priest Adurfarnbag i Farroxzadan supposedly compiled the *Denkard* – a compendium of Zoroastrian doctrine and praxis – in Baghdad in the ninth century, but its final redaction came in the tenth century.[31] Other collections of priestly *responsa* appeared in these centuries.[32] Perhaps the earliest suggestion from within the Good Religion that Zoroaster brought a 'book' appears in the *Zaratusht-nama*, a biography of the Prophet written in New Persian at Rayy during the thirteenth century. It describes Zoroaster as a messenger with a scripture, almost in an Islamic mould.[33]

Muslims seem to have attributed a book to Zoroastrians by the tenth century. The geographer Muhammad ibn Ahmad al-Muqaddasi, writing in approximately 355/966, reported, 'I went into the fire temple of Khūz and asked what their God said in their book. They showed me their manuscripts (*ṣuḥuf*) and explained to me what the Pahlavi text said.'[34] In Abu Hanifa Ahmad ibn Dawud al-Dinawari's (d. 281 or 282/894–895 or before 290/902–903) historical text, *al-Akhbar al-Tiwal*, Zoroaster brings to King Bishtasif [Gushtasp] 'the book which is in the hands of the Magi'.[35] Muhammad ibn Ahmad al-Khwarazmi categorises Zoroastrians with the Hindus, Buddhists and Sabi'ans – People without a Book – in his *Mafatih al-'Ulum*, an encyclopedia of scientific knowledge written approximately 367/977. However, he noted that the Avesta was 'the sacred book of the Zoroastrians which Zarādusht, whom they claim as their prophet, brought'.[36] In the heresiographical text *al-Farq bayn al-Firaq*, Abd al-Qahir ibn Tahir al-Baghdadi (d. 329/1037) attempted to refute the Qadarite philosophy of al-Qasim al-Dimashqi, who argued that the same letters of the alphabet used to write the Qur'an also comprise 'the book of Zoroaster of the Magians'.[37] These vague and sometimes polemical descriptions of Zoroastrian scripture suggest that Muslims generally ascribed a sacred book to the Good Religion by the tenth century.

It does not follow, however, that Muslims considered Zoroastrians to be People of the Book. The Hanafi jurist Abu Bakr al-Jassas (305–370/917–982) argued emphatically that Zoroastrians were not People of the Book because they did not read the Bible or Qur'an.

> Zoroastrians do not profess anything from the books of God revealed to His prophets. Rather, they read the book of Zoroaster. He was a lying would-be prophet (*kāna mutanabbiyan kadhdhāban*). Hence they are not People of the Book . . . They are not now professing anything from the books of God the Exalted.[38]

The political philosopher Abu l-Hasan al-Mawardi (364–450/974–1058) classified Zoroastrians as people with 'the semblance of a book' (Ar., *shubhat kitāb*), as did Muhammad ibn Abd al-Karim al-Shahrastani (479–548/1086–1153), the philosopher of religion.[39] It is rare to find Zoroastrians described as People of the Book outside of a few isolated reports.

Zoroastrians in Hadith

Collections of hadith generally affirm that early Muslims did not consider Zoroastrians to be People of the Book. Nevertheless, a few reports suggest that Zoroastrians had a sacred text. Abd Allah ibn Abbas (68/686–688), for example, states in the *Sunan* of Abu Da'ud Sulayman ibn al-Ash'ath al-Sijistani (202–275/817–889) that the Good Religion was inspired by the devil: 'When the Persians' prophet died, Satan wrote Zoroastrianism for them' (*inna ahla fārisa lammā māta nabiyyuhum kataba lahum iblīsu al-majūsiyya*).[40] While this report does not attribute a book to Zoroastrians, it does imply that their religion was textual. Two reports narrated on the authority of Ali ibn Abi Talib assert that Zoroastrians lost their scripture. Both of them appear in Abu Yusuf Ya'qub ibn Ibrahim's (d. 182/798) *Kitab al-Kharaj*. 'Ali, may God honor him, said: I am the most knowledgeable person about them [Zoroastrians]. They were people of a book that they used to read and a religious tradition that they used to study until it was stricken from their hearts (*Kānū ahla kitābin yaqra'ūnahu wa-'ilmin yadrusūnahu fa-nuzi'a min ṣudūrihim*).'[41]

The second report clarifies the first. It suggests that Zoroastrians lost their book after adopting the doctrine of consanguineous marriage.

> The Zoroastrians were a nation who possessed a religious book which they used to study. One of their kings one day got drunk and took his sister to a place outside of the town. He was followed by four of his priests who witnessed his copulation with his sister. When he sobered [up], he was

> told by his sister that the only way to save himself from being punished by death for what he had done in the presence of the four priests was to declare the act lawful and call it 'Adam's law' because Eve was part of the body of Adam. He followed her advice and ordered accordingly, killing all who were against it. He then threatened to put to fire any objector and this brought them to submit to the new law. The Prophet accepted the jizya from them for their original religious book but did not allow intermarriage and sharing of food with them.[42]

This report has obviously been shaped to appeal to a Muslim audience. The number of witnesses to the rape meets the Qur'anic threshold of four; the origin of humanity is the Semitic duo Adam and Eve rather than the singular Persian Gayomart; and the king punishes with fire, a holy element in Zoroastrianism that would have been polluted thereby. Alternately worded hadith suggested that this incestuous practice entered their books and was never purged.[43] Abu Ubayd did not consider reports from Ali on this issue to be authentic or reliably transmitted.[44] He insisted that they had been invented by those who wished to justify the taxation of Zoroastrians.

Indeed, both hadith are excerpts from larger reports that advocate for the taxation of Zoroastrians. Therefore, fiscal concerns are inseparable from debates about the existence of a Zoroastrian book. There were other issues at stake as well, including the integrity of the Islamic legal system. In the seventh century, Muslim raids on Byzantine and Sasanian territories had led to the collapse or retreat of imperial defences, bringing large populations of non-Arabs and non-Muslims under the jurisdiction of the caliphs. Individual commanders made unique agreements with each city that surrendered.[45] In the centuries afterward, Muslims jurists developed standardised codes of conduct for war and diplomacy based on Qur'anic principles and the example of Muhammad.[46] They stipulated that Muslims must invite non-Muslim adversaries to convert to Islam before combat. People of the Book who refused the invitation could be fought until they submitted to taxation. Communities without a book, by contrast, were not eligible to pay jizya. In theory, their only option was to convert or fight.[47]

The implications of this idealised conception of war were potentially significant. If Zoroastrians lacked a book, they should not have been taxed.

Yet the caliphs had clearly accepted jizya from them. As we will see, some Muslims struggled to reconcile this fact with theoretical norms. Hence the propagation of reports suggesting that Zoroastrians once had a book. Other transmitters suggested that it was the Prophet Muhammad's decision to tax Zoroastrians and that Muslims should follow his example, regardless of whether Zoroastrians had a book.

The Taxation of Zoroastrians

Numerous hadith in Ahmad ibn Yahya ibn Jabir al-Baladhuri's *Futuh al-Buldan* and Abu Yusuf's *Kitab al-Kharaj* suggest that the Prophet Muhammad set the precedent for taxing Zoroastrians when he collected jizya from the people of Bahrayn (a region encompassing most of the eastern littoral of the Arabian Peninsula, whose capital was Hajar). The authors of these two works attempted to resolve questions of taxation by reference to Muhammad's custom. Abu Yusuf did so explicitly at the behest of the Abbasid caliph Harun al-Rashid (r. 170–193/786–809). Al-Baladhuri's work about the Islamic conquests also sought to ground Abbasid fiscal policy in prophetic precedent, especially in the chapters on Yemen and Bahrayn.

Most reports suggest that Muhammad's deputy, al-'Ala' al-Hadrami (d. 14/635 or 21/642), was the first Muslim to tax Zoroastrians.[48] He was governor of Bahrayn from the Prophet's era through the caliphate of Umar.[49] It is not clear when Muhammad first dispatched him to collect tribute from the people of Bahrayn. Al-Baladhuri reported both the year 6 and 8 AH.[50] Yet Abu Ubayd said that Abu Ubayda ibn al-Jarrah was sent to collect tax from Bahrayn and returned with its revenue after the Prophet made peace with the people and appointed al-'Ala' as the *amir*.[51] Al-Baladhuri reported elsewhere that there was no fighting in Bahrayn during the Prophet's lifetime, but that al-'Ala' besieged Zara (a Persian stronghold at Hajar) during the caliphate of Abu Bakr, perhaps in 12/633.[52] The city did not fall until the caliphate of Umar, which makes his administration the logical point at which the question of taxation arose.

While al-'Ala' imposed tax on Bahrayn, he may not have deliberately set a precedent for collecting it from Zoroastrians. Al-Baladhuri preserves a copy of his agreement with the region's inhabitants.

> In the name of God, the Merciful, the Compassionate. These are the terms agreed upon between al-'Alā' al-Ḥaḍramī and the people of Bahrayn. It is agreed that they will save us the trouble of work and divide with us the dates. Whosoever of them fails to keep this, may the curse of God, the angels, and the world altogether be upon him. As for the jizya, al-'Alā' assessed one dinar on every adult.[53]

Significantly, this version of the agreement does not mention the Prophet. Nor does it indicate the religious affiliation of the Bahraynis, even though al-Baladhuri prefaces this report by stating that the population was a mixture of polytheists, Jews and Zoroastrians. The final clause, which sets the rate of jizya at one dinar, appears to have been added after the fact; the treaty mentions only a tribute paid in dates. In fact, the agreement presumes the existence of an agrarian economy at Bahrayn, and consequently asks the people to surrender a portion of their harvest. Its terms resemble those of Khaybar, which Muhammad conquered a year earlier.[54] The jizya clause, by contrast, presumes the existence of a monetised economy, demanding that non-Muslims pay tax in gold coins. If al-'Ala' (rather than Muhammad) secured an unspecified amount of dates (not coinage) as tribute from the people of Bahrayn (undifferentiated by religion), why do many other reports instead suggest that the Prophet accepted jizya from the region's Zoroastrians?

Harmonising Reports

It seems that transmitters edited hadith about Muhammad collecting tax from Zoroastrians at Bahrayn and Yemen in order to harmonise them and thereby create a consistent precedent. For example, the following report appears in al-Baladhuri's account of the conquest of Yemen: 'The Prophet collected jizya from the Zoroastrians of Hajar and the Zoroastrians of Yemen and assessed one dinar or its equivalent in clothes on every adult male or female from the Zoroastrians of Yemen.'[55] This report begins by mentioning Hajar (Bahrayn) because that was supposedly the earliest precedent for taxing Zoroastrians. Then it insists that the Prophet did the same at Yemen, at the rate of one dinar or its equivalent in cloth. As noted above, the report about al-'Ala' accepting jizya from the people of Bahrayn mentions that he did so at the rate of one dinar, despite the fact that his written agreement with them only stipulates a share of their dates. Nearly every report about the collection of jizya at Yemen sets the tax rate at one dinar; no other report about Bahrayn does so. Thus, there appears to have been an attempt to reconcile these accounts by making the same amount due in Hajar as in Yemen.

A hadith in Abu Yusuf's *Kitab al-Kharaj* seemingly confirms that reports about taxing Zoroastrians at Yemen and Bahrayn were harmonised after the fact. Abu Yusuf notes that Muhammad sent a letter to al-Mundhir ibn Sawa, the leader of Bahrayn, inviting his people to convert to Islam. There are two versions of this letter in *Kitab al-Kharaj*. The first version explicitly demands that the Zoroastrians of Bahrayn pay jizya.[56] The second version states that those who refuse to become Muslims (their religion is not specified) must pay one dinar, or the equivalent in Maʿafiri cloth, as jizya. (The content of these letters is analysed in greater depth in Chapter Three.) The stipulation that non-Muslims pay a dinar or its equivalent in cloth was a policy most often associated with Yemen, not Bahrayn. Reports in the tax manuals of Abu Ubayd and Abu Dawud explicitly state that Maʿafiri cloth was a substitute for jizya in Yemen.[57] Indeed, Maʿafiri cloth takes its name from the village of Maʿafir, near the city of Taʿizz in Yemen.[58] Clearly, in the second version of the Prophet's letter, someone has applied information from a hadith about Yemen to a report about Bahrayn, where the Prophet supposedly set the precedent for taxing Zoroastrians.

There is further evidence that reports of taxation from Yemen and Bahrayn were later reconciled or at least confused. In Yahya ibn Adam's (d. 203/818) *Kitab al-Kharaj*, the Prophet instructs Muʿadh ibn Jabal to collect one dinar or its equivalent in cloth from the men and women of Yemen.[59] Most tax collectors stipulated that jizya should only be collected from men. Hence Yahya commented, 'We never heard of jizya imposed on women except in this tradition and in a tradition from ʿAmr on the authority of al-Hasan about the Zoroastrians'.[60] In other words, the only two times this Abbasid-era expert on early Islamic tax policy had ever encountered the notion that women should pay jizya was in this report about Yemen and in a similar report about Zoroastrians. Considering the foregoing evidence, it seems to be more than mere coincidence.

'I Do Not Know How I Will Deal with the Zoroastrians'

Hadith transmitters may have harmonised reports about taxing Zoroastrians because there was not a clear precedent. The caliph Umar was certainly ambivalent about accepting jizya from followers of the Good Religion. According to a report in Abu Bakr Abd al-Razzaq ibn Hammam al-San'ani's (126–211/744–827) *Musannaf*, Umar initially refused to collect it. "Amr ibn Dīnār informed me on the authority of Bajāla al-Tamīmī that 'Umar ibn al-Khaṭṭāb did not want to take jizya from the Zoroastrians until 'Abd al-Raḥmān ibn 'Awf testified that the Messenger of God, may God bless him, took it from the Zoroastrians of Hajar.'[61] Other reports suggest that Umar was simply perplexed.

> The Emigrants (*Muhājirūn*) had a council (*majlis*) in the mosque. 'Umar used to sit in it with them and talk to them about matters from the provinces that came to his attention. One day he said: I do not know how I will deal with the Zoroastrians (*mā adrī kayfa aṣna' bi-l-majūs*). 'Abd al-Raḥmān ibn 'Awf stood and said: I testify that the Messenger of God, may God bless him, said: Follow the custom of the People of the Book with them (*sunnū bihim sunnat ahl al-kitāb*).[62]

Umar's dilemma, which is widely attested in the early Islamic sources, suggests that this prophetic guidance was not widely known. (The report is treated at length in Chapter Three.) If the Prophet had deliberately taxed Zoroastrians at Bahrayn, Yemen and Oman, it seems strange that Umar, one of his closest Companions, would have been unaware of it.[63] The Andalusi jurist Abu Muhammad Ali ibn Ahmad ibn Hazm (384–456/994–1064) sought to preempt this argument by listing many prophetic customs that Umar supposedly did not know. He went so far as to suggest that Umar might have received unwittingly a share of the jizya from the Zoroastrians of Bahrayn.[64]

Numerous hadith suggest that Umar was confused about taxing Zoroastrians, so the relatively few reports suggesting that his immediate predecessor, Abu Bakr, did so in accordance with the Prophet's example appear dubious.[65] They are ostensibly based on a hadith in which the Muslim general Khalid ibn al-Walid invited a Persian governor to pay jizya before the conquest of Iraq. This episode supposedly occurred during the caliphate of Abu Bakr (11–13/632–634). Sarah Bowen Savant has argued that Muslim authors in the Abbasid era shaped narratives about the conquest of Iraq to emphasise that Persians repeatedly rejected opportunities to convert to Islam.[66] This hadith seems to fit the pattern. Abu Ubayd, the Abbasid tax official, invoked the report as proof that Muhammad set a definitive precedent that Abu Bakr dutifully followed. But it fails to explain Umar's dilemma.

Contesting the Taxation of Zoroastrians

Umar's uncertainty about accepting jizya from Zoroastrians reflects a broader debate within the early Islamic community about the propriety of taxing People without a Book. Evidence of this controversy survives in the hadith corpus. The *Sunan* of Abu Da'ud, one of the six canonical Sunni hadith collections, records a tradition in which the *spahbed*, or Sasanian military governor, of Bahrayn visited the Prophet to ask an unspecified question. It is possible to infer the nature of the *spahbed*'s inquiry from Muhammad's answer and from the fact that this story appears in a section of Abu Da'ud's work entitled 'Levying Jizya from Zoroastrians'. Apparently, the *spahbed* (Ar., *al-Usbadhī* or *Asbadhī*) asked Muhammad if his people could submit to the Prophet's authority and retain their religion by paying jizya. As this report contains competing answers to the question, it reveals the struggle within the early Islamic community over the permissibility of taxing Zoroastrians. (The report has been divided into three parts for easier analysis even though it appears as one seamless narrative in *Sunan Abī Dā'ūd*.)

1. Muḥammad ibn Miskīn al-Yamāmī informed us that Yaḥyā ibn Ḥassān informed us that Hushaym informed us that Dāwud ibn Abī Hind told us on the authority of Qushayr ibn 'Amr on the authority of Bajāla ibn 'Abda on the authority of Ibn 'Abbās. He said: A man from the Asbadhiyyin of the people of Baḥrayn—who were the Zoroastrians of Hajar—came to the Messenger of God, may God bless him, and tarried with him. Then he emerged, so I asked him: What have God and His Messenger ruled regarding you all? He said: Evil. I said: How dare you! (*Mah!*) He said: [We must accept] Islam or be killed (*al-islām aw al-qatl*).

2. He [Bajāla] said: 'Abd al-Raḥmān ibn 'Awf said: He [the Prophet] accepted jizya from them.
3. Ibn 'Abbās said: The people adopted 'Abd al-Raḥmān ibn 'Awf's saying and abandoned what I heard from al-Asbadhī."[67]

The layers of this hadith reveal opposing viewpoints about accepting jizya from Zoroastrians. Part One encourages Muslims not to accommodate them. They must fight Zoroastrians like the polytheists of Arabia, presumably because they lack a book. Part Two endorses the taxation of Zoroastrians. It asserts that the Prophet set an example that subsequent generations of Muslims should follow. Part Three affirms that the permissive hadith represents the preferred prophetic precedent based on the consensus of the community.

Neverthless, Muslims remembered the reluctance of some caliphal administrators to accept jizya from Zoroastrians. Abu Musa al-Ash'ari, whom the Prophet sent to spread Islam in Yemen with Mu'adh ibn Jabal (the region's first tax collector), hesitated to tax them.[68] He said, 'Had I not seen my companions collecting the jizya from them – that is, the Zoroastrians – I would not have done it.'[69] At least one Muslim was willing to defend violently the notion that Muhammad taxed Zoroastrians, equating criticism of that policy with defamation of the Prophet.

> When Farwa ibn Nawfal al-Ashja'ī said that it was a grave mistake to accept the jizya from the Zoroastrians who are not People of the Book, he was challenged by al-Mustawrid ibn al-Aḥnāf to recant or be killed for speaking thus against the Prophet, who did accept jizya from the Zoroastrians of Hajar.[70]

Al-Mustawrid was a member of the Banu Tamim, an Arab tribe from Hajar. Tamimis had close relations with the Sasanian Empire before the advent of Islam, and some members of the tribe had converted to Zoroastrianism. A contingent of *asāwira*, or Sasanian heavy cavalry, settled among the Banu Tamim at Basra after defecting during the conquest of Iraq. Another Sasanian regiment, the Ḥamrā', was integrated with the Tamimi forces.[71]

Bajala ibn Abda, who reported Abd al-Rahman's layered statement about the Prophet collecting jizya from the Zoroastrians of Bahrayn, was a Tamimi too. Bajala was the secretary of Jaz' ibn Mu'awiya, a Tamimi who served as governor of Ahwaz. As soon as Umar learned from Abd al-Rahman that the Prophet had taxed Zoroastrians, Umar supposedly wrote to Jaz' instructing him to do likewise.[72] It is no coincidence that these permissive reports are narrated by members of the Banu Tamim. According to Michael Lecker, 'Some, perhaps many, Tamimis stood to benefit from the recognition by the Muslim state of the Zoroastrians as "People of the Book".'[73] The prospect of a self-interested tribe of Persianised Arabs advocating on behalf of Zoroastrians is an important reminder that – as Thomas Sizgorich, Michael Penn and Jack Tannous have demonstrated – sometimes ethnic, religious and imperial boundaries in Late Antiquity were fuzzy.[74] Some Muslims evidently had an interest in the accommodation of Zoroastrians.

Stifling Dissent

Such reports did not persuade everyone, though. Al-Mustawrid's willingness to violently defend the notion that Muhammad taxed Zoroastrians offers some insight into the construction of a normative Islamic discourse on the issue. Advocates of taxation employed several strategies to stifle dissent and delegitimise their critics. First, as we have already seen, they attributed the decision directly to the Messenger of God. Second, like al-Mustawrid, they reframed questions about accepting jizya from Zoroastrians as criticism of the Prophet. Third, proponents of taxing Zoroastrians labelled dissenters as 'Hypocrites'.

The Arabic term 'Hypocrites' (*al-munāfiqūn*), or waverers, denotes Muslims who questioned the Prophet's policies at Medina. They were among Muhammad's harshest critics during his wars with Mecca, so the term is extremely pejorative. The proponents of taxing Zoroastrians found Qur'anic justification for ignoring their opponents by labelling them Hypocrites. This much is evident in the *asbab al-nuzul* literature, which describes the reasons that particular verses of the Qur'an were revealed. According to Abu l-Hasan Ali ibn Ahmad al-Wahidi (d. 468/1076), one of the earliest authors in the genre, the controversy about collecting jizya from Zoroastrians resulted in the revelation of Q 5: 105. The verse reads, 'O you who believe! You are responsible for your own souls. He who errs cannot injure you if ye are rightly guided.' It encourages faithful Muslims to ignore their detractors.

According to al-Wahidi, the context for the revelation of this verse was a letter the Prophet sent to al-Mundhir ibn Sawa, the ruler of Bahrayn, inviting the people of that region to convert to Islam or pay jizya. The population consisted of Arabs (in this context, a synonym for polytheists), Jews, Christians, Sabi'ans and Zoroastrians – the complete roster of religions mentioned in Q 22: 17. Not coincidently, this is the only hadith of which I am aware that claims that there were Sabi'ans or Christians at Bahrayn. Al-Mundhir accepted Islam but wrote to the Prophet that the people of Bahrayn preferred to be taxed. Muhammad responded:

> As for the Arabs, [only accept Islam from them;] otherwise they will have nothing but the sword. As for the People of the Book and the Zoroastrians, accept the jizya from them. When this letter was read to them, the Arabs embraced Islam while the People of the Book and the Zoroastrians agreed to pay the jizya. The Hypocrites among the Arabs said: How strange from Muhammad! He claims that Allah has sent him to fight all people until they surrender to Allah and [that he only accepts jizya] from the People of the Book. But we only see that he has accepted from the idolaters of the people of Hajar that which he had rejected from the Arab idolaters. Allah, exalted is He, then revealed—'O you who believe! You are responsible for your own souls. He who errs cannot injure you if ye are rightly guided [Q 105: 5]'.[75]

These Hypocrites alleged that Zoroastrians were polytheists and therefore ineligible to pay jizya. In other words, Muhammad had violated Qur'anic principles by collecting tax from them. The revelation of Q 105: 5 rejected that notion, urging rightly guided conformists to ignore their faithless detractors. Such reports were undoubtedly intended to stifle dissent.

Early Muslim jurists dismissed questions about the propriety of taxing Zoroastrians. Abu Ubayd noted that legal experts like Rabi'a ibn Abi Abd al-Rahman (d. 135/753) responded curtly to such inquiries. "Abd Allāh ibn Sāliḥ informed us on the authority of al-Layth ibn Sa'd on the authority of 'Amr ibn al-Hārith. He said: I wrote to Rabī'a ibn Abī 'Abd al-Raḥmān asking him about the Zoroastrians. How was jizya fixed on them while the Arab polytheists were left [without recourse]?' Note that the seeming inconsistency of this policy was the same issue registered in the Hypocrites' complaint above. 'He wrote: There is enough for you in the affairs of those who have departed to relieve you of a question of this sort'.[76] For Rabi'a, the taxation of Zoroastrians was a settled issue not worth discussing further.

The Umayyad caliph Umar ibn Abd al-Aziz wrote a similar letter to al-Hasan al-Basri (21–110/624–728), which was preserved by Abu Ubayd.

> Ḥajjāj told us on the authority of Ḥammād ibn Salama on the authority of Ḥumayd. He said: 'Umar ibn 'Abd al-'Azīz wrote to al-Ḥasan asking him: On what basis did the imams (*a'imma*) who preceded us recognise the Zoroastrians marrying their mothers and daughters? He mentioned other things about their matter, naming them. Al-Ḥasan wrote to him: To proceed, aren't you a follower and not an innovator? Peace.[77]

Here Umar's question about consanguineous marriage and 'other things' pertaining to Zoroastrians does not explicitly mention taxation. But in other versions of the letter, al-Hasan al-Basri tells the caliph that Muslims must tolerate the Zoroastrians' polytheism (*shirk*) because they pay jizya.[78] It seems that al-Hasan al-Basri, too, dodged questions about the legality of taxing Zoroastrians.

Finally, the proponents of taxing Zoroastrians urged unquestioning obedience to prophetic precedent. For example, Abu Ubayd credits the second caliph Umar with piously enacting Muhammad's custom as soon as he learned of it:

> Do you not see that 'Umar, when 'Abd al-Raḥmān ibn 'Awf informed him on the authority of the Messenger of God, peace be upon him, that he took it [*jizya*] from them, arrived at that and accepted it from them? . . . When he found the tradition (*athar*) from the Messenger of God, peace be upon him, he obeyed it. He did not ask what was behind it.[79]

The implication is that devout Muslims should do likewise.

Conclusion

Early Muslims generally did not regard Zoroastrians as People of the Book. Qur'anic exegetes did not classify them as such, and the transcription of the Avesta seems not to have been a factor. Rather, transmitters of hadith remembered that Muslims had accepted jizya from the Zoroastrians of Hajar.

Umar's reluctance to tax them suggests that this precedent was not widely known, if it had been consciously made prior to his reign. Taxing People without a Book was controversial because it appeared to violate emerging legal ideals. Members of the Banu Tamim, an Arabian tribe that may have benefited from the integration of Zoroastrians into the caliphate, defended the idea that Muhammad had collected jizya from followers of the Good Religion. Early Muslim jurists, affirming the status quo, circumvented criticism of past practice by dismissing inquiries and promoting pious examples of compliance. They remained ambivalent about the accommodation of Zoroastrians and, as the next chapter argues, sought to limit it.

Notes

1. Abū Ja'far Muḥammad ibn Jarīr al-Ṭabarī, *Tārīkh al-rusul wa-l-mulūk*, ed. M. J. de Goeje (Leiden: Brill, 1964), Secunda Series, vol. 3, 1636; compare Abū Ja'far Muḥammad ibn Jarīr al-Ṭabarī, *The End of Expansion*, trans. Khalid Yahya Blankinship, vol. 25, History of Al-Tabari (Albany: State University of New York Press, 1989), 168.
2. For the dihqan's religious identity, see Choksy, *Conflict and Cooperation*, 82; for the political context of the quote, see Haug, *The Eastern Frontier*, 135.
3. Rose, *Zoroastrianism: An Introduction*, Chapter 9.
4. Stausberg, "Invention of a Canon".
5. As exceptions, see Daniel J. Sheffield, 'In the Path of the Prophet: Medieval and Early Modern Narratives of the Life of Zarathustra in Islamic Iran and Western India' (Ph.D. Dissertation, Harvard University, 2012); Kianoosh Rezania, 'The Dēnkard against Its Islamic Discourse', *Der Islam* 94, no. 2 (2017): 336–62.
6. Jamsheed K. Choksy, 'Zoroastrians in Muslim Iran: Selected Problems of Coexistence and Interaction during the Early Medieval Period', *Iranian Studies* 20, no. 1 (1987): 27.
7. *Encyclopaedia of Islam*, 2nd ed. (Leiden: Brill, 1960), s.v. 'ahl al-kitab'.
8. s.v. 'ahl al-dhimma'.
9. Stausberg, 'Invention of a Canon', 257.
10. Ignaz Goldziher, *Introduction to Islamic Theology and Law*, trans. Andras and Ruth Hamori (Princeton, NJ: Princeton University Press, 1981), 15.
11. Khanbaghi, *The Fire, the Star and the Cross*, 25.
12. Jacques Waardenburg (ed.), *Muslim Perceptions of Other Religions: A Historical Survey* (New York: Oxford University Press, 1999), 6; Guy Monnot, 'Les

religions dans le miroir de l'islam', in *Islam et religions* (Paris: Maisonneuve et Larose, 1986), 123; Guy Monnot, 'Sabéens et idolâtres selon 'Abd al-Jabbār', in *Islam et religions* (Paris: Maisonneuve et Larose, 1986), 91.

13. *EI2*, s.v. 'Madjus' (Michael Morony); Friedmann, *Tolerance and Coercion in Islam*, 72; Saâd Ghrab, 'Islam and Non-Scriptural Spirituality', *Islamochristiana* 14 (1988): 56.
14. Guy Monnot, 'L'echo musulman aux religions d'Iran', *Islamochristiana* 3 (1977): 96.
15. Bürgel, 'Zoroastrians as Viewed in Medieval Islamic Sources', 202.
16. On the Qur'anic definition of believers, see Fred M. Donner, *Muhammad and the Believers: At the Origins of Islam* (Cambridge, MA: Harvard University Press, 2010).
17. Muḥammad ibn Aḥmad al-Qurṭubī, *al-Jāmiʿ li-aḥkām al-Qur'ān*, ed. Aḥmad 'Abd al-'Alīm Baraddūnī (Beirut: Iḥyā' al-Turāth al-'Arabī, 1985), 12:22.
18. al-Ḥusayn ibn Mas'ūd al-Baghawī, *Ma'ālim al-tanzīl*, ed. Muḥammad 'Abd Allāh Nimr, 'Uthmān Jum'ah Ḍumayrīyah, and Sulaymān Muslim Ḥarash (Riyadh, Saudi Arabia: Dār al-Ṭībah, 1993), 5:371.
19. Muḥammad ibn Ya'qūb Fīrūzābādī, *Tanwīr al-miqbās min Tafsīr Ibn 'Abbās*, trans. Mokrane Guezzou, Great Commentaries on the Holy Qur'an 2 (Louisville, KY: Fons Vitae; and Amman, Jordan: Royal Aal al-Bayt Institute for Islamic Thought, 2008), 422–23.
20. Maḥmūd ibn 'Umar Zamakhsharī, *al-Kashshāf 'an ḥaqā'iq ghawāmiḍ al-tanzīl*, ed. Muhammad Alyan Marzuqi (Beirut: Dar al-Kitab al-Arabi, 1966), 3:147.
21. 'Abd Allāh ibn 'Umar Bayḍāwī, *Beidhawii Commentarius in Coranum*, ed. Heinrich Leberecht Fleischer (Osnabrück: Biblio, 1968), 1:629.
22. Ismā'īl ibn 'Umar Ibn Kathīr, *Tafsīr al-Qur'ān al-'aẓīm* (Beirut: Dār al-Jīl, 1988), 3:104.
23. Abū Ja'far Muḥammad ibn Jarīr al-Ṭabarī, *Jāmi' al-bayān fī tafsīr al-Qur'ān*, ed. al-Ḥasan ibn Muḥammad Nīsābūrī (Bayrūt: Dār al-Ma'rifah, 1989), 9:97–98.
24. Jalāl al-Dīn Muḥammad ibn Aḥmad Maḥallī and Jalāl al-Dīn 'Abd al-Raḥmān ibn Abī Bakr Suyūṭī, *Tafsīr al-Jalālayn*, trans. Feras Hamza (Louisville, KY: Fons Vitae, 2008), 308–9.
25. Fakhr al-Dīn Muḥammad ibn 'Umar Rāzī, *Mafātīḥ al-ghayb wa-bi-hāmishih Tafsīr Abī al-Sa'ūd* (Cairo: al-Matba'ah al-Amirah al-Sharafiyah, 1890), 6:173.
26. Alberto Cantera (ed.), *The Transmission of the Avesta* (Wiesbaden, Germany: Harrassowitz, 2012), xiii.

27. Alberto Cantera, *Studien zur Pahlavi-Übersetzung des Avesta*, Iranica 7 (Wiesbaden: Harrassowitz, 2004), 135–62; English summary in Philip Huyse, 'Late Sasanian Society between Orality and Literacy', in Vesta Sarkhosh and Sarah Stewart (eds), *The Sasanian Era*, vol. 3, The Idea of Iran (London: I. B. Tauris, 2008), 144–45.
28. Huyse, 'Late Sasanian Society between Orality and Literacy', 145–48.
29. Xavier Tremblay, 'Ibant Obscuri Uaria Sub Nocte: Les Textes Avestiques et Leurs Recensions Des Sassanides Aux XIIIe s. Ad En Particulier d'après l'alphabet Avestique. Notes de Lecture Avestiques VIII', in Alberto Cantera (ed.), *Transmission of the Avesta* (Wiesbaden, Germany: Harrassowitz, 2012), 117, 131.
30. J. P. de Menasce, 'Questions Concerning the Mazdaeans of Muslim Iran', in Robert G. Hoyland (ed.), *Muslims and Others in Early Islamic Society* (Aldershot: Ashgate, 2002), 331–41.
31. *Encyclopaedia Iranica*, s.v. 'Denkard'; see also Rezania, 'The Dēnkard against Its Islamic Discourse'.
32. J. P. de Menasce, 'Zoroastrian Literature after the Muslim Conquest', in Richard N. Frye (ed.), *Cambridge History of Iran*, vol. 4 (Cambridge: Cambridge University Press, 1975), 543–65.
33. Sheffield, 'In the Path of the Prophet', 35, 249.
34. Quoted in Monnot, 'L'echo musulman aux religions d'Iran', 87.
35. Quoted in Savant, *New Muslims of Post-Conquest Iran*, 154.
36. C. E. Bosworth, 'Al-Khwārazmī on Various Faiths and Sects, Chiefly Iranian', in D. Amin, M. Kasheff, and A. Sh. Shabbazi (eds), *Iranica Varia: Papers in Honor of Professor Ehsan Yarshater*, vol. 30, Acta Iranica (Leiden: Brill, 1990), 10–19.
37. 'Abd al-Qāhir Ibn Ṭāhir al-Baghdādī, *al-Farq bayn al-firaq (Moslem Schisms and Sects)*, trans. Kate Chambers Seelye, reprint of 1920 edition, vol. 1 (New York: AMS Press, 1966), 206; see also *al-Farq bayn al-firaq (Moslem Schisms and Sects)*, trans. Abraham Halkin, vol. 2 (Tel-Aviv: Palestine Publishing Co., 1935), 132.
38. Aḥmad ibn 'Alī al-Jaṣṣāṣ, *Kitāb Aḥkām al-Qur'ān*, ed. Muhammad Sadiq al-Qamhawi (Beirut: Dar al-Ihya al-Turath al-Arabi, 1984), 3:327–328.
39. Friedmann, *Tolerance and Coercion in Islam*, 71.
40. Abū Dā'ūd Sulaymān ibn al-Ash'ath al-Sijistānī, *Sunan Abu Dawud*, trans. Ahmad Hasan (Lahore: Sh. M. Ashraf, 1984), 863–64.
41. Abū Yūsuf Ya'qūb ibn Ibrāhīm al-Kūfī, *Kitāb al-kharāj*, ed. Mahmud Baji (Tunis: Dar Busalamah, 1984), 132; compare *Kitāb al-kharāj*, trans. Adam Ben Shemesh, vol. 3, *Taxation in Islam* (Leiden: Brill, 1969), 88.

42. Abū Yūsuf Ya'qūb ibn Ibrāhīm al-Kūfī, *Taxation in Islam*, 3:88–89; Abū Yūsuf Ya'qūb ibn Ibrāhīm al-Kūfī, *Kitāb al-kharāj*, ed. Taha Abd al-Ra'uf Sa'd and Sa'd Hasan Muhammad (Cairo: al-Maktaba al-Azhariyya lil-Turath, 1999), 1:143.
43. 'Abd al-Razzāq ibn Hammām al-Ḥimyarī al-Ṣan'ānī, *al-Muṣannaf*, ed. Ḥabīburraḥmān A'ẓamī (Bayrūt: Tawzī' al-Maktab al-Islāmī, 1983), 6:70–71.
44. Abū 'Ubayd al-Qāsim ibn Sallām, *Kitāb al-amwāl* (Bayrut: Dar al-Shuruq, 1989), 42; Abū 'Ubayd al-Qāsim ibn Sallām, *The Book of Revenue*, trans. Imran Ahsan Khan Nyazee (Reading: Garnet, 2002), 32, 498.
45. For the most recent treatment of this period, see Hoyland, *In God's Path: The Arab Conquests and the Creation of an Islamic Empire.*
46. On divergent interpretations of these general principles by subsequent generations of exegetes, see Asma Afsaruddin, *Striving in the Path of God: Jihad and Martyrdom in Islamic Thought* (New York: Oxford University Press, 2013).
47. Majid Khadduri, *War and Peace in the Law of Islam* (Baltimore: Johns Hopkins Press, 1955), 75, 80.
48. Abū Yūsuf Ya'qūb ibn Ibrāhīm al-Kūfī, *Kitāb al-kharāj*, 1984, 133.
49. Michael Lecker, 'The Preservation of Muhammad's Letters', in *People, Tribes, and Society in Arabia around the Time of Muhammad* (Aldershot: Ashgate, 2005), 7.
50. Aḥmad ibn Yaḥyá al-Balādhurī, *Kitāb futūḥ al-buldān*, ed. M. J. de Goeje (Leiden: Brill, 2014), 78–79; al-Balādhurī, *The Origins of the Islamic State*, 1:121.
51. Abū 'Ubayd al-Qāsim ibn Sallām, *Kitāb al-amwāl*, 82; Abū 'Ubayd al-Qāsim ibn Sallām, *The Book of Revenue*, 30.
52. al-Balādhurī, *Kitāb futūḥ al-buldān*, 2014, 80; al-Balādhurī, *The Origins of the Islamic State*, 129–30; on Zara, see Michael Lecker, 'The Levying of Taxes for the Sassanians in Pre-Islamic Medina (Yathrib)', *Jerusalem Studies in Arabic and Islam* 27 (2002): 120–23.
53. al-Balādhurī, *Kitāb futūḥ al-buldān*, 1956, 1:95; al-Balādhurī, *The Origins of the Islamic State*, 121.
54. Yaḥyā ibn Ādam, *Kitab al-Kharaj*, trans. A. Ben Shemesh, vol. 1, *Taxation in Islam* (Leiden: Brill, 1967), 39; see also Emon, *Religious Pluralism and Islamic Law*, Chapter 1.
55. al-Balādhurī, *Kitāb futūḥ al-buldān*, 2014, 71; al-Balādhurī, *The Origins of the Islamic State*, 110.
56. Abū Yūsuf Ya'qūb ibn Ibrāhīm al-Kūfī, *Kitāb al-kharāj*, 1999, 1:144; Abū Yūsuf Ya'qūb ibn Ibrāhīm al-Kūfī, *Taxation in Islam*, 3:89.

57. Abū 'Ubayd al-Qāsim ibn Sallām, *The Book of Revenue*, 25; Abū Dā'ūd Sulaymān ibn al-Ash'ath al-Sijistānī, *Sunan Abu Dawud*, 2:863.
58. *EI2*, s.v. 'Ma'afir'.
59. See similar reports in Abū 'Ubayd al-Qāsim ibn Sallām, *The Book of Revenue*, 25.
60. Yaḥyā ibn Ādam, *Kitāb al-kharāj*, ed. Aḥmad Muḥammad Shākir, 2nd ed. (Cairo: al-Maṭba'ah al-Salafīyah wa-Maktabatuhā, 1964), 68–69; Yaḥyā ibn Ādam, *Kitab al-Kharaj*, 1:60.
61. al-Ṣan'ānī, *al-Muṣannaf*, 6:68.
62. al-Balādhurī, *Kitāb futūḥ al-buldān*, 1956, 2:327; al-Balādhurī, *The Origins of the Islamic State*, 424.
63. On Oman, see al-Balādhurī, *The Origins of the Islamic State*, 118.
64. M. J. Kister, 'Social and Religious Concepts of Authority in Islam', *Jerusalem Studies in Arabic and Islam* 18 (1994): 90.
65. Abū 'Ubayd al-Qāsim ibn Sallām, *The Book of Revenue*, 32; Qudāmah ibn Ja'far, *Kitāb al-kharāj*, trans. Adam Ben Shemesh, vol. 2, *Taxation in Islam* (Leiden: Brill, 1965), 42–43.
66. Savant, *New Muslims of Post-Conquest Iran*, Chapter 6.
67. Abū Dā'ūd Sulaymān ibn al-Ash'ath al-Sijistānī, *Sunan Abu Dawud*, 2:864.
68. *EI2*, s.v. 'Abu Musa al-Ash'ari'.
69. Abū 'Ubayd al-Qāsim ibn Sallām, *The Book of Revenue*, 33.
70. Abū Yūsuf Ya'qūb ibn Ibrāhīm al-Kūfī, *Taxation in Islam*, 3:88–89.
71. *EI2*, s.v. 'Tamim'.
72. Abū Yūsuf Ya'qūb ibn Ibrāhīm al-Kūfī, *Taxation in Islam*, 3:88.
73. *EI2*, s.v. 'Tamim'.
74. Sizgorich, *Violence and Belief in Late Antiquity*; Penn, *Envisioning Islam: Syriac Christians and the Early Muslim World*; Tannous, *The Making of the Medieval Middle East.*
75. Abū l-Ḥasan 'Alī Vāḥidī Nīshābūrī, *Al-Wāḥidī's Asbāb al-Nuzūl*, Great Commentaries on the Holy Qur'an 3 (Louisville, KY: Fons Vitae, 2008), 102; see also al-Balādhurī, *The Origins of the Islamic State*, 121.
76. Abū 'Ubayd al-Qāsim ibn Sallām, *Kitāb al-amwāl*, 45; compare Abū 'Ubayd al-Qāsim ibn Sallām, *The Book of Revenue*, 34.
77. Abū 'Ubayd al-Qāsim ibn Sallām, *Kitāb al-amwāl*, 45; Abū 'Ubayd al-Qāsim ibn Sallām, *The Book of Revenue*, 33–34.
78. al-Ṣan'ānī, *al-Muṣannaf*, 6:50–51 #9976.
79. Abū 'Ubayd al-Qāsim ibn Sallām, *Kitāb al-amwāl*, 43–44; Abū 'Ubayd al-Qāsim ibn Sallām, *The Book of Revenue*, 33.

3

Marriage, Meat and the Limits of Accommodation

In the late eighth century, the Abbasid official Abu Yusuf produced a taxation manual called *Kitab al-Kharaj*. In it, he acknowledges that it is permissible for Muslims to tax Zoroastrians, but followers of the Good Religion remained beyond the pale of other forms of intercommunal contact. The section on taking jizya from Zoroastrians begins with this statement:

> The people of *shirk* among the idol worshippers and the fire worshippers and the Zoroastrians are not the equivalent of the People of the Book in terms of slaughtered animals and marriageable women, on account of what came from the Prophet, peace be upon him, regarding that. It is what the community and the practice [agree] upon, and there is no difference of opinion about it. (*Wa-laysa ahl al-shirk min ʿabadat al-awthān wa-ʿabadat al-nīrān wa-l-majūsi fī l-dhabāʾiḥi wa-l-munākaḥati ʿalā l-mithli mā ʿalayhi ahl al-kitāb li-mā jāʾa ʿan al-nabī ṣallā allāhu ʿalayhi wa-sallama fī dhālika wa-huwa alladhī ʿalayhi al-jamāʿatu wa-l-ʿamal wa-lā ikhtilāfa fīhi*).[1]

According to Abu Yusuf (died 182/798), Muslim men should not wed Zoroastrian women nor consume meat butchered by adherents of the Good Religion. By contrast, Muslim men could marry Jewish or Christian women, and those religious communities were capable of slaughtering animals in a ritually acceptable manner, as endorsed by the Qur'an (5: 5).[2] When did this prohibition on marriage and meat originate? What was its significance? What effect might it have had on cross-confessional interaction in early Islamicate history? And was there truly no difference on opinion on the matter?

Ideology and Memory

To answer these questions, one might begin in the realm of memory. Pierre Nora and Maurice Halbwachs have demonstrated the importance of memory in the writing of history.[3] Individuals choose to remember or forget information about the past that helps them to explain the present. Collective memories form the basis of societies as well as religions. Historians may write national narratives that promote patriotism or communal narratives that inspire belief. They could discover 'new' memories to reinforce the status quo or encourage social change. They might forget 'old' memories for the same reasons. In Islamic Studies this phenomenon has been usefully documented by Sarah Bowen Savant and Antoine Borrut.[4] The previous chapter described Muslim efforts to remember prophetic precedents regarding the taxation of Zoroastrians. These precedents helped to justify accepting jizya from People without a Book, a decision that generated some controversy.

Georges Duby (1919–1996), a leading scholar of Memory Studies, argued that controversy often reveals the underlying ideological structures in a society. Changes in the material or political structure of society can quickly become ideological, creating conflict between systems. 'For the historian, the most revealing phase is the moment when conflict comes to an end: victory is followed by repression, and much information can be gathered from the records of investigations, interrogations and sentences which are held in judicial and police archives.'[5] In the study of ideology, Duby advised historians to pay special attention to behavioural manuals, which prescribe conduct and therefore reveal the issues at stake in a given struggle. Yet he acknowledged that it is important to distinguish between 'the mental representations of systems' and actual practice.[6] In other words, scholars must not mistake legal dictum for case law.

These insights inform the current study. While historians lack a judicial archive per se from the early caliphates, hadith collections preserve the competing rulings of jurists and thus expose the latent ideological structures of early Islamicate society. Furthermore, Abu Yusuf's *Kitab al-Kharaj* and sources like it can be compared to behaviour manuals that prescribe conduct. Together they form a judicial archive of sorts, incomplete and subjective but nonetheless useful to the historian of ideology. These sources reveal that most early Muslim jurists sought to limit the accommodation of Zoroastrians to taxation. In an effort to demarcate the boundary between followers of the Good Religion and People of the Book, they prohibited Muslims from marrying Zoroastrians or consuming meat slaughtered by them.

This chapter will explore the origins and implication of this ban, which circulated in conjunction with Abd al-Rahman ibn Awf's statement about the acceptability of taxing Zoroastrians (discussed in Chapter Two). The prohibition seems related to post-prophetic rulings regarding Sabi'ans and Banu Taghlib. Despite Abu Yusuf's statement, early Muslim jurists did not unanimously agree. Abu Thawr deemed it permissible to marry Zoroastrians and eat meat slaughtered by them. His ruling appears to rest on a hadith that urges Muslims to 'follow the custom of the People of the Book' with Zoroastrians. Most jurists interpreted this phrase as a variation of the prophetic permission to tax them. By the third/ninth century, representatives of the major Sunni legal schools had rejected the idea of marrying Zoroastrians or eating meat slaughtered by them. Their successful promulgation of the ban reveals the limits of accommodation.

Origins of a Prohibition

Although Abu Yusuf related many reports regarding the taxation of Zoroastrians, the idea that Muslims ought not to marry them or eat meat slaughtered by them is contained in a single hadith narrated on the authority of al-Hasan ibn Muhammad ibn al-Hanafiyya (d. circa 100/718). Hasan was the grandson of Ali ibn Abi Talib (d. 40/661), the Prophet's cousin and son-in-law. Hasan's father, Muhammad (d. 81/700), was the offspring of Ali's marriage to Khawla al-Hanafiyya. Muhammad was also the half-brother of Husayn, the famous Shi'i Imam and martyr. After the death of Husayn at Karbala, Muhammad ibn al-Hanafiyya became the object, although seemingly not the leader, of a revolt proclaimed at Kufa by Mukhtar against Umayyad authority.[7] It is unclear if Abu Hashim (d. 98/717–718), Hasan's full brother, engaged in politics, but he died without children. Hasan himself appears to have remained politically quiet, perhaps associated with the Murji'ite movement.[8] Hence some devotees of this branch of the Prophet's family looked to Husayn's descendants, Muhammad al-Baqir and Ja'far al-Sadiq (discussed below), for leadership.

Hasan ibn Muhammad did transmit hadith, though, including this influential report about Zoroastrians:

> Qays ibn al-Rabīʿ al-Asadī (died between 165–168/782–785) told us on the authority of Qays ibn Muslim al-Jadalī (d. 120/738) on the authority of al-Ḥasan ibn Muḥammad that he said: The Messenger of God, peace be upon him, made peace with the Zoroastrians of the people of Hajar on the basis of taking jizya from them. It is neither permissible to marry their women nor eat their slaughtered animals (*ghayra mustaḥillin munākaḥata nisāʾihim wa-lā akl dhabāʾiḥihim*).[9]

The last sentence of this report is seemingly the origin of the idea that Muslims should not marry Zoroastrians or eat animals slaughtered by them.

This prohibition is closely associated with Hasan ibn Muhammad. The very next report in Abu Yusuf's work advocates taking jizya from Zoroastrians but does not mention marriage or meat. Significantly, this second report also has a chain of transmission that does not include Hasan.[10] The prohibition is exclusive to reports narrated on the authority of Hasan in other collections as well. These reports allude to a letter that Muhammad wrote to the Zoroastrians of Hajar. Ibn Zanjawayh's (d. 251/855–856) *Kitab al-Amwal* states:

> Ḥumayd informed us that Abū Nuʿaym informed [him] that Sufyān informed [him] on the authority of Qays ibn Muslim [who narrated] on the authority of al-Ḥasan ibn Muḥammad. He said: The Messenger of God wrote to the Zoroastrians of Hajar inviting them to Islam. He accepted it from whomever submitted. Jizya was imposed on whomever refused, except that (*fī an*) a slaughtered animal of theirs is not to be eaten, and a woman of theirs is not to be married.[11]

In Ibn Abi Shayba's *Musannaf*, Hasan narrates that the Prophet wrote to Hajar, inviting its population to convert to Islam. Those who refused had to pay jizya 'on the condition that a slaughtered animal of theirs is not to be eaten and a woman of theirs is not to be married' (*ʿalā an lā tuʾkala la-hum dhabīḥatun wa-lā tunakaḥa la-hum imraʾatun*).[12] In al-Baladhuri's *Futuh al-Buldan*, Hasan reported that jizya would be imposed on Zoroastrians 'without eating their slaughtered animals and marrying their women' (*fī ghayr akl li-dhabā'iḥihim wa-lā nikāḥ li-nisā'ihim*).[13] One of the transmitters in al-Baladhuri's *isnad* is Yahya ibn Adam (d. 203/818), whose own taxation manual curiously does not include this hadith.

Many early Islamic sources contain a copy of the Prophet's letter. It is usually addressed to the Arab ruler of the region, al-Mundhir ibn Sawa. After conquering eastern Arabia in 575, the Sasanians garrisoned soldiers at Hajar and stationed a military commander, or *spahbed* (Ar., *Asbadh*) over the Arab tribes there. One of these tribes was the Banu Tamim.[14] Mundhir, also known as Abd Allah ibn Zayd ibn Abd Allah ibn Darim, was the ruler of the Arabs of Bahrayn (and Oman by some accounts).[15] The Persian governor (*marzubān*) of Hajar was Sībukht. Muhammad wrote to Mundhir – and the governor, according al-Baladhuri – either in the year 6 or 8 AH.[16] Abu Ubayd situated the letter in relation to the missives that the Prophet supposedly dispatched at the same time to the rulers of the Byzantine and Sasanian Empires.[17]

Although the letter does not contain the prohibition, Hasan's report appears to paraphrase parts of the letter. Abu Ubayd preserves three (very different) prophetic letters to Hajar, none of which forbids marrying Zoroastrians or eating the animals they butcher.[18] The version of the letter preserved by al-Tabari does not include the prohibition, but he added in a postscript that their women and slaughtered animals were impermissible.[19] Early Muslim historians generally agreed that Hajar's polytheistic Arabs converted to Islam in response to the letter while the Jewish and Zoroastrian populations declined, preferring to pay tax.[20] The Prophet allegedly coaxed, 'Whoever prays our prayers, and faces our *qibla*, and eats our slaughtered animal, that [person] is a Muslim. Whoever rejects that, *jizya* [will be] imposed on him.'[21] Variant wordings of this report specified that a Zoroastrian who did these things would be considered a 'submitter' (*muslim*), 'secure' (*āmin*) in the 'protection' (*dhimma*) of God and His Prophet.[22] The Jews and Zoroastrians of Hajar ultimately chose jizya. Apparently, among other things, they were unwilling to eat meat butchered by Muslims.

Sahnun ibn Sa'id (d. 240/854), an early Maliki jurist, preserved the most extensive version of the Prophet's letter to Hajar, one that includes some original material but also incorporates most of the variants. It does not mention marrying Zoroastrians or eating meat at all.

> Ibn Wahb on the authority of Maslama on the authority of a man on the authority of Abī Ṣāliḥ al-Sammān on the authority of Ibn 'Abbās said: The Messenger of God, may God bless him, wrote to Mundhir ibn al-[Sāwā], member (*akhī*) of Banī 'Abd Allāh from Ghaṭafān, a great man of the people of Hajar, summoning them to Allāh and to Islām. He accepted Islām and read the letter of the Messenger of God, may God bless him, to the people of Hajar. Some accepted and some declined. He wrote to the Prophet, may God bless him: Verily, I have read your letter to the people of Hajar. The [pagan] Arabs have entered into Islām while the Zoroastrians and Jews declined Islām and proposed the jizya. I await your command regarding them. The Messenger of God, may God bless him, wrote: To the worshippers of God among the [Asbadhiyyin, the retinue of the Sasanian military governor], if you undertake prayer and pay the *zakāt* and act in good faith toward God and His Messenger and pay the *'ushr* of the date palms and half *'ushr* of the seed and do not Zoroastrianize (*lam tumajjisū*) your children, then everything you had before you submitted (*aslamtum*) is yours, except that the fire temple belongs to God and His messenger. If you refuse, jizya is upon you. He read [it] to them. The Jews and Zoroastrians declined Islam and desired the jizya.[23]

This version of the letter emphasises the fiscal obligations incumbent on those who submitted. Zoroastrians allegedly forfeited their fire temple and could not raise their children in the Good Religion.[24] The prohibition, meanwhile, is nowhere to be found.

Sabi'ans and Banu Taghlib

Michael Morony has suggested that the injunction not to marry Zoroastrian women or eat animals slaughtered by followers of the Good Religion originated with early Muslim jurists.[25] The legal experts ruled similarly regarding Sabi'ans, which makes for a fruitful comparison. Exegetes did not know what to make of Sabi'ans, whom the Qur'an mentions favourably alongside Jews and Christians (as well as Zoroastrians in 22: 17).[26] The identity of whatever group the Qur'an had intended was obviously lost within a century. By the second/eighth century, Muslim jurists could not agree on the etymology of their name, let alone their identity.[27] They speculated about Sabi'an beliefs, generally concluding that they worship angels. Unsure of where Sabi'ans lived, the exegetes proposed Syria, Iraq or the Sawad.[28]

According to Abu Ubayd, Zoroastrians set the precedent for taxing Sabi'ans.[29] Was it permissible for Muslims to marry or eat animals slaughtered by Sabi'ans? Baghawi's *Tafsir* noted that while Umar permitted the consumption of animals slaughtered by Sabi'ans, Ibn Abbas did not.[30] Second/eighth-century jurists such as Mujahid (d. 102 or 104/720–721 or 722–723), al-Hasan al-Basri (21–110/624–728) and Ibn Abi Najih (d. 131/749) ruled that Muslims should not marry Sabi'ans nor consume the meat they butcher.[31] Sufyan al-Thawri (d. 161/778) and Ata ibn Abi Rabah (d. 115/773) explained that the group existed legally somewhere in the realm between Zoroastrians and People of the Book. Abu Hanifa (d. 150/767), by contrast, decided that it was permissible because they read Psalms.[32] Abu Ubayd (154–224/770–838) noted that most jurists did not consider Sabi'an women and slaughtered animals to be permissible because the group's beliefs resembled those of Zoroastrians.[33] The idea that Muslims should not marry Sabi'ans or eat their slaughtered animals is the result of post-prophetic debates and comparisons to Zoroastrians.

The judicial archive of memory preserves similar material about the Banu Taghlib. A nomadic, Christian Arab tribe of Mesopotamia, the Banu Taghlib was one of the largest and strongest tribes of pre-Islamic Arabia, displaying great prowess in battle. When Muslim forces overran their territory during the conquest of Iraq, the Banu Taghlib refused to convert to Islam or to pay jizya. They perceived the latter as an insult and were prepared to flee to Byzantine territory to avoid it.[34] The caliph Umar, fearing that their departure would bolster the enemy forces that were engaged with his troops along the Byzantine front, allowed the Banu Taghlib to pay double the rate of *ṣadaqa* – an alms tax paid by Muslims – instead of jizya.[35] Certain reports add that Umar prohibited the Banu Taghlib to baptise or 'Christianise' (*yunaṣṣirū*) their children because of their refusal to pay jizya.[36] In the Abbasid era, the caliph Harun al-Rashid questioned the Banu Taghlib's loyalty and accused them of baptising their children.[37] The idea of not 'Zoroastrianising' children from Muhammad's letter to Hajar is clearly related to reports about the Banu Taghlib.

Ali ibn Abi Talib displays marked hostility toward the Banu Taghlib in Abd al-Razzaq's *Musannaf*. Ali witnessed Muhammad's treaty with them, which they allegedly broke by baptising their children. Ali noted wryly that he would have preferred to fight them.[38] Some reports suggest Umar had prohibited the Banu Taghlib from drinking wine on account of their refusal to pay jizya. Ali reportedly loathed meat prepared by Taghlibis, griping that the only part of Christianity to which they adhered was wine drinking.[39] Muslims also remembered Ali's disdain extending to Christian Arab tribes more generally. He is supposed to have said: 'Do not marry the women of the Christian Arabs and do not eat meat slaughtered by them'.[40] Nurit Tsafrir regards specific reports about the Banu Taghlib to be earlier than generic reports about Arab Christians. The conflation of the two groups is a relatively late misunderstanding.[41]

The ban on Taghlibi women and meat appears to be a product of the late first/early eighth century. The jurist Sa'id ibn Jubayr (d. 95/713–714) stated in al-Baladhuri's *Futuh al-Buldan* on the authority of Ibn Abbas, 'The slaughtered animals of the Christians of the Banu Taghlib are not to be eaten and their women are not to be married. They are neither of us nor of the People of the Book.'[42] Likewise, Ata ibn Abi Rabah (d. 114–115/732–733) ruled that Arab Christians were not People of the Book. The Tribes of Israel (Ar., *Banū Isrā'īl*) had received the Torah from Moses and the Gospel from Jesus, but Arab Christians had embraced the faith after it ceased being divinely inspired. Therefore, Muslim men should not marry Arab Christian women. Muhammad ibn Idris al-Shafi'i (150–204/767–820) agreed. Like Ata, he believed that Arabs could not be People of the Book. Therefore, it was impermissible to marry or eat meat butchered by them. Nevertheless, Muslims could tax Arab Christians.[43]

Most jurists rejected this narrow definition of People of the Book, including the founders of the other major Sunni legal schools and earlier jurists such as al-Hasan al-Basri (d. 110/728), Ikrima (d. 105/723–724), al-Sha'bi (d. 103–110/721–728), Sa'id ibn al-Musayyab (d. 94/713), Ibn Shihab al-Zuhri (d. 124/724) and Qatada ibn Di'ama (d. 117/735).[44] They argued that Jews and Christians were People of the Book regardless of their ethnicity or time of conversion. These juridical debates largely occurred in the second/eighth century. That makes them roughly contemporaneous with Hasan's statement regarding Zoroastrians.

Follow the Custom of the People of the Book

The chain of transmission for Hasan's report is remarkably consistent. It invariably flows from him to Qays ibn Muslim. The *isnad* spreads after that, but often follows a path from Qays ibn Muslim to Qays ibn al-Rabi' and then to Sufyan al-Thawri (d. 161/778). This is the chain of transmission in two of the earliest collections of hadith, Abd al-Razzaq's (d. 211/826) *Musannaf* and Ibn Abi Shayba's (d. 235/849) *Musannaf*. In a fifteenth-century commentary, Badr al-Din al-Ayni claimed that Abd al-Razzaq and Ibn Abi Shayba had transmitted the report on the authority of Ali ibn Abi Talib, although this may simply be an error because Hasan was Ali's grandson, which Ibn Abi Shayba specifically notes in the *isnad*.[45] Harald Motzki has suggested that, absent evidence to the contrary, historians should generally consider the common link in a chain of transmission to be the *terminus ante quem* of a report.[46] If the common link is Qays ibn Muslim, the report dates to the early second/eighth century. There is little reason to doubt its ultimate attribution to Hasan, which potentially pushes it into the first century.

A different but more or less contemporaneous report about Zoroastrians circulated on the authority of Muhammad al-Baqir (57–114 or 117/677–732 or 735), the Prophet's great-great grandson. It urged Muslims to 'follow the custom of the People of the Book with them' (*sunnū bihim sunnat ahl al-kitāb*).[47] Abd al-Razzaq's *Musannaf*, one of the earliest compilations of hadith, also contains this report, although the phrase cannot be found in any version of the Prophet's letter to Mundhir ibn Sawa.[48] Abu Yusuf narrates it in the context of Umar's confusion about taxing Zoroastrians.

> One of the shaykhs told us on the authority of Ja'far ibn Muḥammad on the authority of his father. He said: A tribe was mentioned to 'Umar, may God be pleased with him, that worships fire. They were not Jews or Christians or People of the Book. 'Umar said: I do not know what to do with these. 'Abd al-Raḥmān ibn 'Awf, may God be pleased with him, stood. He said: I testify that the Prophet said: Follow the custom of the People of the Book with them.[49]

This hadith resembles reports about Sabi'ans in its struggle to situate followers of the Good Religion relative to People of the Book. Also, as they had done with Sabi'ans, early Muslims speculated wildly about Zoroastrian beliefs, attributing horse worship to them among other things.[50]

The chain of transmission for this report seems credible. Muhammad al-Baqir was a respected early Muslim jurist and the fifth Imam in the Twelver or Imami Shi'i tradition.[51] Muhammad's son, Ja'far al-Sadiq (*c.* 83–148/702–765), was the Sixth Imam. Beyond Ja'far, the *isnad* spreads to Sufyan al-Thawri, Yahya ibn Sa'id and others, but the common link is always Ja'far. Harald Motzki notes that father-son transmissions are common in Abd al-Razzaq's collection, where the transmission from Ja'far to Muhammad is almost exclusive.[52] Both men were well respected in proto-Sunni legal circles, so the report need not be seen as distinctively Shi'i in nature.[53] It did, however, circulate in at least one source with Alid *isnads* that bless the Prophet's family.[54]

The report's connection to Ali is potentially significant. In Abd al-Razzaq's *Musannaf* Ali deemed himself the most knowledgeable person about taxing Zoroastrians, and ascribed (corrupted) books to them.[55] Both Muhammad al-Baqir and Hasan ibn Muhammad were members of Ali's family, albeit from different branches. The fact that Ali was associated with the case of the Banu Taghlib and the injunction against marrying Arab Christians or eating animals slaughtered by them perhaps explains his descendants' interest or authority in related matters.

Al-Baqir's chain of transmission from the Prophet is incomplete. In the technical terms of later hadith criticism, it is 'severed' or 'unconnected' (*munqaṭi'* or *ghayr muttaṣil*) because neither Umar nor Abd al-Rahman met Muhammad al-Baqir.[56] A defective *isnad* is not uncommon in this era, and Scott Lucas has suggested that early hadith transmitters treated reports narrated by Companions and Successors as equally valid to those from the Prophet.[57] Muhammad al-Baqir was generally considered a reliable narrator of hadith, and the founders of the four main Sunni schools all transmitted reports from him.[58] These reports include chains of transmission that terminate with Muhammad al-Baqir, not the Prophet. Nevertheless, some Medinans accused al-Baqir of transmitting reports on the Prophet's authority despite never having met him.[59] While the report can be reasonably attributed to al-Baqir, its connection to the Prophet is more tenuous.

Later jurists understood 'the custom of the People of the Book' (*sunnat ahl al-kitāb*) to refer to taxation. The Hanafi jurist al-Jassas (d. 370/981) took this phrase to be synonymous with the prophetic permission to collect jizya from Zoroastrians.[60] The Hanbali scholar Abd al-Rahman ibn Muhammad ibn Qudama al-Maqdisi (d. 682/1283) agreed.[61] Makki ibn Abi Talib (d. 437/1045) said al-Shafi'i also limited it to taxation.[62] According to Fakhr al-Din Razi (544–606/1149–1210), the jurists 'agree that the Zoroastrians received the treatment of the People of the Book with regard to taking the jizya from them without eating meat slaughtered by them or marrying their women.'[63] The Hanafi jurist Badr al-Din al-Ayni (d. 855/1451) interpreted it to mean taking jizya and giving security.[64] Despite the apparent consensus, at least one early Muslim jurist used this phrase to argue that it was permissible to marry Zoroastrians and eat meat butchered by them.

Abu Thawr (d. 240/854), an independent jurist of Iraq sometimes associated with the school of al-Shafi'i, was the earliest proponent of this idea. Little information about him survives, meaning that his views on the matter are most readily accessible through later refutations of them. As stated succinctly by the Shafi'i jurist al-Baghawi (d. 516/1122), 'Abu Thawr said their women and slaughtered animals are permissible but most Companions and *'ulamā'* differ from that'.[65] Similarly, the Hanbali scholar Abd al-Rahman ibn Muhammad ibn Qudama al-Maqdisi stated, 'As for Abu Thawr's saying about the permissibility of their women and meat, it differs from the consensus. So do not heed it.'[66] According to Badr al-Din Ayni, Abu Thawr narrated the permission to marry Zoroastrian women on the authority of Hudhayfa.[67] As caliphal governor of Mada'in, the former Sasanian capital at Ctesiphon in Iraq, Hudhayfa ibn al-Yaman was married to a Zoroastrian woman.[68] It is possible that he promoted the idea although I have not been able to locate this hadith.

Ibn Kathir said, by contrast, that Abu Thawr permitted Muslims to marry Zoroastrians on the basis of the phrase *sunnū bihim*. 'It seems that he adheres in general to an incompletely transmitted hadith narrated on the authority of the Prophet that says: "Follow the custom of the People of the Book with them."'[69] Ibn Kathir denied the validity of Abu Thawr's interpretation because Qur'an 5: 5 only permits Muslims to consume the food of People of the Book. The Hanafi jurist al-Jassas (d. 370/981) asked hypothetically if this hadith could be used to argue that Zoroastrians were People of the Book. He concluded that it could not because they do not read either of the two books of God (the Hebrew Bible and New Testament).[70] Abu Thawr's opinion evidently did not prevail.

Zoroastrian Cheese and Boundary Marking

The jurists' ban on marriage and meat was prescriptive, but Duby reminds us that behaviour manuals do not always reflect actual behaviour. Accordingly, it is reasonable to ask what effect the prohibition might have had on intercommunal contact. The case of 'Zoroastrian' cheese is instructive. Michael Cook has argued that Muslim attitudes toward its consumption became progressively more liberal over time.[71] For early Muslims occupying territories of the former Sasanian Empire, cheese was a controversial commodity because Persians made it with rennet – partially curdled milk extracted from the stomach of a slaughtered calf. Not only did most Muslim jurists presume Persians to be Zoroastrians and therefore incapable of valid slaughter, but rennet is a form of carrion, which is forbidden to Muslims by the Qur'an (2: 137, 5: 3, 6: 145, 16: 115). As a result, there are a number of very early hadith in which the Companions of the Prophet express concern about the permissibility of eating Zoroastrian cheese. The caliph Umar is supposed to have instructed Muslim troops headed to Iran in the conquest era to only eat cheese prepared by People of the Book.[72] One early Muslim settler at Basra reportedly stopped eating cheese because he lived among Zoroastrians and feared that it might contain carrion.[73] Despite these reports, three of the four Sunni legal schools ruled that Muslims could eat Zoroastrian cheese.

On what grounds did early Muslim jurists permit the consumption of Zoroastrian cheese? Numerous hadith appeared suggesting that the Prophet had allowed it. For example, when Muhammad encountered a Persian cheese after the conquest of Mecca, he is supposed to have instructed his followers to invoke the name of God and eat.[74] The chains of transmission for these reports generally lead back to Kufa.[75] Jurists of the Hanafi and Hanbali law schools, which were based in Iraq, demonstrated considerable interest in the rules about Zoroastrian cheese, while Hijaz-based Maliki jurists were relatively uninterested. Shafi'i law did not address the issue but, in reports with Kufan *isnads*, Shi'i Imams generally permitted its consumption.[76]

Significantly, this includes reports attributed to Muhammad al-Baqir and Hasan ibn Muhammad.[77]

Iraqi jurists advanced a number of legal arguments to justify the consumption of Zoroastrian cheese. For instance, they argued that any cheese was permissible insofar as Muslims lacked certain knowledge that it contained carrion. If a Muslim simply did not know, he or she could partake. Some jurists suggested that cheese purchased in an Islamicate market was presumed lawful, regardless of the identity of its maker. Others argued that once rennet was combined with additional ingredients, the final product – cheese – was permissible. Some scholars even argued that rennet was not carrion.[78] In short, they found sufficient justification to eat Persian cheese despite the prohibition. Presumably, their permissiveness facilitated commercial and social interaction with Zoroastrians, allowing Muslims to benefit from their useful endeavours.

If early Muslim jurists erred on the side of liberality in the case of cheese, what might have been the intent of the related ban on meat slaughtered by Zoroastrians? David Freidenreich argues that it demarcated the boundary between followers of the Good Religion and People of the Book.[79] The increasing levels of abstraction to which Muslim jurists carried this sort of boundary marking reveals that their concern was not the meat itself but the legal implications of Zoroastrians' lack of an acceptable scripture. For example, the hadith collections of Abu Isa Muhammad ibn Isa al-Tirmidhi (210–279/825–892) and Abu Abd Allah Muhammad ibn Yazid ibn Maja (209–273/824–887) each contain a report that prohibits game killed by a Zoroastrian's hunting dog. Tellingly, both reports speak in the passive voice and neither is attributed to the Prophet or his Companions.[80] They appear to reflect the rulings of early Muslim jurists.

Later Islamic legal literature devoted considerable attention to joint Muslim-Zoroastrian hunting ventures. For example, Abu Hamid Muhammad ibn Muhammad al-Ghazali (450–505/1058–1111) wrote:

> If a Zoroastrian and a Muslim are partners in the act of slaughter, it is prohibited. The same applies if each sends an arrow or a hunting dog at a game animal. But if one of them strikes the animal first, beginning the act of slaughter, its legal status follows that hunter. If the Zoroastrian's dog

> chases the quarry toward the Muslim's dog, who kills it, its meat is permitted. If the Muslim's dog exhausts the quarry but the Zoroastrian's dog then catches it and kills it, the animal is carrion and the Zoroastrian must offer compensation to the Muslim.[81]

Jurists devised increasingly fantastic scenarios: is the game edible if a Muslim hunts alone using a Zoroastrian's dog? What if a Zoroastrian encourages the Muslim's dog to pursue the quarry? And what happens when a Zoroastrian converts to Islam after he releases his dog but before it makes the kill? As Freidenreich notes, 'The pedagogical function of these cases accounts for discussions that are in other respects overly extensive, impractical, and, for most Muslims, hypothetical'.[82] In other words, Muslim jurists were less interested in regulating the behaviour of Muslim hunters than in exploring the implications of the Zoroastrians' peculiar status as People without a Book. They were marking the boundary between communities.

Intercommunal Sex and Marriage

Jamsheed Choksy has emphasised the reciprocal nature of Muslim-Zoroastrian boundary marking.[83] In the realm of interpersonal law, the codes of each community were similar enough that it is possible that Muslim jurists adopted Zoroastrian rules, or vice versa. For example, Zoroastrians prohibited the consumption of meat slaughtered by Muslims.[84] Both Muslim and Zoroastrian jurists condemned interfaith marriage, preventing the children of such unions from inheriting their parents' wealth. Islamic and Zoroastrian law also proscribed extramarital sex between Muslims and Zoroastrians. Although the Qur'an (4: 25) permits Muslim men to have intercourse with their slaves who are People of the Book, several jurists argued that Zoroastrian slaves had to convert to Islam first.[85] Similarly, Zoroastrian law warned men and women against engaging in cross-confessional coitus. Conceiving a child in this manner constituted a grave sin. In the tenth century, the high priest Emed i Ashawahishtan warned: '[If a Zoroastrian man] has sexual intercourse with a woman of another religion and consequently she becomes pregnant, then a sin preventing his soul [from] reaching paradise will result from begetting a child with [a member of] another religion.'[86] The high priest's warning applies to sexual relations with non-Zoroastrians in general, although Muslims were almost certainly the concern.

These rules, too, marked the borders between communities. They allowed individual adherents of the Good Religion to preserve their ritual purity, not to mention the distinctiveness and vitality of the Zoroastrian community.[87] David Nirenberg has noted that fear about the disintegration of Christian-Muslim boundaries in the medieval Kingdom of Aragon led authorities to police the bodies of prostitutes who worked across the confessional divide.[88] Similarly, the only province in which the tenth-century Muslim geographer al-Muqaddasi noted the existence of brothels is Fars – a region of the early Islamic world that presumably would have retained a large Zoroastrian population in that period.[89] Thus, even as jurists clearly defined the sexual limit of their communities, Muslims and Zoroastrians transgressed it.

Blood Price

The blood price (Ar., *diya*) of Zoroastrians is perhaps the most obvious indicator of their inferior status as People without a Book. Blood price was the amount that a perpetrator paid to the victim of a violent crime in lieu of physical retaliation by his or her family. It was a pre-Islamic Arab custom meant to prevent blood feuds between tribes. Under the aegis of Islamic law, blood price became a legal instrument for settling cases of murder and manslaughter. The blood price of non-Muslims – including Zoroastrians – was equal to that of Muslims until the caliphate of Muʿawiya (d. 60/680).[90] He is supposed to have appropriated for the Umayyad treasury half of the blood money awarded to his injured Christian physician. Later, the Umayyad caliph Umar ibn Abd al-Aziz (ruled 99–101/717–720) allegedly declared that a non-Muslim's blood price was half that of a Muslim's.[91] Thus, three of the four major Sunni law schools afforded to Jews and Christians half (or less) of the amount of blood money afforded to Muslim victims. They allocated even lower amounts to Zoroastrians and other People without a Book.[92]

Unlike most scholars, Muhammad ibn Idris al-Shafiʿi (150–204/767–820) considered Zoroastrians to be People of the Book. He reportedly said, 'The Zoroastrians are People of a Book other than the Torah or Gospel. They forgot their book and corrupted it. The Messenger of God permitted the collection of jizya from them.'[93] This point of view reflects the reports in Chapter Two regarding Zoroastrians' supposedly lost book. It also demonstrates one of al-Shafi'i's guiding legal principles – that the custom of the Prophet cannot contradict the Qur'an. Since the sacred text (9: 29) states that jizya should be taken from the People of the Book, and Muhammad accepted it from Zoroastrians, al-Shafi'i concluded that Zoroastrians must be People of the Book.[94] Admittedly, there are contradictory opinions attributed to al-Shafi'i on this point. Yohanan Friedmann suggests that al-Shafi'i's students may have modified his views after his death in order to bring them more in line with their peers who did not consider Zoroastrians to be People of the Book.[95] Even so, the Shafi'i school, in theory, did not offer injured Zoroastrians the same amount of compensation as injured Muslims.

Aptin Khanbaghi views Zoroastrians' low blood price as evidence that 'the *dhimma* did not always apply to them'.[96] That is a fundamental misunderstanding of Islamic law. Zoroastrians had a blood price because of their protected status (*dhimma*), not in spite of it. The lower rate simply reflects the Muslim jurists' failure to recognise a Zoroastrian book of scripture. Like other legal disabilities, blood price differentiated them from Jews and Christians. Sunni jurists also used it to distinguish between males and females, and between Muslims and non-Muslims, in the construction of legal hierarchies.[97] They generally ruled that the latter deserved less blood money than the former.

Abu Hanifa, however, offered Zoroastrians the same blood price as Muslims. The Hanafi school of law, arguably the most influential and widespread in the early Islamic world, afforded all non-Muslims the same blood price. Independent jurists such as Ibrahim ibn Yazid al-Nakha'i (*c.* 50–96/670–717) and al-Sha'bi did as well.[98] The Maliki and Hanbali schools, which guaranteed a Zoroastrian male one-fifteenth the blood price of a Muslim male, were never popular on the Iranian plateau or regions further east, where there were significant Zoroastrian populations. Their rulings, clearly, were boundary markers. The Shafi'i school, on the other hand, was popular in Iran, where it vied with the Hanafi school for influence.[99] Partisans of the two schools competed intensely at Nishapur, for example.[100] But it seems from a close reading of al-Muqaddasi's geographical treatise that Hanafis were generally ascendant across the Iranian plateau in the tenth century.[101] Travis Zadeh asserts that most residents of Transoxiana were Hanafis at the time.[102] Therefore, only one of the three Sunni legal schools that afforded Zoroastrians a lower blood price held sway in provinces with significant Zoroastrian populations, and the dominant Hanafi school offered Zoroastrians the same blood price as Muslims.

Consequently, it is unclear how much practical significance blood price had. A Zoroastrian plaintiff could theoretically sue a Muslim defendant for blood money in an Islamic court. Uriel Simonsohn has demonstrated that Jews and Christians utilised Islamic courts in Egypt and Iraq.[103] However, most of the cases were intra-confessional affairs in which one non-Muslim litigated against another. Jews and Christians sometimes appealed to Muslim authorities after receiving an unfavourable or unenforceable ruling from the leaders of their own religious communities. Since non-Muslims had their choice of venue in such cases, they could pit competing legal schools against each other in search of the most favourable outcome.

By contrast, a case of blood money between a Muslim and a Zoroastrian could not be settled in a non-Muslim court because it was an inter-confessional affair. The Zoroastrian litigant would have to enter a mosque (where court was usually held), risking his or her ritual purity through contact with non-Zoroastrians. He or she would be allowed neither to serve as witness nor present evidence against Muslims in that setting.[104] In the end, a non-Hanafi judge would have to rule in the Zoroastrian's favour for the lower blood price to have any effect. It seems an improbable scenario, similar to the theoretical hunting expeditions described earlier. Considering the Zoroastrians' inherent disadvantage in an Islamic court, it is unlikely that many pursued cases of blood money there. Rather, Muslims used blood price to legally distinguish Zoroastrians from the People of the Book by emphasising their lower standing in the hierarchy of religions.

Conclusion

There are limits to accommodation. In order to emphasise the inferiority of Zoroastrians relative to People of the Book, jurists prohibited Muslim men from marrying Zoroastrian women and eating animals slaughtered by adherents of the Good Religion. This ban, attributed to the Prophet Muhammad, circulated on the authority of Hasan ibn Muhammad, a descendent of Ali.

Muhammad al-Baqir, another member of Ali's family, remembered a different prophetic directive. He reported that Muslims were to follow the same custom with Zoroastrians as with the People of the Book. Abu Thawr interpreted al-Baqir's report to mean that Muslims could wed Zoroastrians and eat meat prepared by them. Most other jurists disagreed, insisting that the report applied to taxation only. They affirmed Zoroastrians' inferiority in the social order. The practical effect of their rulings is difficult to measure. Zoroastrians warranted a lower blood price than Muslims according to most schools of Islamic law, except the Hanafi school that was ascendant in Iran. Iraqi jurists generally permitted the consumption of cheese made by Zoroastrians, even though it might contain the by-products of butchered animals. These examples derive from behaviour manuals and should not be mistaken for case law. Nevertheless, they suggest that some Muslims were keen to interact with followers of the Good Religion despite the latter's social standing. Jurists sought to benefit from the community's useful endeavours while upholding the legal boundary between Zoroastrians and People of the Book. Meat and marriage, then, represent the limits of accommodation in the early caliphates.

Notes

1. Abū Yūsuf Ya'qūb ibn Ibrāhīm al-Kūfī, *Kitāb al-kharāj*, 1999, 1:142; compare Abū Yūsuf Ya'qūb ibn Ibrāhīm al-Kūfī, *Taxation in Islam*, 3:3:66.
2. See also Nurit Tsafrir, 'The Attitude of Sunnī Islam toward Jews and Christians as Reflected in Some Legal Issues', *Qanṭara: Revista de Estudios Arabes* 26, no. 2 (2005): 317–36.
3. Pierre Nora, 'Between Memory and History: Les Lieux de Mémoire', *Representations*, no. 26 (1989): 7–24; Maurice Halbwachs, *On Collective Memory*, ed. Lewis Coser (Chicago: University of Chicago Press, 1992).
4. Savant, *New Muslims of Post-Conquest Iran*; Antoine Borrut, 'Remembering Karbalā: The Construction of an Early Islamic Site of Memory', *Jerusalem Studies in Arabic and Islam* 42 (2015): 249–82.
5. Georges Duby, 'Ideologies in Social History', in Jacques Le Goff and Pierre Nora (eds), *Constructing the Past: Essays in Historical Methodology* (Cambridge: Cambridge University Press, 1985), 158.
6. Duby, 159.
7. Yarshater, *Encyclopaedia Iranica*, s.v. 'Kaysaniya'.

8. Josef van Ess, *Theology and Society in the Second and Third Century of the Hijra. Volume 1: A History of Religious Thought in Early Islam*, trans. John O'Kane (Leiden: Brill, 2016), 202–5.
9. Abū Yūsuf Ya'qūb ibn Ibrāhīm al-Kūfī, *Kitāb al-kharāj*, 1999, 1:142; Abū Yūsuf Ya'qūb ibn Ibrāhīm al-Kūfī, *Taxation in Islam*, 3:66.
10. Abū Yūsuf Ya'qūb ibn Ibrāhīm al-Kūfī, *Kitāb al-kharāj*, 1999, 1:142; Abū Yūsuf Ya'qūb ibn Ibrāhīm al-Kūfī, *Taxation in Islam*, 3:88.
11. Ḥamīd ibn Mukhlid Ibn Zanjawayh, *Kitāb al-amwāl*, ed. Shakir Dhib Fayyad (Riyadh, Saudi Arabia: Markaz al-Malik Faysal lil-Buhuth wa-al-Dirasat al-Islamiyya, 1986), 1:136.
12. 'Abd Allāh ibn Muḥammad Ibn Abī Shaybah, *al-Kitāb al-Muṣannaf fī l-aḥādīth wa-l-āthār*, ed. Kamāl Yūsuf al-Ḥūt (Beirut: Dar al-Taj, 1989), 6:429.
13. al-Balādhurī, *Kitāb futūḥ al-buldān*, 2014, 80; al-Balādhurī, *The Origins of the Islamic State*, 1:123.
14. Michael Lecker, *People, Tribes, and Society in Arabia around the Time of Muḥammad*, Variorum Collected Studies Series (Burlington, VT: Ashgate, 2005), 55, 73.
15. See, for example, Abū 'Ubayd al-Qāsim ibn Sallām, *The Book of Revenue*, 18–21.
16. al-Balādhurī, *Kitāb futūḥ al-buldān*, 2014, 78–79; al-Balādhurī, *The Origins of the Islamic State*, 1:121.
17. The letter to Kisra may, in fact, be conflated with this letter to the Persian governor at Hajar. See Abū 'Ubayd al-Qāsim ibn Sallām, *The Book of Revenue*, 21.
18. Abū 'Ubayd al-Qāsim ibn Sallām, 18–21, 197–98.
19. Abū Ja'far Muḥammad ibn Jarīr al-Ṭabarī, *The Victory of Islam*, trans. Michael Fishbein, vol. 8, History of Al-Tabari (Albany, NY: State University of New York Press, 1989), 142; al-Ṭabarī, *Tārīkh al-rusul wa-l-mulūk*, I, 1600.
20. al-Balādhurī, *Kitāb futūḥ al-buldān*, 2014, 81.
21. al-Balādhurī, 80–81; Abū Yūsuf Ya'qūb ibn Ibrāhīm al-Kūfī, *Kitāb al-kharāj*, 1999, 1:144.
22. Abū Yūsuf Ya'qūb ibn Ibrāhīm al-Kūfī, *Kitāb al-kharāj*, 1999, 1:144; Mālik ibn Anas and 'Abd al-Salām ibn Sa'īd Saḥnūn, *al-Mudawwana al-kubrā* (Bayrūt: Dār al-kutub al-'ilmiyya, 1994), 5:129.
23. Mālik ibn Anas and Saḥnūn, *al-Mudawwana al-kubrā*, 1:529.
24. I have treated the issue of the fire temple elsewhere. See Andrew D. Magnusson, 'Muslim-Zoroastrian Relations and Religious Violence in Early Islamic

Discourse, 600–1100 CE' (Ph.D. Dissertation, University of California at Santa Barbara, 2014), 167–168.

25. Michael Morony, 'Conquerors and Conquered: Iran', in G. H. A. Juynboll (ed.), *Studies on the First Century of Islamic Society* (Carbondale: Southern Illinois University Press, 1982), 81.
26. For more information on Sabi'ans, see François de Blois, 'The 'Sabians' (Sabi'un) in Pre-Islamic Arabia', *Acta Orientalia* 56 (1995): 39–61; Christopher Buck, 'The Identity of the Sābi'ūn: An Historical Quest', *Muslim World* 74, no. 3–4 (1984): 172–86.
27. al-Baghawī, *Tafsīr al-Baghawī*, 102.
28. al-Ṭabarī, *Jāmi' al-bayān fī tafsīr al-Qur'ān*, 357–58.
29. Abū 'Ubayd al-Qāsim ibn Sallām, *The Book of Revenue*, 29, 499; Ibn Zanjawayh, *Kitāb al-amwāl*, 1:135.
30. al-Baghawī, *Tafsīr al-Baghawī*, 102; see also al-Qurṭubī, *al-Jāmi' li-aḥkām al-Qur'ān*, 434–35.
31. Ibn Kathīr, *Tafsīr al-Qur'ān al-'aẓīm*, 99–100.
32. Ibn Kathīr, 99.
33. Abū 'Ubayd al-Qāsim ibn Sallām, *The Book of Revenue*, 499.
34. al-Balādhurī, *Kitāb futūḥ al-buldān*, 2014, 182; al-Balādhurī, *The Origins of the Islamic State*, 285.
35. *EI2*, s.v. 'Taghlib' (Michael Lecker).
36. al-Ṣan'ānī, *al-Muṣannaf*, 6:50.
37. Muḥammad ibn al-Ḥasan Shaybānī, *The Islamic Law of Nations: Shaybānī's Siyar*, trans. Majid Khadduri (Baltimore: Johns Hopkins Press, 1966), 34–35.
38. al-Ṣan'ānī, *al-Muṣannaf*, 6:50.
39. al-Ṣan'ānī, 6:72.
40. al-Ṣan'ānī, 6:72.
41. Freidenreich, *Foreigners and Their Food*, 266, footnote #47.
42. al-Balādhurī, *Kitāb futūḥ al-buldān*, 2014, 181–82; al-Balādhurī, *The Origins of the Islamic State*, 284.
43. Friedmann, *Tolerance and Coercion in Islam*, 65–66.
44. Friedmann, 61–62.
45. Badr al-Dīn Maḥmūd ibn Aḥmad ibn Mūsā al-'Aynī, *al-Bināya sharḥ al-hidāya*, ed. Amin Salih Sha'ban (Beirut: Dār al-Kutub al-'Ilmīyah, 2000), 5:44; Ibn Abī Shaybah, *al-Kitāb al-Muṣannaf*, 6:429.
46. Harald Motzki, 'Dating Muslim Traditions: A Survey', *Arabica* 52, no. 2 (2005): 240.

47. Ibn Abī Shaybah, *al-Kitāb al-Muṣannaf*, 6:429 #32651.
48. al-Ṣanʿānī, *al-Muṣannaf*, 6:68 #10025.
49. Abū Yūsuf Yaʿqūb ibn Ibrāhīm al-Kūfī, *Kitāb al-kharāj*, 1999, 1:143; Abū Yūsuf Yaʿqūb ibn Ibrāhīm al-Kūfī, *Taxation in Islam*, 3:88.
50. Abū ʿUbayd al-Qāsim ibn Sallām, *The Book of Revenue*, 19–20.
51. There is one possible exception. Ibn Kathir also claims to have it from Zayd ibn Wahb, but only in some manuscripts. See Ismāʿīl ibn ʿUmar Ibn Kathīr, *Tuḥfat al-ṭālib bi-maʿrifat aḥādīth-Mukhtaṣar Ibn al-Ḥājib.*, ed. Abd al-Ghani ibn Humayd ibn Mahmud Kubaysi (Beirut: Ibn Hazm, 1996), 290. While there are reports narrated by Ibn Wahb on the Zoroastrians of Hajar, such as the one preserved by Sahnun above, they do not contain this specific phrase.
52. Harald Motzki, 'The Muṣannaf of ʿAbd Al-Razzāq al-Ṣanʿānī as a Source of Authentic Aḥādīth of the First Century A.H.', *Journal of Near Eastern Studies* 50, no. 1 (1991): 7.
53. Arzina Lalani, *Early Shi'i Thought: The Teachings of Imam Muhammad al-Baqir* (London: I. B. Tauris, 2000), 96.
54. al-Haytham ibn Kulayb al-Shāshī, *Musnad al-Shāshī*, ed. Mahfuz al-Rahman Zayn Allah (Medina: Maktabat al-Ulum wa-l-Hikam, 1989), 1:257–258.
55. al-Ṣanʿānī, *al-Muṣannaf*, 6:70–71.
56. ʿUthmān ibn ʿAbd al-Raḥmān Ibn al-Ṣalāḥ al-Shahrazūrī, *An Introduction to the Science of the Hadith (Kitab Maʿrifat Anwāʿ ʿilm al-Ḥadīth)*, trans. Eerik Dickinson (Reading: Garnet, 2006), 143.
57. Harald Motzki, *The Origins of Islamic Jurisprudence: Meccan Fiqh before the Classical Schools*, trans. Marion H. Katz (Leiden: Brill, 2002), 241–42; Scott Lucas, 'Where Are the Legal Hadith? A Study of the Musannaf of Ibn Abi Shayba', *Islamic Law & Society* 15 (2008): 298.
58. Lalani, *Early Shi'i Thought*, 98–100.
59. Lalani, 100.
60. al-Jaṣṣāṣ, *Kitāb Aḥkām al-Qur'ān*, 3:327.
61. ʿAbd al-Raḥmān ibn Muḥammad Ibn Qudāmah, *al-Mughnī wa-l-Sharḥ al-kabīr ʿalá matn al-Muqniʿ*, ed. Muḥammad Rashīd Riḍá, Reprint of 1922 Cairo edition (Bayrūt: Dār al-Kitāb al-ʿArabī, 1972), 396.
62. Makkī Ibn Abī Ṭālib, *Al-Hidāya ilā Bulūgh al-Nihāya* (Shariqa: Kulliyyat al-Dirāsāt al-'Ulyā wa-l-Baḥth al-'Ilmī, Jāmi'at Shāriqa, 1429), 3:608, https://al-maktaba.org/book/31728.
63. Rāzī, *Mafātīḥ al-ghayb*, 373.
64. al-ʿAynī, *al-Bināya sharḥ al-hidāya*, 5:44.

65. al-Ḥusayn ibn Masʿūd al-Baghawī, *al-Tahdhīb fī fiqh al-Imām al-Shāfiʿī*, ed. Adil Ahmad Abd al-Mawjud (Beirut: Dār al-Kutub al-ʿIlmīyah, 1997), 5:378.
66. Ibn Qudāmah, *al-Mughnī wa-l-Sharḥ al-kabīr ʿalá matn al-Muqniʿ*, 396.
67. al-ʿAynī, *al-Bināya sharḥ al-hidāya*, 45. I have not been able to locate this hadith.
68. Aḥmad ibn Muḥammad Khallāl, *Aḥkām ahl al-milal min al-jāmiʿ li-masāʾil al-Imām Aḥmad ibn Ḥanbal* (Beirut: Dār al-Kutub al-ʿIlmīyah, 1994), 1:162; compare Friedmann, *Tolerance and Coercion in Islam*, 186.
69. Ibn Kathīr, *Tafsīr al-Qurʾān al-ʿaẓīm*, 2:20.
70. al-Jaṣṣāṣ, *Kitāb Aḥkām al-Qurʾān*, 3:327.
71. Michael Cook, 'Magian Cheese: An Archaic Problem in Islamic Law', *Bulletin of the School of Oriental and African Studies* 47 (1984): 462.
72. Cook, 455.
73. Muḥammad Ibn Saʿd, *Al-Ṭabaqāt al-Kubrá*, al-Ṭabʿah 1 (Bayrūt, Lubnān: Dār al-Kutub al-ʿIlmīyah, 1990), 7:77.
74. Cook, 'Magian Cheese,' 449.
75. Cook, 461.
76. Cook, 456.
77. Cook, 457, 461; compare Freidenreich, *Foreigners and Their Food*, 164.
78. Cook, 'Magian Cheese', 457–60.
79. Freidenreich, *Foreigners and Their Food*, Chapter 10.
80. *Jamiʿ al-Tirmidhi* #1466; *Sunan Ibn Maja* #3330.
81. Quoted in Freidenreich, *Foreigners and Their Food*, 151.
82. Freidenreich, 150.
83. Choksy, *Conflict and Cooperation*, 122–27.
84. Choksy, 'Zoroastrians in Muslim Iran', 24.
85. Abū Yūsuf Yaʿqūb ibn Ibrāhīm al-Kūfī, *Taxation in Islam*, 3:66.
86. Quoted in Choksy, *Conflict and Cooperation*, 124.
87. For more information on Zoroastrian conceptions of purity, see Choksy, *Purity and Pollution in Zoroastrianism.*
88. Nirenberg, *Communities of Violence*, Chapter 5.
89. Muḥammad ibn Aḥmad Muqaddasī, *Aḥsan at-taqāsīm fī maʿrifat al-aqālīm (The Best Divisions for Knowledge of the Regions)*, trans. Basil Anthony Collins (Reading: Garnet, 1994), 380.
90. al-Ṣanʿānī, *al-Muṣannaf*, 10:95–6.
91. *EI2*, s.v. 'diya'.

92. Antoine Fattal, *Le Statut légal des non-musulmans en pays d'Islam* (Beyrouth: Impremiere catholique, 1958), 117–18.
93. Friedmann, *Tolerance and Coercion in Islam*, 75.
94. Friedmann, 75.
95. Friedmann, 74 footnote #79.
96. Khanbaghi, *The Fire, the Star and the Cross*, 25.
97. Friedmann, *Tolerance and Coercion in Islam*, 47–50.
98. Friedmann, 50.
99. Wilferd Madelung, *Religious Trends in Early Islamic Iran*, Bibliotheca Persica, no. 4 (Albany, NY: Persian Heritage Foundation, 1988), Chapter 3.
100. Richard W. Bulliet, *The Patricians of Nishapur: A Study in Medieval Islamic Social History* (Cambridge, MA: Harvard University Press, 1972).
101. Muqaddasī, *Best Divisions for Knowledge, passim.*
102. Travis Zadeh, *The Vernacular Qur'an: Translation and the Rise of Persian Exegesis* (London: Institute of Ismaili Studies, 2012), 306.
103. Uriel Simonsohn, 'Communal Boundaries Reconsidered: Jews and Christians Appealing to Muslim Authorities in the Medieval Near East', *Jewish Studies Quarterly* 14, no. 4 (2007): 328–63; see also *A Common Justice.*
104. Antoine Fattal, 'How Dhimmis Were Judged in the Islamic World', in Jacques Waardenburg (ed.), *Muslim Perceptions of Other Religions: A Historical Survey* (New York: Oxford University Press, 1999), 96–99; compare Emon, *Religious Pluralism and Islamic Law*, 136–41.

4

Salman's Charter as a Site of Memory

In the wake of the Bombay Riot of 1851, Sorabjee Jamsetjee Jejeebhoy published a slender volume entitled *Tuqviuti-Din-i-Mazdiasna* ('The Virtues of the Zoroastrian Religion').[1] Sorabjee was a member of the Parsi, or Indian Zoroastrian, community and the son of Jamsetjee Jejeebhoy, the wealthy merchant, philanthropist and Baronet of India.[2] Sorabjee undoubtedly intended its publication to ease tensions between Muslims and Parsis after weeks of sectarian violence in Bombay. The book included a charter (N.P., *'ahd-nāma*) that the Prophet Muhammad had supposedly granted to the family of Salman al-Farisi in the seventh century.[3] Salman was a Companion of the Prophet and a former Zoroastrian. The charter, written in Arabic, offered various fiscal and legal privileges to Salman's brother and his descendants.[4] The Prophet gave them full autonomy over their lands and fire temples, and urged Muslims to treat them kindly, regardless of whether they converted to Islam. Muhammad warned that Muslims who contravened his instructions would face divine retribution. This ahd-nama, sealed by the Prophet and witnessed by several of his Companions – including Salman – is dated Rajab of year 9 AH, or 631 CE.

This document routinely surfaces in the Parsi community of Mumbai during moments of interreligious tension as a panacea. Sorabjee Jamsetjee Jejeebhoy translated the ahd-nama into Gujarati in the wake of the sectarian Bombay Riot of 1851. The Iran League, a Parsi organisation dedicated to improving ties between Muslims and Zoroastrians in Iran and India, funded the first English translation in 1925.[5] Jamshedji Saklatwalla rose to the charter's defense in 1938 after an editorial in a Bombay newspaper questioned its authenticity.[6] In 1991 the periodical *Parsiana* featured an acrimonious exchange between Ervad Darius Sethna and an Iranian scholar, Ali Jafarey. Sethna did not recognise Jafarey's conversion from Islam to Zoroastrianism. As noted previously, conversion is a contentious issue in modern Zoroastrianism, particularly among Parsis.[7] After Jafarey published an article questioning the use of bull's urine in Zoroastrian rites of purificiation, Sethna suggested that Jafarey, whom he still considered to be a Muslim, would be ineligibile for such rites anyway. Sethna contemptuously urged Jafarey to study his own religion (Islam) and its scripture (the ahd-nama) instead.[8] Just a few years later, in 1995, Mithoo Coorlawala offered the charter as an answer to religious extremism. She argued, 'In our fundamentalist times they [the charter and related documents] carry an important message of conciliation and co-existence'.[9] As expressed by Coorlawala, the ahd-nama offers hope to members of the Parsi community for better relations with Muslims in India and beyond.

With the exception of Jafarey, these authors assume that the charter is authentic. They generally praise the Prophet Muhammad's tolerance of the Good Religion and lament the failure of subsequent Muslims to follow his example. The ahd-nama supposedly bears little relation to Zoroastrians' lived experience in the early caliphates; rather, it is imagined as the antithesis of their history.[10] Acceptance of the charter's authenticity, then, seems almost predicated on the belief that medieval Muslims mistreated Zoroastrians, forcing them into India, Islam, or decline. Interest in the document is also rooted in anxiety about the present – including legitimate concerns about sectarian strife in contemporary Iran and India – with an eye toward a more harmonious future.[11] Hence Parsi authors encourage Muslims to return to the Prophetic ideals expressed in the charter, thereby improving the lot of contemporary Zoroastrians.

Salman's charter has, in other words, become a site of memory. Historians of memory, such as Maurice Halbwachs and Pierra Nora, emphasise that history is not simply a record of the past; people choose to remember and forget ideas, events and individuals as it suits their needs in the present. Interest groups, nations and families might even hold shared interpretations of the past, resulting in collective memories. Halbwachs emphasises that the collective memory of religious communities is no different.

> [A]lthough religious memory attempts to isolate itself from temporal society, it obeys the same laws as every collective memory: it does not preserve the past but reconstructs it with the aid of the material traces, rites, texts, and traditions left behind by that past, and with the aid moreover of recent psychological and social data, that is to say, with the present.[12]

Communities might develop these artefacts into sites of memory (*lieux de mémoire*). They can be physical or symbolic places that specific groups, often minorities, regularly visit in order to reflect on historical episodes that they imbue with contemporary significance but that are not recognised or no longer spontaneously commemorated by the broader society and therefore in danger of being forgotten. Sites of memory have enormous 'capacity for metamorphosis, an endless recycling of their meaning and an unpredictable proliferation of their ramifications'.[13] Therefore the careful historian must decode them in order to determine what people value in the present by the things they choose to remember and forget about the past.

Salman's charter is a text that has become a site of memory. Recent scholarship has demonstrated the diverse ways that Muslims chose to remember Salman.[14] This chapter is concerned specifically with the ahd-nama and its reception in medieval Islamdom. Whence the charter's content? What does it reveal about how Muslims remembered Zoroastrians? Who preserved this document and why? While Parsis remember that Muslims ignored its stipulations, Persian histories reveal that Muslims were keenly interested in the ahd-nama. Salman's relatives, Abbasid scribes and Indo-Iranian rulers all made copies. It is more difficult to say whether they abided by its precepts, but the charter remains a site of memory for reflection on Muslim–Zoroastrian relations in the Middle East and South Asia.

The Origins of the Charter

The ahd-nama is probably not authentic. The document contains a number of anachronisms that belie its alleged origins. Mohammad Reza Torki has noted ten suspicious elements in it.[15] For example, the Iranian province of Fars, in which Salman's family presumably lived when Muhammad wrote the charter, had not yet been conquered by the Muslims in 9/631. Likewise, many of the laws from which Muhammad frees Salman's family were not introduced until a century or more after the Prophet's death. It is also curious that the charter bears a *hijri* date as that calendar was not in use during Muhammad's lifetime. Yet the ahd-nama's occasional spelling errors, its awkward invocation of blessings on the Prophet in a third-person voice while he is speaking in the first person, and the fact that manuscript copies of it are written in *nasta'liq* script are not proofs of forgery.[16] These errors and anachronisms can be attributed to later scribes, not the original author.[17]

The likelihood that Salman's charter is inauthentic makes it more, not less, interesting to the historian of memory as Sarah Bowen Savant has aptly noted. However, there has been little attempt to uncover its origins. Previous analyses that suggested it was of South Asian origin or relatively recent date are not supported by the evidence.[18] The ahd-nama hails from the medieval Middle East, although there are distinct Indian recensions of the text.[19] Mohammad Reza Torki traced it to Persian histories such as *Tarikh-i Guzida* (730/1330) and *Mujmal al-Tawarikh wa 'l-Qisas* (*c.* 528/1126). A fourteenth-century anecdote states that the Sufi master Abu Ali al-Farmadi (407–477/1016–1084) preserved Salman's charter in one of his books from the eleventh century.[20] The ahd-nama also exists in Abu Nu'aym Ahmad ibn Abd Allah al-Isfahani's (336–430/948–1038) *Dhikr Akhbar Isfahan*.[21] The oldest extant version appears in Abu Muhammad Abd Allah ibn Muhammad ibn Ja'far ibn Hayyan's (274–369/887–979) *Tabaqat al-Muhaddithin bi-Isbahan*.[22] Yet the anonymous author of *Mujmal al-Tawarikh* admits to copying it from Hamza ibn al-Hasan al-Isfahani's (280–350/893–961) *Ta'rikh Isfahan*. Unfortunately, that work is now lost, so the charter's precise origin is uncertain.[23] According to Muhammad ibn Hindushah Nakhjavani (*c.* 679/1280–768/1366), an Ilkhan-era master scribe, 'in the days of the Arab government' the ahd-nama 'was sent to Fars'.[24] The implication is that the charter originated outside of Iran and during the early Abbasid caliphate.

St Catherine's Firman

Salman's charter resembles other writs supposedly issued by the Prophet Muhammad to various non-Muslim communities throughout the Middle East. These documents granted certain privileges to these communities, often exempting them from taxation and freeing them from legal restrictions. As Muhammad was illiterate, they are usually written by Ali and stamped with the Prophet's handprint or seal. Christian, Jewish and Samaritan communities in Egypt, Palestine, Syria, Anatolia and Iraq possessed such texts.[25]

A well-studied document of this sort resides at St Catherine's Monastery in the Sinai Peninsula of Egypt. The Prophet Muhammad supposedly granted it after a delegation from the monastery visited him at Medina in 10/631. This writ is often called a *firmān*, a term usually associated with Ottoman-era chancelleries, indicating its relatively late origins. Stamped with the Prophet's hand, this firman limits the tax liability of Christians, holds their churches inviolable, prohibits outside interference in ecclesiastic appointments and exempts them from military service.[26] Scholars have rightly questioned its authenticity. Like Salman's charter, the St Catherine's firman contains a number of anachronisms. For instance, it bears a *hijri* date even though that calendar was not in use during the Prophet's lifetime, and frees Christians of laws that Muslims had not yet devised. The firman includes a list of Muslim witnesses, two of whom were not Muslims at that time.[27] The similarities between the documents suggest that they belong to the same genre of literature.

It is doubtful that the St Catherine's firman is a genuine Prophetic charter from the seventh century. Jean-Michel Mouton argues that it was probably forged by the monks at the monastery during a period of crisis in the Fatimid era.[28] Exactly what that crisis was remains unclear. The most likely scenario is the imposition of direct Muslim rule over the monastery in the twelfth century. St Catherine's had been largely autonomous before the First Crusade, but the Muslim authorities in Cairo sought to secure the Sinai Peninsula after the Franks conquered Palestine in 1099.[29] As a result, contact between the Fatimids and the monks increased, and two mosques were built – one inside the monastery and the other over the site of a church atop Mount Sinai.[30] The firman may have been a reaction to Fatimid encroachment on the monastery's autonomy during the Crusades.

St Catherine's firman seems to have been modelled on the Treaty of Najran, forged centuries earlier on behalf of Iraqi Christians. The Treaty of Najran (Ar., *ṣulḥ Najrān*) purports to be an agreement that the Prophet Muhammad made in 2/623 with the people of Najran, a region in the Arabian Peninsula near the present border between Saudi Arabia and Yemen. There are competing accounts in Islamic sources of how the treaty came to be, so it is difficult to say more than that about its origins.[31] Like Salman's charter and the St Catherine's firman, the Treaty of Najran grants autonomy to Najranis in their religious affairs, exemption from taxation and conscription and freedom from laws regulating the behaviour of non-Muslims in public. Unlike Salman's charter, which reserves these privileges for Salman's family, the Treaty of Najran extends them to all Christians everywhere. At least, one version of the Treaty of Najran does so.

There are in fact two versions of the Treaty of Najran – one preserved in Christian sources, the other in Muslim sources. The content of each is quite different. For example, the Muslim version of the Treaty of Najran, found in the works of Abu Ubayd (154–224/770–838) and al-Baladhuri (d. 279/892), contains a relatively simple list of rights and privileges afforded to the Najranis by the Prophet in exchange for their submission. Negotiated by the civil and military leaders of Najran, its terms applied only to Najranis.[32] The terms of submission are plausible enough that the Muslim version of the Treaty of Najran may reflect an actual agreement that the Prophet made in the seventh century. The Christian version of the Treaty of Najran, on the other hand, is more expansive. Like the St Catherine's firman, its privileges extend to all Christians everywhere. It was supposedly negotiated by a delegation of Christian dignitaries from Najran. This treaty heaps praises on Christians, offering them far more rights than responsibilities. Its form, diction and content are extremely elaborate. The Christian version of the Treaty of Najran is found in Bar Hebraeus' *Chronicon Ecclesiasticum* and the anonymous Nestorian history known as the *Chronicle of Séert*.[33] The St Catherine's firman is nearly identical to the Christian version of the Treaty of Najran in the *Chronicle of Séert*.[34] The ahd-nama, as will be demonstrated below, more closely resembles the Muslim version.

Antoine Fattal assumed that a Christian priest must have fabricated the Christian version of the Treaty of Najran because it was discovered by a monk named Habib at *Bayt al-Hikma* (The House of Wisdom), the Abbasid library at Baghdad, in 265/878–879.[35] Louis Massignon argued that a prominent Muslim family, the Banu Makhlad, forged it. The Banu Makhlad had once been Nestorian Christians – indeed, one branch of the family remained so – and served as viziers and governors in the early Abbasid caliphate. Massignon speculated that the Banu Makhlad retained some sympathy for their Nestorian family members and former co-religionists, and therefore invented the Treaty of Najran to relieve them of the harsh strictures imposed on non-Muslims by the Abbasid caliph al-Mutawakkil.[36] As Najranis, the Banu Makhlad naturally modelled the Christian version of the Treaty of Najran on the agreement that the Prophet had with their ancestors. As government administrators, they had little difficulty producing a credible forgery. Indeed, the Treaty of Najran proved so convincing that it became the model for myriad charters in the possession of non-Muslim communities throughout the Middle East.[37] In Nora's terms, these were sites of memory where people remembered an alternative past that addressed their needs in the present.

Khabar Salman

The ahd-nama relates to a second genre of literature, which Louis Massignon called *Khabar Salman* (Salman's Narrative). Khabar Salman is a collective term for several lengthy reports about the life and conversion to Islam of Salman al-Farisi. Although the details differ slightly, they share the same basic outline. They are also very early, hailing from the first and second Islamic centuries, contemporaneous with the first biographies of the Prophet Muhammad. In fact, Ibn Ishaq and Ibn Sa'd, two of the earliest transmitters of the *sira*, are among the earliest transmitters of Khabar Salman. There were already seven or eight distinct recensions of Khabar Salman circulating by 175/792.[38]

Khabar Salman connects Muhammad to Jesus of Nazareth through Salman's contact with one of Jesus' long-lived Apostles. As a boy, Salman unexpectedly meets the unnamed Apostle (*waṣī*), who introduces him to esoteric knowledge and asceticism. In some versions of the story, the Apostle also relays writings that are destined for Muhammad. On his deathbed, the Apostle urges Salman to seek out a new mentor in another city for further instruction. Salman finds the new mentor, usually a monk or an ascetic, and studies with him until that man too passes away. The process then repeats itself as Salman searches out his next mentor. In one version of the story, the mentors greet Salman by name when they meet him, for it has been prophesied that a Persian will visit them seeking knowledge. They teach Salman about the coming of a future messenger of God named Muhammad. They also teach him the signs by which he will recognise this messenger (either Muhammad's pious conduct or the physical seal of prophethood between his shoulders). Salman's mentors instruct him in proto-Islamic worship, which includes reciting the *shahada* and performing *salat*, and he spends years – centuries in some versions – studying with each one. His journeys take him to the major patriarchal seats of the eastern Mediterranean (Alexandria, Antioch, Constantinople and Jerusalem) or beyond. The last monk announces the advent of Muhammad and sends Salman to Arabia. Salman is enslaved along the way by treacherous Bedouin and sold to a Jewish person at Medina. There he meets Muhammad. Salman recognises in him the sign of the long-awaited Prophet and converts to Islam. The story ends with Muhammad's Companions pooling their resources to purchase Salman's freedom.[39]

Salman's manumission by the Companions is an element common to all versions of Khabar Salman.[40] An official deed of manumission (Ar., *mukātaba*) accompanies it in later texts. The deed, written by Ali, describes the terms of sale to Muhammad and transfers Salman's clientage to the Prophet. The list of witnesses appended to it includes Abu Bakr, Umar, Hudhayfa ibn al-Yaman, Abu Dharr al-Ghifari, al-Miqdad ibn al-Aswad, Bilal and Abd al-Rahman ibn Awf. The deed bears the date 'Jumādā al-Ūlā, the year of the emigration of Muḥammad to Madīna' (1/622).[41]

Although it is dated to the first year of the *hijri* calendar – an anachronism not lost on al-Khatib al-Baghdadi (d. 463/1071)[42] – Salman's deed of manumission resembles a fourth/tenth-century contract of sale (*sharṭ*). Comparing it to the oldest surviving manual on contract law, the *Kitab al-Buyu'* of the Egyptian scholar Abu Ja'far Ahmad ibn Muhammad al-Tahawi (d. 321/933), it is clear that Salman's deed of manumission resembles a standardised Hanafi contract of sale. The deed begins, as it should, with the phrase *hādhā mā* and subsequent clauses follow in roughly the recommended order; it explicitly precludes future claims against the object of sale (in this case, Salman); and the date and witness list are properly situated. These features were supposed to make the contract unassailable.[43] Thus, the simple story of Salman's manumission by the Companions had, just a century and a half later, produced a legally binding contract of sale to the Prophet. Not coincidently, this embellishment of Khabar Salman appeared only after the standardisation of such contracts in Hanafi law.

Salman's deed of manumission and charter are closely associated. They appear side by side in several Iranian histories, including *Dhikr Akhbar Isfahan*, *Mujmal al-Tawarikh* and *Tarikh-i Guzida*.[44] It is significant that every medieval Muslim text that preserves Salman's charter also preserves his deed of manumission.[45] The two documents may have been composed at roughly the same time. Since Salman's deed of manumission adheres to the norms of a contract of sale, and al-Tahawi's tenth-century *Kitab al-Buyu'* is the oldest surviving work on that subject, the late ninth or early tenth century is a reasonable estimate, which coincides with its first appearance in *Tabaqat al-Muhaddithin bi-Isbahan*.

Both the charter and deed of manumission are linked to Khabar Salman. An abbreviated version of Khabar Salman precedes them in *Mujmal al-Tawarikh* and *Tarikh-i Guzida*. In *Dhikr Akhbar Isfahan*, the deed and charter appear in the midst of several hadith narrated on the authority of Ubayd al-Muktib. According to Massignon, Ubayd al-Muktib (died 140?/757–8?) was one of the earliest transmitters of Khabar Salman.[46] In fact, a version of Khabar Salman, narrated on Ubayd's authority, appears in *Dhikr Akhbar Isfahan* immediately before Salman's deed of manumission and charter. Following immediately after them in the text is a hadith, also narrated on the authority of Ubayd, describing the deed of manumission as a physical object that the Prophet pressed into Salman's hand. Thus, in *Dhikr Akhbar Isfahan*, the deed and charter are literally sandwiched between traditions from Ubayd al-Muktib, even though neither document is transmitted on his authority. Their placement demonstrates the connection between the ahd-nama and Khabar Salman. Both were sites of memory about Salman's putative Zoroastrian origins.

The Content of Salman's Charter

The ahd-nama is a composite document that draws inspiration from more than one source. Some of its content is unique. For instance, the substantial theological excursus in the middle of the text, which varies in length and complexity between the Iranian and Indian recensions, appears to be original. Nevertheless, it is possible to identify at least two sources of the charter's content – the Treaty of Najran and a derivative document called the Treaty of Khaybar.

A significant portion of the ahd-nama derives from the Muslim version of the Treaty of Najran, the agreement that the Prophet made with a tribal delegation from southern Arabia. Unlike the Christian version, described above, the Muslim version closely resembles a conquest-era treaty. Some of the language is nearly identical between them. For example, the ahd-nama begins with the Prophet promising Salman's family the protection of God and Muhammad (*dhimmat Allāh wa-dhimmat Muḥammad*).[47] The Treaty of Najran, by contrast, promises Najranis '*jiwār Allāh wa-dhimmat Muḥammad*'.[48] *Jiwār* and *dhimma* are synonyms, though Milka Levy-Rubin notes that *jiwār* was typically used in the earliest conquest treaties to describe the protection granted to conquered populations. The term *amān* replaced it in later Muslim discourse, and *jiwār* was not used in relation to non-Muslims thereafter.[49] This fact indicates that the Muslim version of the Treaty of Najran is older than the ahd-nama. The authors of Salman's charter borrowed terminology and updated it when necessary. Another example of analogous phrasing is the protection offered to Salman's family. In the ahd-nama it extends to 'their lives and wealth in the land on which they reside' (*dimā'ihim wa-amwālihim fī l-arḍ allatī yuqīmūna fīhā*).[50] The protection afforded to Najranis covers 'their souls, religious communities, lands, and wealth' (*anfusihim wa-millatihim wa-arḍihim wa-amwālihim*).[51]

The ahd-nama further stipulates that Muhammad 'has relieved [Salman's family] of trimming their forelocks, the jizya, conscription, and the tithe' (*qad rafa'tu 'an-hum jazz al-nāṣiya wa-l-jizya wa-l-ḥashr wa-l-'ushr*).[52] The Treaty of Najran simply states that Najranis 'shall not be conscripted nor tithed' (*lā yuḥsharūn wa lā yu'sharūn*).[53] There was much confusion about the meaning of the term *al-ḥashr* ('conscription') in subsequent copies of the ahd-nama.[54] Some medieval copyists misread it as *al-khums* ('one-fifth [of the spoils of war]') or *al-khayr* ('goodness'). Consequently, in *Tarikh-i Guzida* Muhammad relieves Salman's family of 'the jizya and the good and the bad' (*al-jizya wa-l-khayr wa-l-sharr*).[55] Other scribes made sense of *al-ḥashr* by adding other words that gave it a religious meaning. Thus, in Indian recensions of the text, the Prophet relieves Salman's family of the jizya until the Resurrection (*al-jizya ilā al-ḥashr wa-l-nashr*).[56] When compared to the Treaty of Najran, however, the error of such readings is obvious.

The charter demands that Muslims give Salman's family preferential treatment. The Treaty of Najran, on the other hand, denies the Najranis any special status on account of their agreement with the Prophet. In Najran's relations with other tribes, there was supposed to be strict 'parity (*naṣaf*) between them. They neither mistreat nor are mistreated by Najran (*ghayr ẓālimīn wa-lā maẓlūmīn bi-Najrān*).'[57] The ahd-nama changes this concept slightly. Salman's family is 'not to be mistreated nor imposed upon' (*ghayr maẓlūmīn wa-lā muḍayyaq alayhim*).[58] While it was incumbent on Muslims 'to protect them and please them and not impose hateful and odious things on them', there is no insistence that Salman's family reciprocate. The ahd-nama rejects the Treaty of Najran's insistence on parity between tribes by elevating Salman's family above others.

Perhaps the ahd-nama's most obvious similarity to the Treaty of Najran is the section on financial obligation. Najranis famously wove fine garments, and the Treaty of Najran demanded that Christians pay a regular tribute to Muslims in textiles. A *ḥulla* was a two-piece suit of clothing, comprised of a cape-like piece that draped over the shoulders (*ridā'*) and an apron-like loincloth that attached around the waist (*izār*).[59] The concept of a tribute paid in hulla also appears in the charter, but the roles of the respective parties are reversed. Salman's ostensibly Zoroastrian family now collects hulla from Muslim authorities. This stipend was to be paid on account of God's fondness for Salman: 'They must give from the Muslims' treasury each year 200 ḥulla in the month of Rajab and 100 ḥulla in Dhū-l-Ḥijja. Salman deserves (*istaḥaqqa*) that from us because God prefers (*faḍḍala*) Salman over many of the believers.'[60] Another recension of the charter sets the stipend at 200 hulla and 100 ounces (presumably of silver).[61] The idea that Zoroastrians deserve payment is remarkable considering the contentious debates among Muslims about taxing Zoroastrians encountered in Chapter Two. However, Muhammad supposedly paid ten ounces to each member of a delegation from the Banu 'l-Harith tribe of Najran.[62] That report, which emerges out of the larger story of the Treaty of Najran, may be the root of the idea that Salman's family deserves a stipend.

The Treaty of Najran required the Najranis to give 2,000 hulla per year to the Prophet. The tribute was to be paid in semi-annual installments of 1,000 hulla during the months of Safar and Rajab. That represented a substantial sum, even in the days of the Prophet. In later Islamicate history, hulla were fabulously ornate, woven with fine silk and decorated with embroidery (*ṭirāz*). They were roughly equivalent to the *khil'a*, or robe of investiture, bestowed by the caliph on governors and nominally subordinate rulers. Such robes carried immense monetary and symbolic value.[63] The garments of seventh-century Arabia were likely more humble, but they were valuable. According to the Treaty of Najran, each hulla had to be worth at least one ounce.[64] That sum was enough that later generations of Najranis struggled to pay the tribute. After the conquest of Arabia, the caliph Umar ibn al-Khattab had resettled the Najranis on marginal land in Iraq, and many of them converted to Islam, leaving the remainder to plead with successive caliphs – Rashidun, Umayyad and Abbasid – to lighten their financial obligation. They met with some success. The Umayyad caliph Umar ibn Abd al-Aziz reduced the impost to 200 hulla annually, as did the first Abbasid caliph, al-Saffah. According to al-Baladhuri, during the reign of Harun al-Rashid, the amount was fixed in writing at 200 hulla.[65]

That Muslims should literally pay tribute to Salman's family is a clear reversal of the meaning and intent of the Treaty of Najran. Yet it is also evidence that the ahd-nama derives from the Treaty. The 2,000 hulla of the Treaty of Najran became 200 in Salman's charter, perhaps reflecting Harun al-Rashid's adjustment of the rate. Even the mistaken demand for 200 hulla in Safar and 100 in Rajab – a corruption of the original formula of 2,000 hulla paid in two installments of 1,000 – reflects the wording of an alternate version of the Treaty of Najran.[66] The assertion that Salman's family has a right (*istaḥaqqa*) to such a stipend echoes the Treaty of Najran's concern for the rights (*ḥuqūq*) of Najranis.[67] The Treaty of Najran is the primary source of the charter's content.

A Similar Charter

The Treaty of Khaybar also resembles the ahd-nama. Muhammad ibn Hindushah Nakhjavani, a fourteenth-century Iranian master scribe, reported that Abu Ali al-Farmadi (407–477/1016–1084) knew of a charter written 'in the same style' (N.P., *bar hamīn oslūb*) as Salman's. It was addressed to Huyayy ibn Akhtab. These two charters were reproduced by the scribes of Nakhjavani's day out of reverence for Ali, who had originally transcribed both.

> [Abū ʿAlī al-Fārmadī] has studied a copy of [Salmān's] charter as well as a charter which refers to [the Prophet Muḥammad], may God bless and grant him salvation, written by the Commander of the Faithful, may God bless him, to Ḥuyayy ibn Akhṭab, who was the ruler (*wālī*) of Khaybar, in the same style as Salmān's previously mentioned charter . . . [T]he copying and memorizing of these two charters is one of the great glories of the scribes who, like the Commander of the Faithful ʿAlī . . ., were in charge of writing.[68]

Huyayy ibn Akhtab was the leader of the Jewish Banu 'l-Nadir tribe of Medina and, according to biographers of the Prophet, a persistent antagonist of Muhammad. He reportedly plotted the Prophet's assassination when Muhammad once visited him with an inadequate security detail. The Prophet expelled the Banu 'l-Nadir from Medina on account of this conspiracy.[69] Considering the overt hostility between the two men, it seems odd that Muhammad would issue a charter to Huyayy, especially one like Salman's. There are two agreements associated with Huyayy in the Muslim sources, although he was in fact a party to neither: the Prophet's defence pact with the Banu Qurayza and the Treaty of Khaybar. One is presumably the charter written 'in the same style' as the ahd-nama.

Defence Pact

Muhammad's fraught relations with the Jewish populations of Medina is a topic that has attracted much scholarly attention.[70] Eschewing the essentialising claims about it made by anti-Jewish and anti-Muslim polemicists, I admit that the full story cannot be detailed here. Suffice it to say, according to the Prophet's biographers, Huyayy agitated against Muhammad even after the Banu 'l-Nadir had been expelled from Medina. He returned to the city in secret, encouraging the Banu Qurayza to betray the Prophet at the Battle of the Trench in 5/627. They allegedly did not aid Muhammad during the battle, and the Prophet laid siege to their strongholds in retaliation. When the Banu Qurayza finally surrendered, Muhammad had Huyayy executed for treason, along with all of the tribe's adult males.[71] Despite the tension between them, al-Baladhuri reports that Huyayy 'made a pact with the Messenger of God that he would not aid anyone against [Muhammad], and made God guarantor of it'.[72] This report is strangely out of place in al-Baladhuri's chapter on the Banu Qurayza, a tribe to which Huyayy did not belong. Moreover, the defence pact appears in al-Baladhuri's work *after* Huyayy was expelled from Medina for supposedly attempting to assassinate the Prophet. Surely Muhammad would not have negotiated a treaty of mutual defence with the man who just tried to have him killed. Yet Abu Ubayd affirms that they had an agreement that predated the battle.[73]

In reality, Muhammad had a defence pact with the tribes of Medina, including the Banu Qurayza, but Huyayy was not a signatory of it. Abu Ubayd and al-Baladhuri have confused the various treaties comprising the so-called Constitution of Medina. Other Muslim historians, such as al-Waqidi and al-Tabari, transmitted these separate agreements as a single document.[74] When the Prophet arrived at Medina in 1/622, several tribes accepted him as their arbiter, and agreed to articles of confederation. This portion of the Constitution of Medina does not provide for the common defence and therefore predates the defence pact.[75] R. B. Serjeant has convincingly argued that Muhammad negotiated the defence pact just before the Battle of the Trench, approximately 5/627. The defence pact only covered those tribes remaining in Medina at that time. Huyayy could not have signed the pact because his tribe had been expelled from Medina *before* the Battle of the Trench. Thus, Muslim historians have confused the earlier portions of the Constitution of Medina, which included Huyayy and the Banu 'l-Nadir, with the later defence pact, which did not.[76]

By contrast, the Banu Qurayza were part of the defence pact. All of the early Islamic sources agree that there was a special agreement between them and the Prophet that went beyond the original articles of confederation. Nevertheless, Huyayy induced the Banu Qurayẓa to violate the defence pact at the Battle of the Trench; he is said to have personally torn up their copy of it.[77] As a result, Huyayy is commonly associated with the defence pact in the Muslim sources. While the defence pact could be the charter written 'in the same style' as the ahd-nama, its wording does not resemble Salman's charter, nor does any part of the larger Constitution of Medina. Therefore, neither is likely the document that al-Farmadi saw.

Treaty of Khaybar

Considering the dissimilarity between the defence pact and the ahd-nama, Nakhjavani must be referring to the Treaty of Khaybar, an agreement that Muhammad allegedly made with that city after conquering it. Nakhjavani described it as addressed 'to Huyayy b. Akhṭab who was the ruler of Khaybar' (Pers., *jehat-e Ḥuyayy b. Akhṭab kī wālī Khaybar būd*).[78] In fact, Huyayy was not present at the surrender of Khaybar, having been executed two years earlier at the Battle of the Trench. He was wrongly associated with the Treaty of Khaybar, as with the defence pact, because of his ties to that city. Huyayy was not from Khaybar, but he fled there after the Banu 'l-Nadir were expelled from Medina. Ibn Hisham claims that he subsequently became a leader of that city.[79] The Prophet besieged Khaybar in 7/628, and its inhabitants surrendered on terms. Huyayy obviously did not negotiate those terms, but his association with the Treaty is perhaps understandable considering that Muhammad captured Huyayy's daughter, Safiyya, at Khaybar. She then became one of the Prophet's wives.[80]

It should be noted that a document called the Treaty of Khaybar does not exist in early Muslim sources. Ibn Hisham preserved an antebellum letter from the Prophet to the Jews of Khaybar, but it does not resemble Salman's charter.[81] Al-Baladhuri simply described the terms of the city's surrender.[82] Yet at some later date a Treaty of Khaybar came into circulation among Jewish communities in the Middle East because a copy of it was preserved among the papers at the Cairo Geniza.[83] The unnamed document, narrated by a Jewish convert to Islam, is written in Judeo-Arabic and addressed to 'Hanina [Huyayy] and the people of Khaybar and Maqna'. Muhammad, dictating to Ali, granted them certain privileges and exempted them from various impositions – including jizya – even though al-Baladhuri reported none of them as terms of submission.[84] Salman is listed as a witness in the Geniza document, which bears a precise date: Friday, the third day of Ramadan, 5 AH. Hartwig Hirschfeld noted long ago that this date is incorrect. The third of Ramadan fell on a Monday in the year 5. However, he notes that the third of Ramadan fell on a Friday in the year 9, when Muhammad is supposed to have dispatched other letters.[85] The ahd-nama is dated 9 AH, although it does not specify the day or month.

The Treaty of Khaybar was in wide circulation by the medieval period, used by Jews throughout the Middle East to claim exemption from jizya.[86] The charter was quite popular in Yemen, where there existed in Hebrew a certificate to that effect known as *Kitab Dhimmat al-Nabi*.[87] The Jews of Damascus possessed a similar document, though the famous Muslim jurist Ibn Taymiyya rejected its authenticity. Nevertheless, the Fatimid caliph al-Hakim is supposed to have recognised the Khaybaris' exemption from the jizya.[88] There was certainly more than one version of the Treaty, too, since a copy presented to the Abbasid vizier in the eleventh century was deemed a fraud because it was dictated to Muʿawiya ibn Abi Sufyan, who was not yet a Muslim at the siege of Khaybar.[89] It seems that the Treaty of Khaybar was invented *post facto* to ease the tax burden of Jewish communities that could claim Arabian descent.

The content and wording of the Treaty of Khaybar strongly resembles that of Salman's charter. It is undoubtedly the document that Nakhjavani said was written 'in the same style' as Salman's charter. While both derived from the Treaty of Najran and are clearly patterned after each other, it is difficult to say which came first.[90] As will be seen, the content of each reflects ghiyar regulations that sought to visually distinguish Muslims from non-Muslims.

Ghiyar

Like the Treaty of Khaybar, Salman's charter presumes the existence of laws regulating the appearance and conduct of non-Muslims (Ar., *ghiyār*). Milka Levy-Rubin has postulated that early Muslim jurists devised laws to differentiate Muslims from others in places where they lived in close proximity. There was not initially a consistent, comprehensive policy towards non-Muslims because individual treaties had been negotiated with specific cities at the time of the conquest. As a result, non-Muslims theoretically lived under whatever terms their ancestors had agreed to generations earlier. These terms tended to be relatively liberal, offering considerable autonomy in religious and social affairs in exchange for loyalty and some form of remuneration, be it tribute or service in kind.[91]

The conquest-era arrangements worked for decades, so long as the number of Muslims remained small and both Muslims and non-Muslims preferred to live in separate areas or distinct cities. As demographics shifted and cities became more integrated, however, intercommunal contact increased, and it became more difficult to distinguish Muslims from non-Muslims. Early Muslim jurists proposed various legal codes in an attempt to standardise and thereby replace the original treaties. Levy-Rubin suggests that they may have been inspired by Sasanian codes but more research is needed to prove it definitively.[92] Regardless, the intent was to more clearly differentiate Muslims from others.

These legal codes became a convenient means of suppressing practices that Muslims deemed objectionable and, later, of humiliating non-Muslims. The stipulations of ghiyar varied, and jurists such as Abu Yusuf (d. 182/798) and al-Shafi'i (d. 204/820) proposed different laws. The most infamous set of rules, known as the Pact of Umar (*shurūṭ 'Umar*), did not exist until centuries later but was attributed to the second caliph, Umar ibn al-Khattab (ruled 13–23/634–644). There is some debate about which caliph was the first to enforce particular ghiyar restrictions. Sources commonly suggest it was Umar, or his namesake, the Umayyad caliph Umar ibn Abd al-Aziz, or even the Abbasid caliph al-Mutawakkil.[93] The distinctive terminology used to describe seemingly similar types of prohibited clothing, for example, makes it difficult to say with certainty. It is also unclear precisely where and how such laws might have been enforced by caliphal authorities. What is evident is that rules circumscribing the worship, dress and prestige of non-Muslims were part of Islamic juridical discourse by the eighth century. They circulated side by side with the Treaty of Najran in the *Siyar* of the Hanafi jurist Muhammad al-Shaybani (132–189/750–805), for example.[94]

Salman's charter was clearly written in response to ghiyar, again indicating its likely Abbasid-era origins. Through the ahd-nama, the Prophet Muhammad frees Salman's family from many common stipulations.

> I have relieved them [Salman's family] of trimming their forelocks, jizya, conscription, the tithe, and the rest of the burdens and inconveniences. (*Qad rafa'tu 'an-hum jazz al-nāṣiya wa-l-jizya wa-l-ḥashr wa-l-'ushr wa-sā'ir al-ma'ūn wa-l-kulaf.*)[95]

Indian recensions of the charter specifically add the wearing of the *zunnar* (discussed below) to that list. They also include the following paragraph:

> They [Salman's family] have complete control over fire temples, including their domains and wealth. Do not prohibit them from [wearing] luxurious clothing, or riding [animals], or building homes and stables, or carrying biers, or adopting whatever they adopt in their religion and sects. (*Aydīhum muṭlaqatun ʿalā buyūt al-nīrān wa-ḍiyāʿihā wa-āmwālihā wa-lā yamnaʿūnahum min al-libās al-fākhir wa-l-rukūb wa-bināʾ al-dūr wa-l-iṣṭabl wa-ḥaml al-janāʾiz wa-ittikhādh mā yattakhidhūna fī dīnihim wa-madhāhibihim.*)[96]

Ghiyar prohibited or regulated all of these behaviours, and the Treaty of Khaybar granted exemptions to its bearers similar to those mentioned in the ahd-nama. A brief analysis of the Treaty of Khaybar's contents, based on Hartwig Herschfeld's English translation of the Geniza version, will follow in order to demonstrate its similarity to Salman's charter.

Dress and Grooming

The core of ghiyar was the dress code. Various rules stipulated that non-Muslims should not wear particular articles of clothing or seek to imitate Muslim styles. They also had to wear the *zunnār* (also known as *minṭaqa*).[97] A belt or girdle that tied around the waist, it was a visual marker of their legal status. Non-Muslims were obliged to wear the *zunnar* over their clothing in public.[98] The ahd-nama granted Salman's family a reprieve. Surprisingly, the *zunnar* is not mentioned in the Treaty of Khaybar.

Non-Muslims sometimes had to wear certain colours or affix distinctive patches to their clothing. The prescribed colours varied by time and place or the sect to which a person belonged. The Treaty of Khaybar, for example, permits Huyayy's family to wear striped and coloured garments, particularly in white, yellow and brown.[99] Beyond distinguishing non-Muslims from Muslims, these rules also acted as sumptuary laws. For instance, fabrics that doubled as status markers, such as silk, were sometimes forbidden to non-Muslims.[100] Hence, Salman's charter allows Salman's family to wear luxurious clothing. The dress code was neither universally nor consistently applied. Indeed, the tenth-century geographer al-Muqaddasi reported that the Zoroastrians and Christians of Shiraz brazenly flouted it – at the very time and place in which the ahd-nama appeared.[101]

Ghiyar often required non-Muslims to groom differently than Muslims. Therefore, the ahd-nama relieves Salman's descendants of trimming their forelocks. The Treaty of Khaybar liberates Jews from this practice as well.[102] The trimming of forelocks as a form of punishment has a long pedigree in ancient Near Eastern societies.[103] Men generally wore their hair long in pre-Islamic Arabia, so trimmed forelocks marked a freed captive. It was an act of merit for a warrior to release a captive, but the victor would cut the prisoner's hair first in order to mark the victory. The freed man was then expected to pay the champion for his clemency. This custom persisted in early Islamic history. Like freed captives, non-Muslims were required to trim their forelocks and pay the jizya as a token of their subjugation.[104] Trimmed forelocks visually distinguished them from Muslims.

Taxes

Salman's charter frees his family from two taxes, jizya and tithe (*'ushr*). The precise meaning of these two terms varied over time but, by the Abbasid era, the jizya was generally an annual head tax on non-Muslims, while the tithe was an annual ten per cent tax on the agricultural produce of Muslims (or a lesser rate on the products and wares of Muslim and non-Muslim artisans and merchants). In earlier periods the meaning of these terms was more fluid. Among other things, both terms were used to describe the land tax (*kharāj*) paid by all cultivators, regardless of religious affiliation.[105] Thus, this portion of the charter could refer to a general tax on agricultural production rather than a Muslim tithe, or it may indicate there were fiscal benefits across communal boundaries for claiming descent from Salman. The Treaty of Khaybar mentions all three forms of taxation.[106]

The jizya, or poll tax, is an infamous marker of non-Muslim status. Al-Shafi'i included it in his proposed ghiyar regulations. He set the rate at one dinar per man annually.[107] The rate of jizya was usually graduated according to ability to pay – often one, two or four dinars (or the equivalent of twelve, twenty-four or forty-eight dirhams). It was collected from all adult males, with the exception of slaves, clergy and the insane. Tax dodgers could be fitted with a lead seal about their necks like slaves.[108] As Moshe Gil has demonstrated, the Cairo Geniza preserves a petition by the Jewish community of Tiberias for financial relief on the basis of the Treaty of Khaybar.[109]

Fire Temples

The charter offered Salman's family complete control over their fire temples. That was a real concern because Muslims and Zoroastrians initially worshipped together in many Iranian towns. Subsequent generations of Muslims appropriated Zoroastrian sacred space in places such as Rayy, Herat and Bukhara. Some proponents of ghiyar held that non-Muslims could not build new houses of worship nor repair old ones.[110] Zoroastrians were also concerned at times for the safety of their sacred fires and the sanctity of their temples in Dezpul, Istakhr and Nishapur, which later Islamic sources claim to have violated. Such claims are treated at length in Chapter Five.[111] The Treaty of Khaybar, by contrast, does not assert authority over Jewish houses of worship. That is surprising because the Treaty of Najran, its model, specifically protects churches (*bīʿ*).[112]

Riding Animals

Indian recensions of the ahd-nama grant Salman's family permission to ride beasts of burden and to build stables. These were significant concessions because security concerns and sumptuary laws may have otherwise prohibited them from doing so. Indeed, every major edict issued by the caliphs on the subject of ghiyar between the early eighth and the mid-ninth century regulated non-Muslims' use of riding animals, saddles or stirrups.[113] These laws illustrate the concern about farming equipment being diverted to the battlefield. Thus, the Treaty of Khaybar permits Huyayy's descendants to use saddles and carry weapons in the same clause.[114] Restricting the use of relatively expensive riding implements such as saddles and stirrups – and even the ability to ride a horse, elevated above Muslim pedestrians – had the intended side effect of limiting non-Muslim prestige. Such laws were supposed to curb conspicuous consumption.

Funerals

The charter affords Salman's family the privilege of carrying biers. As Zoroastrians consider physical contact with dead matter to be particularly defiling, preparing and conveying a corpse had to be finely orchestrated in order to avoid pollution, which may explain why the author of the ahd-nama specified it.[115] Some Zoroastrians in the pre-modern era had the distinctive custom of leaving their dead exposed to the elements in a large, open-air enclosure known as a Tower of Silence (N.P., *dakhma*). Here the corruptible elements of the body were devoured by scavenging animals so as not to pollute the earth.[116] Zoroastrians at times hired Muslims to dispose of corpses, although Zoroastrian law sought to prevent it.[117] Today, Zoroastrian funerary practices have changed significantly in both Iran and India.[118]

Muslims have developed over the centuries their own distinctive burial customs, including precise rules regarding funeral processions, carrying biers and interring bodies in the earth.[119] Differentiating regulations sometimes prohibited non-Muslims from raising their voices during processions and from burying their dead near Muslims.[120] According to the Treaty of Khaybar, Muslims were supposed to make room for Jewish funerals provided they did not trespass on a sacred spot, such as a mosque.[121] Perhaps the ahd-nama permits Salman's family to carry biers because there was an attempt to limit cross-confessional contact at cemeteries. As Leor Halevi notes, some early Muslim jurists were reluctant to participate in non-Muslim funerals, although we know that Jews and Christians attended Muslim funerals. Indeed in the conversion of Zoroastrians there was something of a trope.[122] The fact that carrying biers is mentioned only in Indian recensions of Salman's charter might suggest later or more localised concerns. For example, the Turkmen rulers of fifteenth-century Mosul required Christians to drag, rather than carry, corpses to burial.[123]

Reception of the Text

Although Salman's charter sought to liberate Salman's Zoroastrian descendants from ghiyar, early Islamic sources do not reveal whether it was effective. They do, however, show that there was keen interest in the document for centuries among Muslim rulers, scribes and merchants from Iran to India. The charter originally surfaced in southwestern Persia in the tenth century, among people who claimed descent from Salman. According to the anonymous author of *Mujmal al-Tawarikh* (who took his information from Hamza al-Isfahani), Salman's descendants in Shiraz possessed the charter.[124] Abu Bakr Ahmad ibn Ali al-Khatib al-Baghdadi (d. 463/1071) noted that Salman had three daughters in Isfahan, dismissively adding that 'some group had claimed that they were part of their offspring'.[125] The author of *Tabaqat al-Muhaddithin* likewise mentioned that

> someone who took an interest in this matter mentioned that Salman has a group [of relatives] from his father's brother, Māhādhar Farrūkh, scattered across the lands. There is a group of them in the city of Shiraz, in the Persian districts, whose leader is a man named Ghassān ibn Zādhān ibn Shādhawayh ibn Māhbandād ibn Māhādhū [sic] Farrūkh, brother of Salmān ibn Badakhshān.[126]

Although described as relatives, these people were perhaps devotees of Salman, the so-called Salmaniyya. The report immediately preceding the one about Salman's relatives includes the claim that he lived for 350 years.[127] That belief belongs to the cult of memory that developed posthumously around Salman. For Muslims, and especially Persians, there was much about his life to celebrate. Salman was a Companion of the Messenger of God and an honorary member of the Prophet's household (*ahl al-bayt*).[128] He was the first Persian convert to Islam, the hero of the Battle of the Trench, and the first governor of Mada'in, former seat of the Sasanian Empire.[129] Among Muslim mystics, Salman was larger than life. He was a proto-Sufi; the Gate (*bāb*) to esoteric knowledge; the *Sīn* of the Mysterious Letters of the Qur'an; an incarnation of the Divine.[130]

Not surprisingly, this Shirazi family passed down Salman's charter within its ranks. *Dhikr Akhbar Isfahan* states that in the eleventh century it was 'in the possession of a grandson (*sibṭ*) of Ghassān'.[131] Based on the genealogy given above, Ghassan would have been Salman's great-great-great nephew. His confessional identity is unclear. Ghassan is a non-sectarian Arabic name. Names carried great religious significance in medieval Islamicate societies and were often indicators of religious affiliation. Speaking of naming patterns among Iranian converts to Islam during this period, Richard Bulliet states:

> Whereas in the earliest stages of conversion [which began with the conquest in the seventh century] identification as a friend of the Arabs was desirable, and somewhat later religiously ambiguous (though not threateningly Zoroastrian) names came briefly into vogue for protective coloration, once Islam was unquestioningly there to stay and rapidly growing stronger with

> a bandwagon effect . . ., it became increasingly desirable to display publicly one's conversion and give ostentatiously Muslim names to one's sons. Names that might be mistaken for Christian or Jewish names steadily lost popularity, and nonreligious Arabic names were even less desirable in what was increasingly an Iranian Muslim society.[132]

The Arabic name Ghassan, while not obviously affiliated with any religion, is distinct from the Persian names that precede it in the family tree.

Salman's charter generated interest beyond his putative family. Hamza al-Isfahani included it in his history 'so that there would be a copy' (N.P., *tā āz yek rū-yi bāshad*).[133] As previously noted, the eleventh-century Sufi master Abu Ali al-Farmadi studied the ahd-nama, and Muhammad Hindushah Nakhjavani added that fourteenth-century Ilkhanid scribes memorised it as an act of devotion to the Prophet's scribe, Ali.[134]

In the twelfth century, a Seljuk sultan summoned one of Salman's descendants to his court in order to view the charter. The anonymous author of *Mujmal al-Tawarikh* reports:

> I heard from a well-known, reliable source that in the time of Sulṭān Muḥammad [ibn Malik Shah] (ruled 498–511/1105–1118), may God have mercy on him, that one of [Salman's relatives] was brought under escort from Shīrāz to Iṣfahān with only the money and clothing that were on him. He sought a private audience with the sultan and gave him the aforementioned charter, still on parchment, to read. [The sultan] kissed it and wept and gave this man many things, and [the man] returned to his home. [The sultan] made a copy of it and the original was returned to its place.[135]

Although the Seljuk ruler ostensibly rewarded this man as a tribute to the Prophet's pious example, Sultan Muhammad is remembered for his harsh treatment of non-Muslims in Baghdad.[136] *Mujmal al-Tawarikh* was written just seven years after the sultan's death, during the turbulent reign of his adolescent son and successor, Mahmud. It was during Mahmud's reign that the Seljuk confederation began to collapse. Sultan Muhammad was the last of the Seljuk rulers to wield universal authority over Iraq and western Iran.[137] This story probably reveals some longing for his unified reign.

Parsis discovered the ahd-nama in Gujarat in the seventeenth century. Nanabhai Punjiya, the leader of the Parsi community at Surat, describes encountering it when Sayyid Musa, a devout and enterprising relative of Shah Jahan (1037–1068/1628–1658), the Mughal ruler of India, moved to that city 'seeking prosperity'.

> The humble servant, Nānā Bahā son of Pūnjiyā son of Piyān the Pārsī, and supporters of the . . . household . . . visited [Sayyid Musa] out of devotion. After a while, mention was made of the religion and *madhhab* of these forlorn Parsis (N.P., *bī kasān fārsiyān*). The eloquent, pious sayyid explained, 'In our library there is a book called *Tārīkh bar Guzīda*. The charter (*'ahd-nāma*) that the Messenger . . . has given to the nephew of Salmān-i Fārsī, may God be pleased with him, has been written in that book, written in the handwriting of the Commander of the Faithful, 'Alī ibn Abī Ṭālib.' He ordered the retrieval of the book from his library. In front of the *majlis*, they read what was written . . . The servant asked to copy that book, expecting (*tavvaqu'*) those honorable sayyids and esteemed shaykhs and qadis of Islam and the muftis of mankind to certify (*mozayyan va monavvar kardand*) the charter and the handwriting.[138]

This story presumably explains how the Parsi community first acquired a copy of Salman's charter.

A relatively late anecdote suggests that Salman's family at one time enjoyed the fiscal benefits promised in the ahd-nama. According to the nineteenth-century *Farsnama-yi Nasiri*, the Prophet Muhammad instructed the Companions to exempt Salman's family from the jizya once they conquered Kazarun, near Shiraz. A tribe in Kazarun that claimed descent from Salman had a copy of these instructions, which bore the Prophet's seal. One of these descendants was a Muslim named Abu Ishaq al-Kazaruni (352–426/963–1033).

> Among the notables of this Salmani tribe was the Rightful Master, Guide of the Eternal Ones, Shaykh Abū Isḥāq Ibrāhīm ibn Shahriyār ibn Mihriyār the Kāzarūnī. Throughout his life, he used to take the alms (*ṣadaqat*) of the honorable Salmān from the treasury that was in the hands of the Abbasid caliphs, and apportion it for the Salmānī tribe.[139]

These alms seem to be the stipend promised in the ahd-nama. Thus, the author of the *Farsnama-yi Nasiri* remembered that Abu Ishaq abided by the terms of the charter.

The *Farsnama-yi Nasiri* is an extremely late source for information about Abu Ishaq al-Kazaruni, who had lived centuries earlier, and the shaykh's medieval hagiography does not include this information about the charter.[140] It celebrates his career in other ways. Abu Ishaq was a Sufi master, the founder of an order that eventually spread to Anatolia and India. His *khanqah*, or Sufi lodge, was renowned for its charity. Abu Ishaq was famous for recruiting volunteers to fight the Byzantines, and his own prowess on the battlefield and zeal as a missionary were proverbial.[141] He reportedly converted to Islam 24,000 Zoroastrians from Kazarun – an impossible feat, considering that the city probably did not have that many residents.[142] Yet the author chose to remember him in the nineteenth century as a pious man who claimed the prophetic favour that Salman's family merited.

Conclusion

Despite its alleged origins, and resonance in South Asia, the ahd-nama first appeared in works on the history of Isfahan during the tenth century. It sits in dialogue with Khabar Salman, and bears similarity to the Treaties of Khaybar and Najran, indicating that Zoroastrians in Persia were subject to the same codes of ghiyar as Jews and Christians elsewhere and that different communities employed similar means in an attempt to circumvent them. Whether they were successful or not is harder to say. It is clear, however, that Muslims took great interest in the charter over generations. Salman's relatives in Shiraz preserved it on parchment during the tenth century; a Sufi master studied it in the eleventh century; and the Seljuk sultan procured a copy in the twelfth century. Ilkhanid scribes memorised the text; Mughals shared it with Parsis in early modern India; and Qajars imagined its implementation. In Nora's terms, Salman's charter was a site of memory. It helped pre-modern Muslims to remember Salman and the example of the Prophet. The ahd-nama has also been a location where Parsis lament the mistreatment of their ancestors. After the Bombay Riot of 1851, it offered the prospect of reconciliation. The charter is, in other words, a place for remembering, forgetting and contesting histories of Muslim–Zoroastrian relations.

Notes

1. For more information on this riot, see Andrew D. Magnusson, 'A History of Violence? Islam, British Orientalism, and the Bombay Riot of 1851', in Justin Quinn Olmstead (ed.), *Britain in the Islamic World: Imperial and Post-Imperial Connections* (London: Palgrave Macmillan, 2019), 3–26.
2. On Sorabjee, see Jal H. Wadia, *Sir Jamsetjee Jejeebhoy Parsee Benevolent Institution Centenary Volume* (Bombay: Mody Printing Press, 1950), 125–32; and H. D. Darukhanawala, *Parsi Lustre on Indian Soil*, vol. 1 (Bombay: G. Claridge, 1939), 261; on Jamsetjee, see Jesse S. Palsetia, *Jamsetjee Jejeebhoy of Bombay: Partnership and Public Culture in Empire* (New Delhi: Oxford University Press, 2015).
3. Sorabjee Jamsetjee Jejeebhoy, *Tuqviuti-Din-i-Mazdiasna* (Bombay: Jam-i-Jamsheed Press, 1851), 1–11.
4. The name of Salman's brother varies in the sources, even between versions of the ahd-nama. See Clément Huart, 'Selman du Fars', in *Mélanges Hartwig Derenbourg, 1844–1908* (Paris: E. Leroux, 1909), 297–310.
5. Nariman, *The Ahad Nameh*. On the Iran League, see Marashi, *Exile and the Nation*, Chapter 2.
6. Jamshedji Edulji Saklatwalla, *A Contribution on the Life, Time, Identity & Career of Salman-al-Faresi, Alias Dasturan Dastur Dinyar* (Bombay: Central Printing Works, 1938), 1–10.
7. Ringer, *Pious Citizens*, 63; for a more recent popular take on the issue, see Walker, 'The Last of the Zoroastrians'.
8. Ervad Darius Sethna, 'Reader's Forum', *Parsiana* 13, no. 10 (1991): 3–4.
9. Mithoo Coorlawala, *Ahd-Namaha: Covenants of Faith* (Bombay: K. R. Cama Oriental Institute, 1995), Preface.
10. R. P. Dewhurst, 'Review: Ahad Nameh', *Journal of the Royal Asiatic Society of Great Britain and Ireland*, no. 4 (1925): 785–87.
11. Coorlawala, *Ahd-Namaha: Covenants of Faith*, Preface; Nariman, *The Ahad Nameh*, Preface.
12. Halbwachs, *On Collective Memory*, 119.
13. Nora, 'Between Memory and History', 12–13.
14. Savant, *New Muslims of Post-Conquest Iran*, Chapter 2; Choksy, *Conflict and Cooperation*, Chapter 1. Savant's book also treats Salman's charter, which I discovered only after my dissertation was complete. While I have since benefited from her insights, and some of our conclusions are complementary,

my analysis of Salman's charter represents an independent and original assessment.

15. Moḥammad Rezā Torkī, *Pārsā-yi Pārsī: Salmān Fārsī beh Revāyat-i Motūn-i Fārsī* (Tehrān: Sherkat-i Inteshārāt-i 'Ilmī va Farhangī, 2008), 152–54.
16. Louis Massignon and Jamshedji Maneckji Unvala, *Salman Pak and the Spiritual Beginnings of Iranian Islam* (Bombay: Bombay University Press, 1955), ii; Burzine K. Waghmar, 'A Note on Parsi Islamology', in H. N. Modi (ed.), *Third International Congress Proceedings: K. R. Cama Oriental Institute* (Bombay: K. R. Cama Oriental Institute, 2001), 252–53.
17. Compare Abū Nu'aym Aḥmad ibn 'Abd Allāh al-Iṣfahānī, *Kitāb dhikr akhbār Iṣfahān*, ed. Sven Dedering, vol. 1 (Leiden: Brill, 1931), 52–54; Anonymous, *Mujmal al-tawārīkh wa-'l-qiṣaṣ*, eds Iraj Afshar and Mahmoud Omidsalar (Tehran: Talayah, 2001), 88–89; Ḥamd Allāh Mustawfī Qazvīnī, *Ta'ríkh-i-Guzída*, ed. E. G. Browne (Leiden: Brill, 1910), vol. 2, xv–xvi; 1, 227; Islamic MS 2556/7, India Office, British Library.
18. Dewhurst, 'Review: Ahad Nameh', 786.
19. Indian recensions of the text can be found in Jejeebhoy, *Tuqviuti-Din-i-Mazdiasna*; 'I.O. Islamic Ms. 2556/7' (November 14, 1802), India Office, British Library.
20. Torkī, *Pārsā-yi Pārsī*, 150.
21. al-Iṣfahānī, *Kitāb dhikr akhbār Iṣfahān*, 1:52–54.
22. Abū l-Shaykh 'Abd Allāh ibn Muḥammad Iṣfahānī, *Ṭabaqāt al-muḥaddithīn bi-Iṣbahān*, ed. 'Abd al-Ghafur 'Abd al-Haqq Husayn Balushi (Beirut: Mu'assasat al-Risālah, 1987), 1: 231–34; Savant, *New Muslims of Post-Conquest Iran*, 83.
23. Anonymous, *Mujmal al-tawārīkh wa-'l-qiṣaṣ*, 2001, 88–89; Jürgen Paul, 'The Histories of Isfahan: Mafarrukhi's Kitab Mahasin Isfahan', *Iranian Studies* 33, no. 2 (2000): 118.
24. Muḥammad ibn Hindūshāh Nakhjavānī, *Dastūr al-kātib fī ta'yīn al-marātib*, ed. Ăbdülğärim Ăli oghlü Ălizadă (Moscow: Danish, 1964), 70–71.
25. Fattal, *Le statut légal*, 30–31; Moshe Gil, *A History of Palestine, 634–1099* (Cambridge: Cambridge University Press, 1992), 152–53; Abū 'l-Fatḥ ibn Abī 'l-Ḥasan al-Sāmirī, *The Kitāb al-Tarīkh of Abu 'l-Fath*, trans. Paul Stenhouse (Sydney: University of Sydney, 1985), 242–46.
26. For the Arabic text of the St Catherine's firman, see B. Moritz, *Beiträge zur geschichte der Sinaiklosters im mittelalter nach arabischen quellen* (Berlin: Verlag der Königlich-Preussische Akademie der Wissenschaften, 1918), 6–8; for an

English translation see Heinz Skrobucha, *Sinai* (London: Oxford University Press, 1966), 58.

27. Jean-Michel Mouton, *Le Sinaï médiéval: Un espace stratégique de l'Islam* (Paris: Presses Universitaires de France, 2000), 107–8; Fattal, *Le statut légal*, 32.
28. Jean-Michel Mouton, 'Les Musulmans a Sainte-Catherine au Moyen Âge', in Dominique Valbelle and Charles Bonnet (eds), *Le Sinaï durant l'antiquité et le Moyen-Âge: 4000 ans d'histoire pour un désert* (Paris: Éditions Errance, 1998), 178–81.
29. Skrobucha, *Sinai*, 62.
30. Mouton, *Le Sinai Medieval*, 112; Skrobucha, *Sinai*, 62.
31. Fattal, *Le statut légal*, 23–24.
32. Abū 'Ubayd al-Qāsim ibn Sallām, *Kitāb al-amwāl*, 280–81; al-Balādhurī, *Kitāb futūḥ al-buldān*, 1956, 76–78.
33. Fattal, *Le statut légal*, 27; Addai Scher (ed.), *Histoire nestorienne (Chronique de Séert) Deuxième Partie (II)*, vol. 13, no. 4, Patrologia Orientalis (Paris: Firmin-Didot, 1919), 600–18; see also British Library Ms. ADD 4854.
34. Mouton, 'Les Musulmans a Sainte-Catherine au Moyen Âge', 177.
35. Scher, *Histoire nestorienne*, 601.
36. Louis Massignon, 'La politique islamo-chrétienne des scribes nestoriens de deir qunna à la cour de bagdad au IXe de notre ère', in Youakim Moubarac (ed.), *Opera minora* (Beirut: Dar-el-Maaref, 1963), 250–57.
37. See, for example, British Library Ms. ADD 4854.
38. Massignon and Unvala, *Salman Pak*, 7.
39. The outline given here is derived from MS Or. 885 Qissat Salman wa Islamihi, University of Leiden. See also Abū Bakr Aḥmad ibn 'Alī al-Khaṭīb al-Baghdādī, *Tārīkh Baghdād aw madīnat al-salām*, ed. Muḥammad Sa'īd 'Urfī (Bayrut: Dar al-Kitab al-'Arabi, 1966), 1:163–171; and 'Abd al-Malik Ibn Hishām and Muḥammad Ibn Isḥāq, *The Life of Muhammad: A Translation of Ishāq's Sīrat rasūl Allāh*, trans. Alfred Guillaume (London: Oxford University Press, 1955), 95–98.
40. Massignon and Unvala, *Salman Pak*, 9.
41. al-Iṣfahānī, *Kitāb dhikr akhbār Iṣfahān*, 1:52.
42. al-Khaṭīb al-Baghdādī, *Tārīkh Baghdād*, 1:170–171.
43. Jeanette A Wakin, *The Function of Documents in Islamic Law: The Chapters on Sales from Tahawi's Kitab al-Shurut al-Kabir* (Albany, NY: State University of New York Press, 1972), 38–63.

44. Anonymous, *Mujmal al-tawārīkh wa-'l-qiṣaṣ*, 2001, 89a–90a; Mustawfī Qazvīnī, *Ta'ríkh-i-Guzída*, vol. 2, pp. xv–xvi and vol. 1, p. 227 Browne misprinted the pages of Volume 1 in which Salman's charter appear but corrected the error in Volume 2. Thus the page numbers for the charter are non-sequential and its content is disbursed across both volumes.
45. The reverse is not always true. Al-Baghdadi preserves the deed of manumission but not the charter. Nevertheless, he took the deed from Abu Nu'aym who preserved both. See *Tārīkh Baghdād*, 1:170.
46. Massignon and Unvala, *Salman Pak*, 7.
47. al-Iṣfahānī, *Kitāb dhikr akhbār Iṣfahān*, 1:53.
48. al-Balādhurī, *Kitāb futūḥ al-buldān*, 1956, 77.
49. Levy-Rubin, *Non-Muslims in the Early Islamic Empire*, 33–34.
50. al-Iṣfahānī, *Kitāb dhikr akhbār Iṣfahān*, 1:53.
51. al-Balādhurī, *Kitāb futūḥ al-buldān*, 1956, 77.
52. al-Iṣfahānī, *Kitāb dhikr akhbār Iṣfahān*, 1:53.
53. al-Balādhurī, *Kitāb futūḥ al-buldān*, 1956, 78.
54. Edward William Lane, *An Arabic-English Lexicon* (London: Williams and Norgate, 1863), s.v. 'ḥashara'. It should be noted that another meaning of this verb is 'to disperse or expel'. Imran Nyazee translates it so in his version of the Treaty of Najran. See Abū 'Ubayd al-Qāsim ibn Sallām, *The Book of Revenue*, 188. However that seems to be a projection of the Najranis' later expulsion by 'Umar into their original agreement with the Prophet.
55. Mustawfī Qazvīnī, *Ta'ríkh-i-Guzída*, 1:227; Anonymous, *Mujmal al-tawārīkh wa-'l-qiṣaṣ*, ed. Muhammad Taqi Bahar (Tehran: Khavar, 1939), 244, footnote #14; Ḥusayn Taqī l-Nūrī Ṭabarsī, *Nafas al-Raḥmān fī faḍā'il Salmān*, ed. Jawad Qayyumi al-Jazah'i al-Isfahani (Iran: Muassasat al-Afaq, 1990), 180.
56. Jejeebhoy, *Tuqviuti-Din-i-Mazdiasna*, 6; I.O. Islamic Ms. 2556/7, 409a.
57. al-Balādhurī, *Kitāb futūḥ al-buldān*, 1956, 78.
58. al-Iṣfahānī, *Kitāb dhikr akhbār Iṣfahān*, 1:53.
59. Fattal, *Le statut légal*, 23.
60. al-Iṣfahānī, *Kitāb dhikr akhbār Iṣfahān*, 1:53.
61. Ṭabarsī, *Nafas al-Raḥmān fī faḍā'il Salmān*, 180. For more information on ounces, see Lane, *An Arabic-English Lexicon*, s.v. 'riṭl'. At some point the exchange rate was one ounce=40 dirhams. The dirham was a silver coin.
62. *Encyclopedia of Islam*, 2nd ed., s.v. 'Banu 'l-Harith b. Ka'b'.
63. See Dominique Sourdel, 'Robes of Honor in Abbasid Baghdad during the Eighth to Eleventh Centuries', in Stewart Gordon (ed.), *Robes and Honor: The*

Medieval World of Investiture (New York: Palgrave, 2001), 137–47; and Gavin Hambly, 'From Baghdad to Bukhara, From Ghazna to Delhi: The Khil'a Ceremony in the Transmission of Kingly Pomp and Circumstance', in Stewart Gordon (ed.), *Robes and Honor: The Medieval World of Investiture* (New York: Palgrave, 2001), 193–222.

64. al-Balādhurī, *Kitāb futūḥ al-buldān*, 1956, 77.
65. al-Balādhurī, 76–81.
66. al-Balādhurī, 76. The proper formula derived from the Treaty of Najran (200 hulla in two installments of 100) is given in some manuscript copies of the ahd-nama. See MS. Pers. D 96 or MS. Clarke 8 of the Bodleian Library, University of Oxford.
67. al-Balādhurī, 77. This phrase was not translated by Hitti.
68. Nakhjavānī, *Dastūr al-kātib fī ta'yīn al-marātib*, 71.
69. Muḥammad ibn 'Umar al-Wāqidī, *The Life of Muhammad: al-Wāqidī's Kitāb al-maghāzī*, trans. Rizwi Faizer (New York: Routledge, 2011), 178.
70. For recent, concise, scholarly treatment of the issue, see Gordon Newby's and Mark Cohen's respective chapters in Abdelwahab Meddeb and Benjamin Stora (eds), *A History of Jewish-Muslim Relations: From the Origins to the Present Day* (Princeton: University Press, 2013), 39–71.
71. al-Wāqidī, *The Life of Muhammad*, 252; Ibn Hishām and Ibn Isḥāq, *The Life of Muhammad: A Translation of Ishāq's Sīrat rasūl Allāh*, 464–66.
72. al-Balādhurī, *The Origins of the Islamic State*, 41.
73. Abū 'Ubayd al-Qāsim ibn Sallām, *The Book of Revenue*, 167; R. B. Serjeant, 'The Sunnah Jami'ah, Pacts with the Yathrib Jews and the Tahram of Yathrib: Analysis and Translation of the Documents Comprised in the So-Called "Constitution of Medina"', *Bulletin of the School of Oriental and African Studies* 41 (1978): 31–32.
74. Serjeant, 'The Sunnah Jami'ah, Pacts with the Yathrib Jews and the Tahram of Yathrib', 8.
75. Said Arjomand, 'The Constitution of Medina: A Sociolegal Interpretation of Muhammad's Acts of Foundation of the Umma', *International Journal of Middle East Studies* 41, no. 4 (2009): 556–60.
76. Serjeant, 'The Sunnah Jami'ah, Pacts with the Yathrib Jews and the Tahram of Yathrib', 25, footnote 71.
77. al-Wāqidī, *The Life of Muhammad*, 223. W. Montgomery Watt doubts whether there ever was a physical copy of the agreement. See Encyclopedia of Islam, s.v. 'Kurayza'.

78. Nakhjavānī, *Dastūr al-kātib fī ta'yīn al-marātib*, 71.
79. Ibn Hishām and Ibn Isḥāq, *The Life of Muhammad: A Translation of Ishāq's Sīrat rasūl Allāh*, 438.
80. Ibid., 511.
81. Ibid., 256.
82. He does, however, preserve a copy of the Prophet's treaty with Maqna, an Arabian city with a Jewish population. Maqna is named in the Geniza copy of the Treaty of Khaybar. Baladhuri's Treaty of Maqna does not resemble the Geniza's Treaty of Khaybar, although Baladhuri describes similar terms of submission for both cities. See al-Balādhurī, *The Origins of the Islamic State*, 1:93–94; al-Balādhurī, *Kitāb futūḥ al-buldān*, 2014, 59–60.
83. Hartwig Hirschfeld, 'The Arabic Portion of the Cairo Genizah at Cambridge', *Jewish Quarterly Review* 15, no. 2 (1903): 167–81.
84. The Prophet did give special dispensation for the Khaybaris to continue cultivating their date palms in exchange for half of the produce. See al-Balādhurī, *The Origins of the Islamic State*, 47.
85. Hirschfeld, 'The Arabic Portion of the Cairo Genizah at Cambridge', 172.
86. Gil, *A History of Palestine, 634–1099*, 151–53; Chase F. Robinson, *Empire and Elites after the Muslim Conquest: The Transformation of Northern Mesopotamia* (New York: Cambridge University Press, 2000), 9.
87. S. D. Goitein, *A Mediterranean Society: The Jewish Communities of the Arab World as Portrayed in the Documents of the Cairo Geniza*, vol. 2 (Berkeley: University of California Press, 1967), 386–87.
88. Ismā'īl ibn 'Umar Ibn Kathīr, *al-Bidāya wa 'l-Nihāya*, vol. 14 (Bayrut, Lubnan: Dar al-Kutub al-'Ilmiya, 2001), 19; Gil, *A History of Palestine, 634–1099*, 152.
89. Richard N. Frye, 'Islamic Book Forgeries from Iran', in Richard Gramlich (ed.), *Islamwissentschaftliche Abhandlungen: Fritz Meier zum sechzigsten Geburtstag* (Wiesbaden: F. Steiner, 1974), 106–9; reprinted in 'City Chronicles of Central Asia and Khurasan: The Ta'rix-i Nisapur', in *Islamic Iran and Central Asia (7th–12th Centuries)* (London: Variorum Reprints, 1979), 405–20.
90. Hartwig Hirschfeld estimates the date of the Geniza copy of the Treaty of Khaybar to be the tenth century, precisely the time frame for the emergence of Salman's charter. See 'The Arabic Portion of the Cairo Genizah at Cambridge', 174.
91. Milka Levy-Rubin, *Non-Muslims in the Early Islamic Empire: From Surrender to Coexistence* (New York: Cambridge University Press, 2011), Chapter 2.
92. Levy-Rubin, *Non-Muslims in the Early Islamic Empire*, 127, 143.

93. Luke Yarbrough, 'Origins of the Ghiyār', *Journal of the American Oriental Society* 134, no. 1 (2014): 113–21.
94. Muḥammad ibn al-Ḥasan Shaybānī, *Siyar*, ed. Majid Khadduri (Beirut: al-Dar al-Muttahida Li-l-Nashr, 1975), 267; Shaybānī, *The Islamic Law of Nations*, 277–78.
95. al-Iṣfahānī, *Kitāb dhikr akhbār Isfahān*, 1:53.
96. Jejeebhoy, *Tuqviuti-Din-i-Mazdiasna*, 7; I.O. Islamic Ms. 2556/7, 409b–410a.
97. For a recent discussion of the *zunnar* and its significance, see Sahner, *Christian Martyrs under Islam: Religious Violence and the Making of the Muslim World*, Chapter 1.
98. Levy-Rubin, *Non-Muslims in the Early Islamic Empire*, 172–75.
99. Hirschfeld, 'The Arabic Portion of the Cairo Genizah at Cambridge', 170–71.
100. On the general disapproval of silk in the hadith, see Richard W. Bulliet, *Cotton, Climate, and Camels in Early Islamic Iran: A Moment in World History* (New York: Columbia University Press, 2009), 47–49.
101. Levy-Rubin, *Non-Muslims in the Early Islamic Empire*, 110–11.
102. Hirschfeld, 'The Arabic Portion of the Cairo Genizah at Cambridge', 170.
103. Ignaz Goldziher, *Muslim Studies*, trans. S. M. Stern (Chicago: Aldine, 1968), 171.
104. Meïr Bravmann, 'The Ancient Arab Background of the Qur'ānic Concept al-Ğizyatu an Yadin', *Arabica* 13 (1966): 307–14.
105. *Encyclopedia of Islam*, 2nd ed. s.vv. 'Djizya', 'Kharadj' and ''Ushr'.
106. Hirschfeld, 'The Arabic Portion of the Cairo Genizah at Cambridge', 170–71.
107. Levy-Rubin, *Non-Muslims in the Early Islamic Empire*, 175.
108. Chase F. Robinson, 'Neck-Sealing in Early Islam', *Journal of the Economic and Social History of the Orient* 48, no. 3 (2005): 401–41.
109. Gil, *A History of Palestine, 634–1099*, 151–53.
110. Levy-Rubin, *Non-Muslims in the Early Islamic Empire*, 171, 175.
111. The specific examples of Rayy, Dezpul and Istakhr are treated in Magnusson, 'Muslim-Zoroastrian Relations and Religious Violence', 144–81.
112. Shaybānī, *Siyar*, 276; Shaybānī, *The Islamic Law of Nations*, 279.
113. Arthur Tritton, 'Islam and the Protected Religions', *Journal of the Royal Asiatic Society of Great Britain and Ireland*, no. 3 (1927): 480–81.
114. Levy-Rubin, *Non-Muslims in the Early Islamic Empire*, 172.

115. Choksy, *Purity and Pollution in Zoroastrianism*, 107–10; Boyce, *A Persian Stronghold of Zoroastrianism*, 110; for more information on contemporary Zoroastrian death rites, see pp. 148–151.
116. Boyce, *Zoroastrians, Their Religious Beliefs and Practices*, 157–58.
117. Leor Halevi, *Muhammad's Grave: Death Rites and the Making of Islamic Society* (New York: Columbia University Press, 2007), 77; Choksy, 'Zoroastrians in Muslim Iran', 24.
118. Walker, 'The Last of the Zoroastrians'; Fozi, *Reclaiming the Fravahar*, 153–54; Marashi, *Exile and the Nation*, 38.
119. In addition to Halevi, see Frederick Mathewson Denny, *An Introduction to Islam* (Upper Saddle River, NJ: Pearson Prentice Hall, 2006), 283.
120. Levy-Rubin, *Non-Muslims in the Early Islamic Empire*, 172.
121. Hirschfeld, 'The Arabic Portion of the Cairo Genizah at Cambridge', 171.
122. Muhammad Qasim Zaman, 'Death, Funeral Processions, and the Articulation of Religious Authority in Early Islam', *Studia Islamica* 93 (2001): 45; Halevi, *Muhammad's Grave*, 79.
123. Thomas A. Carlson, *Christianity in Fifteenth-Century Iraq* (Cambridge: Cambridge University Press, 2018), 43–44.
124. Anonymous, *Mujmal al-tawārīkh wa-'l-qiṣaṣ*, 2001, 89b–90a.
125. al-Khaṭīb al-Baghdādī, *Tārīkh Baghdād*, 170.
126. Iṣfahānī, *Ṭabaqāt al-muḥaddithīn bi-Iṣbahān*, 230–31.
127. Iṣfahānī, 230.
128. 'Paradise yearns for Salman more than Salman for Paradise'. See Jejeebhoy, *Tuqviuti-Din-i-Mazdiasna*, 8.
129. *Encyclopedia of Islam*, 2nd ed., s.v. 'Salman al-Farisi'.
130. *Encyclopedia of Islam*, 2nd ed., s.v. 'Salmaniyya'.
131. al-Iṣfahānī, *Kitāb dhikr akhbār Iṣfahān*, 1:52.
132. Bulliet, *Conversion to Islam in the Medieval Period*, 68–69.
133. Anonymous, *Mujmal al-tawārīkh wa-'l-qiṣaṣ*, 2001, 89a.
134. Nakhjavānī, *Dastūr al-kātib fī ta'yīn al-marātib*, 71.
135. Anonymous, *Mujmal al-tawārīkh wa-'l-qiṣaṣ*, 2001, 90a.
136. Levy-Rubin, *Non-Muslims in the Early Islamic Empire*, 110.
137. *Encyclopedia of Islam*, 2nd ed., s.vv. 'Muhammad b. Malik-Shah' and 'Mahmud b. Muhammad b. Malik-Shah'.
138. 'I.O. Islamic Ms. 2556/7', 418a–420a. Notice that here as in many later copies of the ahd-nama, the charter is written to Salman's nephew rather than his brother.

139. Ḥasan Ḥusainī Fasā'ī, *Fārsnāma-i Nāṣirī*, ed. Mansur Rastgar Fasa'i, vol. 2 (Tihran: Mu'assasa-i Intisharat-i Amir Kabir, 1988), 1437; quoted in Torkī, *Pārsā-yi Pārsī*, 148.
140. Maḥmūd ibn 'Us̱mān, *Kitāb-i Firdaws al-murshidīyah fī asrār al-ṣamadiyah (Die Vita des Scheich Abu Ishaq al-Kazaruni in der persischen Bearbeitung)*, ed. Friedrich Max Meier (Leipzig: Kommissionsverlag F. A. Brockhaus, 1948).
141. Harry Neale, *Jihad in Premodern Sufi Writings* (New York: Palgrave Macmillan, 2017), 1–2; Neguin Yavari, 'Conversion Stories of Shaykh Abu Ishaq Kazaruni (963–1033)', in Guyda Armstrong and Ian Woods (eds), *Christianizing Peoples and Converting Individuals* (Turnhout, Belgium: Brepols, 2000), 225–46.
142. Annemarie Schimmel, 'The Ornament of the Saints: The Religious Situation in Iran in Pre-Safavid Times', *Iranian Studies* 7, no. 1–2 (1974): 95.

5

Fire Temple Desecration and Triumphal Tales of Violence

Local histories of Iranian cities, composed in the early Islamic era, often include one or more accounts of fire temple desecration. Why did Perso-Muslim authors preserve them? What do such tales reveal about the nature of Muslim–Zoroastrian relations after the conquest of Iran? How should modern historians interpret them? Much of the secondary literature presumes that they are indicative of hostility between Muslims and Zoroastrians.[1] Yet if tales of fire temple desecration, intertwined as they often are with tales of mosque construction, seem ideally suited to undermine the idea of accommodation in post-conquest Iran, it is because they were designed to do so. Medieval Muslims wrote them to explain the victory of Islam over Zoroastrianism through the appropriation of sacred space. Tales of fire temple desecration, in other words, are not disinterested historical accounts; they are triumphal narratives of religious supersession.[2]

To properly interpret such accounts, the careful historian of interreligious encounter must bear several caveats in mind when analysing them. First, early Muslims narrated tales of fire temple desecration for a variety of purposes. Even if the moral seems apparent, these stories should not be read presumptively or in isolation. They must be evaluated against the information available in other sources. Second, instances of fire temple desecration should not be isolated from the multiple contexts in which they occur. Muslims and Zoroastrians lived in direct contact for centuries in many communities. A sound understanding of the local dynamics at play in a given place and at a given time is necessary to properly interpret intercommunal violence. Third, these tales tend to exaggerate the numerical and political strength of early Islamic communities in Iran – or project the founding of these communities far into the past – in order to claim that Muslims were dominant (and Zoroastrians subservient) from the earliest days of their arrival. This is particularly true of stories purporting to describe the construction of the first mosque in a town. Since these tales can be rhetorical, it is important to read them critically.

Interpreting Fire Temple Desecration

Early Muslims chose to remember tales of fire temple desecration for a variety of reasons. Since these stories are usually embedded in Islamic texts dedicated to other topics, it is imprudent to take them at face value or ignore the work they are doing in a particular text. For example, according to Ahmad ibn Yahya al-Baladhuri's *Ansab al-Ashraf*, Ziyad ibn Abihi (d. 53/673), the Umayyad Viceroy of the East, ordered his deputy, Ubayd Allah, to destroy Zoroastrian temples.

> Ziyād charged 'Ubayd Allāh ibn Abī Bakrā with extinguishing the fires and demolishing their temples, and seizing whatever offerings were gathered there that the Zoroastrians brought, as well as the wealth intended for their maintenance. He ended up with, they say, 40 million dirhams. Before the year was over, he squandered it and was indebted.[3]

The assumption that Ubayd Allah destroyed many fire temples is based on the claim that he amassed 40 million dirhams from the campaign.[4] Admittedly, 40 million dirhams is an astronomical sum. It is twenty times the amount that Ubayd Allah reportedly extracted as tribute from the Zunbil, a ruler in Afghanistan, that same year.[5] However, it is clear from the other stories in this section of *Ansab al-Ashraf* that al-Baladhuri intended this report to demonstrate Ubayd Allah's profligacy, not the number of fire temples he destroyed.

Ubayd Allah was a notorious spendthrift. He reportedly once paid 30,000 dirhams for a drink of water.[6] Therefore, al-Baladhuri's report about the fire temples may have been intended to emphasise Ubayd Allah's extravagant lifestyle and the evanescence of wealth. His supposed decadence is almost certainly a trope, even if it does reflect the fact that tribal connections permitted men of humble origin, like Ziyad and Ubayd Allah, to profit immensely from the administration of the early caliphate.[7] Perhaps that was even the point: Ubayd Allah was perceived as nouveau riche and reckless with money, so Muslim authors fostered that image of him. The 40 million dirhams accumulated during his campaign of fire temple desecration seem to be part of a carefully crafted caricature. It does not necessarily reflect the number of temples plundered.

In reality, the scope of Ubayd Allah's campaign was quite limited. Ziyad appointed him governor of Sistan in 51/671–2. *Tarikh-i Sistan*, a local history of that province, suggests that it was in connection with this appointment that Ziyad ordered Ubayd Allah to destroy fire temples.[8] Ubayd Allah did so during his march to assume the governorship of Sistan. Therefore, his assault on Zoroastrian sacred space did not extend beyond Fars and Sistan – the two provinces that he passed through on his way east – and the brief period between his appointment as governor of Sistan and his assumption of that post.[9]

According to Amr ibn Bahr al-Jahiz's *Kitab al-Hayawan*, Ubayd Allah targeted three fire temples along the way, but ultimately sacked only one. Al-Jahiz (160–255/776–869) reports that Ubayd Allah went first to the city of Jur (also known as Firuzabad) in Fars province, intending to extinguish its sacred fire.

> While extinguishing it, ['Ubayd Allāh] was told: 'There is no fire more esteemed by the Zoroastrians than the fire at Kariyān of Dārābjird. If you extinguish it, no one will resist (Ar., *yamtaniʿu*) you; while if you extinguish their lowly fire [at Jūr], they will resist (*imtanaʿū*) it and prepare for war.' So he departed for Kariyān and began with it.[10]

Apparently persuaded by this counterintuitive counsel, Ubayd Allah spared the temple at Jur and proceeded to Kariyan.

His reluctance to extinguish the fire at Jur might reflect the Muslim authorities' tenuous control over the region. Jur was the second-to-last city in Fars to submit to Muslim rule.[11] Ardashir I, the founder of the Sasanian Empire, had built it as an imperial capital in the third century.[12] Although emperors no longer resided there by the seventh century, Jur remained a loyal Sasanian stronghold.[13] Muslim forces drove the Sasanian monarch, Yazdagerd III, out of the city just two decades before Ubayd Allah arrived.[14]

Jur was also a major cultic centre. According to Abu l-Hasan ibn Ali ibn al-Husayn al-Mas'udi (275–345/890–956), its fire temple hosted an annual festival and procession.[15] Therefore, Ubayd Allah's fear that Jur's inhabitants would have violently resisted any attempt to extinguish their fire was probably well founded. Perhaps that is the reason he abandoned the effort.

Al-Jahiz is also correct that Zoroastrians greatly esteemed the fire temple at Kariyan. It housed one of the three imperial fires of Sasanian Zoroastrianism – the Adur Farnbag, or Fire of the Priests. Al-Baladhuri described the region as 'the fountain of [the Zoroastrians'] knowledge and religion'.[16] Al-Mas'udi wrote in the tenth century: 'The Zoroastrians venerate this fire beyond any other fire or temple'.[17] In fact, the Muslim geographer Ahmad ibn Muhammad ibn al-Faqih al-Hamadhani reported that Zoroastrians regarded the Adur Farnbag so highly that they took precautions against the possibility that Muslims might extinguish it. 'When the Arabs ruled, the Zoroastrians feared that [this fire] would be extinguished so they split it into two parts – the part in Kariyān and the part carried to Fāsā. They said that if one was extinguished, the other would remain.'[18] The effort that Zoroastrians made to preserve this fire belies the claim that no one would resist its desecration.

When Ubayd Allah arrived at Kariyan, its inhabitants barricaded themselves inside the citadel. According to al-Jahiz, one ill-tempered Persian who remained outside the walls used to pass by Ubayd Allah's camp daily. When Ubayd Allah commented on the Persian's foul temperament, an Arab soldier asked how much he would pay to have the man imprisoned. Ubayd Allah offered 4,000 dirhams, but the soldier convinced him to raise it to 5,000 – perhaps another example of Ubayd Allah's profligacy. According to al-Jahiz, the Persian 'did not resist' (Ar., *mā imtana'a*) when the soldier seized him, which may fulfil the earlier prediction that no one would resist the destruction of the fire at Kariyan. The soldier threw the Persian to the ground and the people trampled him to death. Only then did the citadel surrender. The Muslim forces reportedly extinguished the temple's sacred flame and massacred the Zoroastrian herbads, or priests.[19]

The reason for Ubayd Allah's assault on the temple is not stated, although it seems to have been part of an attempt by the Umayyad Viceroy of the East to eliminate a rival centre of power in what was once the heartland of Sasanian

Iran. Kariyan was located near Darabjird, a rebellious region dominated by a Zoroastrian priest known in Islamic sources as 'the Herbad' (Ar., *al-hirbadh*). He and his supporters surrendered to caliphal armies more than once. The Herbad sued for peace when Muslim forces initially arrived in the region, but he rebelled shortly thereafter, and Darabjird had to be forcibly conquered in the mid-seventh century. Ubayd Allah's assassination of the Herbad appears to be the culmination of that effort.[20]

The final stop on Ubayd Allah's campaign of fire temple destruction was Sistan. *Tarikh-i Sistan* reports that when the Zoroastrians and local aristocracy learned of his intention to destroy their fire temple, they threatened to revolt. The Muslims of Sistan intervened, arguing that destroying the fire temple violated Islamic law (Ar., *sharī'a*). They wrote directly to the Umayyad authorities in Damascus for advice. The court allegedly urged Ubayd Allah to desist:

> 'You should not [destroy the fire temple], since they and their places of worship are protected by treaty . . . In this case, it is not obligatory [to destroy it] since the synagogue is to the Jews and the church is to the Christians as the fire temple is to the Zoroastrians. How could we differentiate between all of the protected people and their houses of worship? . . . If our Prophet, peace be upon him, desired that, . . . he would have uprooted unbelief and religions other than Islam, but he did not. He did not uproot them and even made peace with them through the *jizya* . . .' So ['Ubayd Allāh] ignored [Ziyād's] decree.[21]

The reference to Islamic law in this story is a bit anachronistic, but *Tarikh-i Sistan* was written several centuries after Ubayd Allah's arrival, so such projections are not unexpected. While this source may not accurately depict Muslim–Zoroastrian relations in this period, it nonetheless reflects how later Muslims in the region remembered them.[22] In other words, the author of *Tarikh-i Sistan* chose to remember that fire temples were the equivalent of other houses of worship, and that local Muslims protected them.

Contextualising Fire Temple Desecration

While the extent of Ubayd Allah's destructive acts may have been exaggerated, other accounts of temple desecration seem credible. They too must be carefully assessed to determine the precise meaning of such violence. A firm grasp of the historical context and the identity of the perpetrators is necessary to truly understand the significance of violence.[23] For instance, Abrun the Turk's destruction of the fire temple at Furdujan, near Qom, in 282/895–6 is frequently cited as an example of the persecution of Zoroastrians by Muslims.[24] Ibn al-Faqih's early-tenth-century geographical work, *Kitab al-Buldan* describes this episode as follows:

> [The fire] in this temple remained in this village until, in the year 282, Abrūn al-Turk[25] came there. He was governing Qom (Ar., *kāna yatawallā Qom*). He aimed his mangonels and catapults at the village until he conquered it. He destroyed the walls of the village, sacked the temple, extinguished the fire, and carried the brazier to the city of Qom. The fire has been out since that day.[26]

There is little reason to doubt this account of desecration, but previous scholarship has failed to properly contextualise it. Context matters, particularly when interpreting intercommunal violence. This is as true of the Shepherds' Crusade in fourteenth-century Europe as it is of fire temple desecration in ninth-century Iran. The Shepherds' Crusade of 1320 was a popular movement initiated by pastoralists to defend the Kingdom of Aragon against the Muslims of Granada. The shepherds marched to Paris to invite the king of France to lead them on crusade, but he refused to grant them an audience. In response, they pillaged royal institutions and attacked Jews. These attacks continued throughout France and into Iberia as the shepherds crossed the Pyrenees.[27]

Due to the religious overtones of the Shepherds' Crusade and the devastating effect that it had on France's Jewish population, some historians of Judaism have interpreted this incident as evidence of the growing intolerance toward Jews in fourteenth-century Europe. Others view it through the lens of atrocities committed against Jews in Nazi Germany. From that perspective, the Shepherds' Crusade is but one step in the long march of European intolerance that culminated in the Holocaust. By contrast, David Nirenberg argues that violence against Jews during the Shepherd's Crusade was contingent and particular to that time and place, not part of a pattern of regular persecution against Jews. Furthermore, Jews fared differently on either side of the Pyrenees. When the shepherds initially targeted Jews in France, the king condemned the violence and attempted to contain it. Nevertheless, he did not intervene when accusations that Jews had colluded with lepers in poisoning wells sparked further violence in 1321. In that case, the municipal authorities justified attacks on lepers and Jews as defence of the realm. The king did not challenge that logic and many Jews fled to Aragon for safety. The king of Aragon staunchly defended the Jews against the shepherds in 1320, and accusations against lepers during the poisoning scare of 1321 did not result in violence against Jews in Aragon.[28]

Nirenberg draws two conclusions about religious violence from these facts. First, religious violence must be understood in its local context because even the same violent act can have distinct meanings depending on where and when it occurs. Second, rather than viewing religious violence in hindsight as part of a progressive march toward some tragic end, each act must be understood at the time and in the place that it occurred. Although historians know the end from the beginning, they must resist the urge to impose that knowledge on the past.

Applying Nirenberg's ideas and methodology to Abrun's destruction of the fire temple at Furdujan reveals that this incident may not have been motivated exclusively by anti-Zoroastrian fervour. Abrun was not the regular governor of Qom but had been posted to that city by the Abbasid caliphs. *Tarikh-i Qom* describes him as the city's *amīr*, which implies that he was not a political administrator but a military commander.[29] Al-Tabari confirms that Abrun was 'an officer of the central authorities', meaning the Abbasid caliphate at Baghdad. He was also the brother of Kayghalagh.[30] A mid-ranking member of the caliph's Turkish guard, Kayghalagh mediated on behalf of the Abbasid caliph al-Muhtadi during a troop revolt at Samarra in 256/869–70.[31] Apparently the brothers were promoted for their loyalty because Kayghalagh served as governor of Rayy from 262–264/875–878 while Abrun was set 'over' Qazwin (Ar., *alayhā*) in 266/879–880.[32] Abrun was at Rayy two decades later, where he was killed in 289/902 during an uprising against the harsh governor there.[33] Thus, Abrun seems to have been a soldier and Abbasid appointee, governing the region martially.

The caliphs needed a loyal commander at Qom because al-Jibal, the province to which it belonged, was a hotbed of revolt in the late ninth century. To the north, Tabaristan and Gilan spawned successive Alid rebellions. Al-Jibal was overrun numerous times as the struggle of the Tahirids, Saffarids and Samanids for control of Khurasan spilled over into neighbouring provinces. To the south, the caliph had given begrudging recognition to the Saffarids' seizure of Fars, even as Saffarid armies pressed further west towards the very heart of the caliphate. In Jibal, the Dulafids – who ruled the province hereditarily on behalf of the Abbasids – were showing signs of independence.[34] This unrest appears to be the reason that the caliph, al-Muʿtadid, sent his son, al-Muktafi, in 281/894–895 to preside over the region directly. Abrun likely assumed command of Qom at this time, just a year before his attack on the fire temple.

Previously members of the local al-Ashʿari family had governed Qom until a rogue slave soldier named Wasif captured the city in 278/892.[35] Muhammad ibn Abi l-Saj, Wasif's master, had expelled him from Baghdad for waging war on rival troops. When summoned to return, Wasif refused, wreaking havoc across Khuzistan instead.[36] It was apparently at this time that he seized Qom and ruled it for three years, 279–281/892–895. The Dulafids, who ruled most of al-Jibal on behalf of the Abbasids, were too preoccupied with a succession crisis to immediately respond. Umar Dulafi finally fought Wasif in 281/894–895 but could not defeat him.[37] Later that year, the Abbasid caliph al-Muʿtadid escorted his son, the future caliph al-Muktafi, to al-Jibal, installing him at Rayy as governor over the northern cities of the province, such as Qazwin and Qom. Although al-Tabari does not make the connection, the arrival of the caliph and his son in al-Jibal may have been the reason that Wasif suddenly and inexplicably quit Qom in 281/894–895, despite his recent victory over Umar Dulafi.[38] In 282/895–896 the caliph launched a campaign to kill the leaders of the unreliable Dulafid clan, capture their territories and seize their wealth. That same year, Abrun, the Abbasid general, besieged Furdujan and sacked the fire temple. Therefore, the context for that attack is the Abbasids' attempt to reassert authority over an unruly province.

Qom's frequent tax revolts may also have played a role in Abrun's assault on the fire temple. The city had to be subjugated by the central authorities five times in the ninth century before taxes could be collected.[39] The inhabitants of Qom had complained about their tax rate from the very first survey of the land in 189/804–805. As a result, there were five more surveys in the ninth century and two more in the early tenth century. The residents of Qom endured a total of eight separate tax assessments in a little over a century.[40] Abrun seized Qom in 282/895–896, just two years before the sixth assessment. As described by Anne Lambton, the sixth assessment came after the 'people of Qom had complained of the extortionate treatment of the tax-collectors who had followed one another in Qom in rapid succession, each raising the demand'.[41] Indeed, the fifty-seven years between the fifth and sixth assessments was the longest period in the ninth century without an adjustment of Qom's tax burden. To make matters worse, there was a severe drought at Rayy in 281/894–895. The resulting famine was so bad that, according to al-Tabari, the people resorted to cannibalism.[42] Since Qom is relatively close to Rayy, it undoubtedly suffered the same famine. The local populace's penchant for rebellion, combined with a recent famine and extortionate levels of taxation, suggests that the desecration of the fire temple at Furdujan may have occurred amidst a tax revolt.

A piece of circumstantial evidence supports the assertion that Abrun attacked the fire temple during a tax revolt. *Tarikh-i Qom*, the earliest surviving history of the city, notably does not contain an independent account of Abrun's assault. That source simply quotes information from Ibn al-Faqih's *Kitab al-Buldan* without adding any detail. It seems odd that a local historian would know less about this incident than an itinerant geographer. However, *Tarikh-i Qom* does preserve local lore about an instance of fire temple desecration at Furdujan during the caliphate of Abd al-Malik, nearly two centuries earlier.

> They also say that the Muslims – in the caliphate of 'Abd al-Mālik ibn Marwān, when Ḥajjāj ibn Yūsuf was the governor and viceroy of the two Iraqs – took *kharāj* from the people of this village [Furdujān] and warred with them and conquered this village and broke into the fire temple. There were two golden doors. They pried them off and carried them before Ḥajjāj. He sent them to Mecca to hang at the entrance of the Ka'ba. Only God knows (*Allāhu a'lam*).[43]

Several elements of this story are curious. First, Muslims were not in a position to tax Zoroastrians when they arrived in Qom, probably in 94/712–713, after the caliphate of Abd al-Malik (65–86/685–705). Rather, the local

Zoroastrian ruler allowed them to occupy villages in exchange for defending the frontier.[44] Second, the attackers supposedly sent the temple's golden doors to al-Hajjaj, the Umayyad Viceroy of the East. But the first Muslims came to Qom after instigating a revolt against al-Hajjaj at Kufa.[45] Therefore, it is unlikely that they would have honoured him with such a tribute. Finally, this tale ends with the Arabic phrase, 'Only God knows' (*Allāhu a'lam*), which is commonly used by Muslim authors to express uncertainty about competing narratives of the same event.[46]

This story is more intelligible as a local memory of Abrun's desecration of the fire temple. By the ninth century Muslims governed Qom and could tax Zoroastrians. In fact, the central authorities in Baghdad made the city its own tax district in the early ninth century.[47] Furthermore, the inhabitants of Qom regularly rebelled against their tax burden during Abrun's era. Muslims plundered goods from the temple in both stories. However, only in *Tarikh-i Qom* is the loot sent to al-Hajjaj, a detail that demonstrates the attackers' loyalty to the viceroy. Even though these attacks ostensibly occurred centuries apart, they appear side by side in *Tarikh-i Qom*, which would explain the author's use of the phrase *Allāhu a'lam* to express uncertainty about competing narratives of the same event. In short, this curious report of fire temple desecration makes more sense as a local memory, albeit confused, of the attack on Furdujan in the late ninth century.

This incident is firmly rooted in a local context that makes its contingent nature apparent. Religious antagonism may indeed have been a motivating factor behind the assault on the fire temple, but it is difficult to tell from this anecdote alone. Certainly there were broader concerns about the imposition of caliphal authority in the region and unfair rates of taxation. While undoubtedly devastating for the Zoroastrian population of Furdujan and its subsequent relations with the regional government, this attack should not be seen as part of a broader history of Muslim persecution against Zoroastrians. Its singular nature demands deeper analysis.

Inventing Fire Temple Desecration

As the previous example illustrates, Muslims sometimes invented tales of fire temple desecration to exaggerate the numerical and political strength of early Islamic communities in Iran. They also fabricated them to enhance the reputation of a town, mosque or pious ancestor. Research on the history of Islam in South Asia has uncovered a triumphal Muslim narrative of temple desecration. Indo-Muslim sources are replete with accounts of Muslim rulers destroying Hindu temples to build mosques atop them. Yet most of these accounts are highly rhetorical or difficult to substantiate. Richard Eaton estimates that of the 60,000 temples supposedly destroyed by Muslims in South Asia from 1192–1729, only eighty can be established with certainty. Nevertheless, contemporary Hindu nationalists cite the higher numbers to 'demonstrate a persistent pattern of villainy and fanaticism on the part of premodern Indo-Muslim conquerors and rulers'.[48] The fact that medieval Muslims promoted this discourse of religious supersession only enhances the caricature.

Muslim historians used triumphal narratives to bolster the reputation of their rulers. Jihad was an important rallying cry in medieval South Asia against enemies both internal and external, Muslim and non-Muslim. The legitimacy of a ruler depended to a large extent on his success on the battlefield, and court historians were not above inventing victories for a patron. Such tales often mention the destruction of an enemy's shrine, because sacred sites were emblems of political authority. Consequently, Mughal rulers even celebrated the destruction of their Muslim rivals' mosques![49] Sometimes these claims were pure fabrication. A sixteenth-century Hindu temple in Andhra Pradesh bears the inscription of a Muslim commander in the service of the Qutb Shahs declaring that he damaged the edifice and built a mosque there. Yet there is no surviving evidence of that attack, and another inscription at the site claims that just five years later a representative of the same Qutb Shahs endowed this Hindu temple with revenue from a local village.[50]

Since some claims of temple desecration are rhetorical, scholars must scrutinise them to determine their reliability. They must weigh competing narratives of an event and consider the authors' motives in constructing or preserving them. Otherwise, they risk being duped by their own sources. In 1992, sectarian violence erupted in India over unsubstantiated claims that the Mughal emperor Babur had destroyed a Hindu temple at Ayodhya centuries earlier. Hindu nationalists, defying a court order, demolished the Babri Masjid, the mosque that Babur supposedly built atop the ruins of a temple to the god Ram. Riots between Hindus and Muslims ensued. The tragic irony is that there probably was not an ancient temple on the site. That claim first surfaces in a nineteenth-century colonial gazetteer. What historians have confirmed, however, is that Ayodhya developed as a centre of Ram worship in the Mughal era and through the patronage of Muslim rulers.[51] Tales of temple desecration, verifiable or not, have powerful resonance in the present.

In Iran, as in India, rhetorical claims of temple desecration are often embedded in tales of mosque construction. For example, Abd Allah ibn Amir, a Companion of the Prophet, supposedly built a mosque atop a fire temple at Bam in 30/651–652.[52] There are two stories about the origin of the mosque in *Tarikh-i Kirman*, a nineteenth-century history of that province written by Ahmad Ali Khan Vaziri. He was the descendant of a minor official in the Qajar dynasty whose family had lived in Kirman since the twelfth century. Although *Tarikh-i Kirman* is an extremely late source for such information, Vaziri cites the *Bam-nama*, a lost history of the city written in the thirteenth century by Tahir al-Din ibn Shams al-Din.[53] It mentions the destruction of the fire temple.

> The author of the *Bam-nāma* says: 'At the same time an old man, one of the new Muslims who was completely devoted to Manṣūr al-Dīn [ibn Jaradīn, a local Muslim leader who reportedly remained in Kirman after the initial conquest in order to convert Zoroastrians], offered a piece of gold to 'Abd Allāh b. 'Āmir for someone to remove the fire temple and build a Friday mosque in its place. He granted the old man's wish to build a mosque on four pillars. Today there is no trace of that mosque.'[54]

Unfortunately, the *Bam-nāma* is no longer extant so it is difficult to properly contextualise this quote or to determine its reliability. By the author's own admission, there is not archaeological evidence to support it. The claim that a fire temple existed on the site seems purely rhetorical.

In fact, Vaziri narrates a second story of the mosque's origins that does not mention a fire temple at all. As he does not cite a source, it is presumably more recent.

> ['Abd] Allāh-i 'Āmir left Mujāshi' ibn Mas'ūd with 1,000 men in Gavāshir and entered Bam on the way to Khurāsān. Manṣūr al-Dīn had been in Nasā Narmāshīr inviting the people to Islam but hadn't made progress

> on account of his small entourage. He joined with ʿAbd Allāh-i ʿĀmir and constructed a large compound further away from the Zoroastrians of that district who used to vex the Muslims and speak ill of their religion. ʿAbd Allāh sent for a large group of the insurgents of that troublesome faction, and many of the people of Bam and Narmāshīr entered into the glory of Islam and built a mosque that is called the Mosque of the Honorable Messenger. He had with him a piece of wood from the tree under which the Believers swore allegiance to the Honorable Seal [of the Prophets], peace be upon him. The sublime truth in the glorious Qur'ān declares: 'Truly God was pleased with the believers when they swore allegiance to you under the tree . . .' to the end of the verse [Sūrat al-Fatḥ, 48:14]. He placed it in the *miḥrāb*. Today, which is the year 1291 [1874–1875], that mosque with the same well-known name is outside of the city of Bam.[55]

It is significant that in this story Abd Allah did not built the mosque on the site of a Zoroastrian temple. Rather, he moved the small band of Muslims further away from the Zoroastrians in order to decrease the interaction between them. This second account better reflects the struggle of a Muslim minority living on the eastern frontier of the Islamic world in the mid-seventh century.[56]

In this second story, the reputation of the mosque at Bam is not literally and symbolically built on the ruins of a fire temple. Rather, the mosque's claim to fame is that it hosts a Prophetic relic. Local Iranian historians boasted of similar connections to Muhammad as part of a conscious effort to place their otherwise marginal cities within the mainstream of Islamic history. Muslims living on the fringes of the medieval Islamic world – that is, geographically distant from its centres of political power and religious authority – inserted themselves into the central narrative of the faith through religious relics, contact with the Companions, or visions of the Prophet Muhammad. Mimi Hanaoka describes this as a discourse of 'centering the periphery' in Islamic history.[57]

Tārīkh-i Kirmān locates Bam within the central narrative of Islamic history in two ways. First, it makes Abd Allah ibn Amir the builder of the Mosque of the Honorable Messenger. As a Companion of the Prophet, two-time governor of Basra and subjugator of Fars and Khurasan, Abd Allah had a certain cachet in early Islamic Iran. *Kitab Ahval-i Nishapur* ascribes supernatural power (Ar., *baraka*) to him on account of his interaction with Muhammad as a child.[58] However, it is unlikely that Abd Allah ever visited Bam, let alone constructed its first mosque. 'The shaykhs of Kirman' boasted that he marched through their province on his way to conquer Nishapur, and the southern route to Khurasan did pass through Kirman. However, al-Tabari reports that Abd Allah in haste took the shorter but more dangerous route through the deserts of eastern Iran, skirting the province.[59] Therefore, it is unlikely that Abd Allah 'entered Bam on the way to Khurāsān', as *Tarikh-i Kirman* suggests, because that would have taken him in the wrong direction. Instead, Abd Allah sent his subordinate Mujashi' to conquer the city.[60] Yet the notion that Abd Allah had once passed through Bam spawned the related notion that he was buried there. In fact, Abd Allah died in Mecca.[61] He may have never visited Bam, which makes it extremely unlikely that he built its first mosque.

Tarikh-i Kirman also places the Mosque of the Honorable Messenger in the mainstream of Islamic history through a Prophetic relic that Abd Allah placed in its prayer niche. In 628, the Prophet Muhammad attempted a pilgrimage to Mecca with 1,400 of his followers but was diverted to Hudaybiyya by hostile Meccan forces. A rumour spread that the future caliph Uthman had been killed while negotiating on Muhammad's behalf with the Meccans. To prevent the Muslims from fleeing in panic, the Prophet asked them to swear allegiance to him. Their pledge to adhere to whatever terms Muhammad negotiated with the Meccans at Hudaybiyya became known as the Pledge of Good Pleasure (Ar., *bay'at al-riḍwān*) because the Qur'an declared that it pleased God.[62] It was also known as the Pledge of the Tree because the Prophet administered the oath under a tree.

Abd Allah supposedly installed a piece of that tree in the mosque at Bam. Not only is it unlikely that he visited the city, but it is unlikely that he had such a relic. Abd Allah was not at Hudaybiyya; he was just two years old at the time. His father, Amir, would not become a Muslim until Muhammad conquered Mecca in 630.[63] Sometime later, the second caliph Umar is supposed to have felled the tree at Hudaybiyya because it became a site of veneration.[64] Yet the remote probability that Abd Allah could have acquired a piece of that tree is, in some sense, irrelevant. The intent of the 'centering the periphery' genre is to enhance the reputation of an otherwise marginal place. A Prophetic relic installed by Abd Allah, regardless of its authenticity, serves this function for the Mosque of the Honorable Messenger at Bam.

The story of fire temple desecration seems to have done similar work in an earlier era. It proclaimed the triumph of Islam over Zoroastrianism at Bam. Kirman boasted a substantial Zoroastrian population in the thirteenth century, when the *Bam-nama* was likely composed. Therefore, the author of that work, Tahir al-Din, had reason to proclaim the supersession of Islam in his home town because Muslims were still in contact – and perhaps competition – with Zoroastrians there. It may be that the size and influence of the Zoroastrian community had decreased sufficiently by the nineteenth century that the narrative of temple desecration no longer had the same resonance for its Muslim audience.[65] As it became less imperative to assert Islam's dominance over Zoroastrianism, a second story about the origin of the mosque came into circulation. This revised story dropped the trope of violence, inserting peripheral Bam into the mainstream of Islamic history through a Prophetic relic. It was a Muslim-centred story for Bam's increasingly Muslim population. Both tales were invented to enhance the reputation of the local mosque.

The Fire Temples of Bukhara

Three brief examples from Bukhara further illustrate the importance of critically reading tales of desecration. All of them derive from a single source, *Tarikh-i Bukhara*, the twelfth-century Persian abridgement of an Arabic history of the city written in 332/943–944 by Muhammad ibn Jaʿfar al-Narshakhi. The author alleges that Muslims confiscated several sacred sites in that Central Asian city. The first and most credible is that Qutayba ibn Muslim built a mosque atop a fire temple when he conquered Bukhara's citadel in 94/712–713.[66] The occupying forces secured the most defensible spot in the city and worshipped within it, as they had done at Nishapur.[67] However, regarding the location of the mosque, the text simply states: 'That site was an idol house' (N.P., *ān mawḍiʿ but-khāna būd*).[68] The idol house mentioned here could be a Buddhist shrine rather than a Zoroastrian fire temple.[69] While certainly an act of appropriation, it is not an incontrovertible instance of fire temple desecration.

Villas of the Kashkathan

Scholars attribute the disappearance of fire temples in Bukhara to the rise of mosques generally.[70] Yet a specific example from *Tarikh-i Bukhara* suggests that economic factors may have been as pertinent. One of the more prosperous groups at Bukhara was the Kashkathan. They were Magians, practitioners of a Cental Asian cult of fire distinct from Sasanian Zoroastrianism, who reportedly left the city rather than live alongside Muslims. The Kashkathan built estates and several fire temples on the outskirts of town.

> Muḥammad ibn Ja'far al-Narshakhī has related in the book that Qutayba ibn Muslim came to Bukhārā and seized Bukhārā. He ordered the people of Bukhārā to give one half of their own houses and estates to the Arabs. There was a tribe in Bukhārā called the Kashkathān . . . Qutayba insisted on the division of their houses and means. They left everything to the Arabs and built 700 villas outside of the city. Nowadays those villas have become desolate and most have become part of the city. Two or three villas, which they call the Villas of the Magians (Pers., *maghān*) have remained on that site. Magians used to be there. The fire temples of the Magians used to be numerous in this district. At the gate of these Magian villas used to be lovely, verdant gardens. Their estates are extremely expensive.[71]

The expanding city eventually swallowed the estates and fire temples that were once outside its boundaries.

The value of these properties increased after the Samanids made Bukhara their capital. The fire temples of the Kashkathan appear to have been casualties of the courtiers' desire for proximity to the ruler. According to *Tarikh-i Bukhara*:

> We heard the following in the days of the *amīr* Ḥamīd [ruled 331–343/943–954]: 'The reason that the estates of the Villas of the Magians are so expensive is that the rulers have settled in Bukhara. The slaves and relatives of the ruler wanted to purchase those estates to the extent that the price of each *jift* of these estates became 4,000 dirhams.'[72]

It is unclear if the villas were already derelict. They may have been abandoned before the tenth century as members of the *dihqan* class moved to the city.[73]

One piece of evidence in support of that theory is that Muslims pilfered the gates of the Kashkathan villas to expand Bukhara's congregational mosque in the early tenth century.[74] When the congregational mosque collapsed shortly thereafter, one of these gates was utilised in the construction of another mosque. The repurposing of building material was not a select dishonour reserved for Magians. Muslims at Bukhara reused their own dilapidated structures. When the old congregational mosque in the fortress deteriorated, it became the tax bureau.[75]

Thus, *Tarikh-i Bukhara* attributes the disappearance of the Kashkathans' fire temples not to the rise of mosques but specifically to demand for land during the Samanid era. Since it seems that villas and fire temples disappeared simultaneously, this episode betrays no particular animosity toward Magians. The drastic shift in property values also does not appear to be religiously significant. Market forces were at work when prices rose in the tenth century as the Samanid rulers established themselves in this district, and again when the value of their estates dropped precipitously after the Samanid era. The Persian translator of *Tarikh-i Bukhara*, Abu Nasr Ahmad al-Qubavi, declared in 574/1178–1179, 'In our days these estates of the Villas of the Magians are such that they give them away for free and nobody wants [them]'.[76] The vagaries of the real estate market, rather than the construction of mosques, seem responsible for the disappearance of the fire temples of the Kashkathan at Bukhara.

Temple of Makh

Richard Frye noted that the Mosque of Makh at Bukhara used to be a Zoroastrian place of worship.[77] It is possible, however, that the Mosque of Makh was not built atop a fire temple at all. There are two stories about the origins of this mosque, only one of which claims that it was the site of a fire temple. The tale of desecration comes from *Tarikh-i Bukhara*. It relates that Makh was a pre-Islamic ruler of the city who established a bazaar where merchants could sell idols during the festival season.

> This site became a fire temple thereafter. On the day of the bazaar, as soon as the people had assembled, everyone entered the fire temple and venerated the fire. That fire temple remained in place until the time of Islam, when the

> Muslims seized power. They built that mosque on that site. Today it is one of the esteemed mosques of Bukhārā.[78]

This tale of destruction does not appear in the original *History of Bukhara* written in Arabic by al-Narshakhi in the tenth century. Muhammad ibn Zufar ibn Umar added it when he abridged the Persian translation of that text in the twelfth century. He borrowed the story from Abu l-Hasan Abd al-Rahman ibn Muhammad al-Nishapuri's book, *Khaza'in al-'Ulum*. That source is now lost, so there is no telling how old the story is.[79]

Abd al-Karim ibn Muhammad al-Sam'ani's *Kitab al-Ansab*, a twelfth-century biographical dictionary of hadith transmitters, preserves a different story about the Mosque of Makh. The entry under the name *al-Makhi* reads as follows: 'This eponym (Ar., *nisba*) belongs to a man among the Zoroastrians named Makh. He converted to Islam and turned his house into a mosque in Bukhara. It is called the Mosque of Makh.'[80] Al-Sam'ani attributes its origin to the willing renovation of a former Zoroastrian's house, not the Islamic conquest. Al-Sam'ani travelled to Bukhara at least twice during his lifetime to gather hadith, so his knowledge of the mosque's history is plausible, and he would have less reason to embellish the history of its mosque than a local resident.[81] Al-Sam'ani died in 562/1166, before Muhammad ibn Zufar abridged *Tarikh-i Bukhara* in 574/1178–1179, meaning that his story is technically the older of the two.[82] According to Frye, the Soviet archaeologists who excavated the Mosque of Magok-Attar dated it to the ninth century.[83] In general, that time frame favours al-Sam'ani's tale of conversion over *Tarikh-i Bukhara*'s tale of conquest. This example emphasises the importance of reading competing accounts in juxtaposition.

Conclusion

The interpretations offered here are suggestive of the types of work that accounts of fire temple desecration did in early Islamic history.[84] To propose that some such tales from early Islamicate history have been exaggerated, taken out of context or invented is not to deny that others may be reliable. The appropriation of sacred space was common in Late Antiquity, and there is archaeological evidence for the transformation of Zoroastrian temples into mosques, especially in later periods.[85] Nevertheless, Perso-Muslim authors preserved stories of temple desecration to demonstrate the supersession of Islam, so scholars must contextualise even the most credible claims, consider the writer's intent and compare sources of information against each other. This approach reveals that the motives for such violence were often complex and not easily reducible to religious animosity alone, as seen in Abrun's assault on the fire temple near restive Qom. It also shows that Muslims sometimes fabricated them to create a larger-than-life persona for famous progenitors such as Ubayd Allah ibn Abi Bakra or Abd Allah ibn Amir. They used these stories to enhance the prestige of peripheral places by inserting those places into the mainstream of Islamic history at, for example, Bam. Tales of fire temple desecration represent a sort of collective memory of interreligious encounter. The medieval authors of Persian local histories generally favoured them over tales of accommodation because they wanted to remember the superiority of Islam and project its dominance over Zoroastrianism far into the past.

Notes

* An earlier version of this chapter appeared in A. C. S. Peacock, *Islamisation: Comparative Perspectives from History* (Edinburgh: Edinburgh University Press, 2017), 102–117.

1. For a representative sample, see Boyce, *Zoroastrians, Their Religious Beliefs and Practices*; Frye, *Golden Age of Persia*; Morony, 'Conquerors and Conquered: Iran'; Choksy, *Conflict and Cooperation*; Rose, *Zoroastrianism: An Introduction*; Khanbaghi, *The Fire, the Star and the Cross.*
2. The best studies of this phenomenon are in South Asian history. See, for example, Azfar Moin, 'Temple Destruction in India and Shrine Desecration in Iran and Central Asia', *Comparative Studies in Society and History* 57, no. 2 (2015): 467–96; Romila Thapar, *Somanatha: The Many Voices of a History* (London: Verso, 2005); and Richard H. Davis, *The Lives of Indian Images* (Princeton, NJ: Princeton University Press, 1997).
3. Aḥmad ibn Yaḥyá al-Balādhurī, *Ansāb al-ashrāf*, ed. Muhammad Hamidullah, vol. 1 (Cairo: Dar al-Ma'arif, 1959), 494.
4. Hugh Kennedy, *The Great Arab Conquests: How the Spread of Islam Changed the World We Live In* (Philadelphia: Da Capo, 2007), 184, 195; Boyce, 'Zoroastrianism in Iran after the Arab Conquest', 230; Morony, *Iraq after the*

Muslim Conquest, 257; Alfred Kremer, *Culturgeschichte des Orients unter den Chalifen*, vol. 2 (Wien: W. Braumuller, 1875), 164.

5. Anonymous, *Tārikh-e Sistān*, trans. Milton Gold (Roma: Istituto italiano per il Medio ed Estremo Oriente, 1976), 75.
6. al-Balādhurī, *Ansāb al-ashrāf*, 1:498.
7. Kennedy, *Great Arab Conquests*, 195; Morony, *Iraq after the Muslim Conquest*, 257.
8. Anonymous, *Tārikh-e Sistān*, ed. Muhammad Taqi Bahar (Tihran: Kitabkhanah-i Zavvar, 1935), 92; Anonymous, *Tārikh-e Sistān*, 74.
9. Bahā' al-Dīn Muḥammad ibn al-Ḥasan Ibn Ḥamdūn, *al-Tadhkirah al-Ḥamdūnīyah*, ed. Iḥsān 'Abbās, vol. 2 (Bayrut: Ma'had al-Inma al-'Arabi, 1983), 268.
10. 'Amr ibn Baḥr al-Jāḥiẓ, *al-Ḥayawān*, ed. Abd al-Salam Muhammad Harun, vol. 4 (Cairo: Maktabat Mustafa al-Babi al-Halabi wa-Awladuh, 1938), 480. The text reads 'Dar Harith' instead of 'Darabjird', which is clearly an error.
11. Martin Hinds, 'The First Arab Conquests in Fars', in Jere Bacharach, Lawrence Conrad and Patricia Crone (eds), *Studies in Early Islamic History* (Princeton, NJ: Darwin Press, 1996), 224.
12. For an archaeological study of this site, see Huff, 'Formation and Ideology of the Sasanian State in the Context of Archaeological Evidence'.
13. Kennedy, *Great Arab Conquests*, 182.
14. al-Ṭabarī, *Tārīkh al-rusul wa-l-mulūk*, 5:2863; Anonymous, *Tārikh-e Sistān*, 63.
15. Abū l-Ḥasan ibn 'Ali b. al-Husayn al-Mas'ūdī, *Murūj al-dhahab wa-ma'ādin al-jawhar*, eds Abel Pavet de Courteille, Charles Barbier de Meynard, and Charles Pellat, vol. 2 (Bayrut: al-Jami'ah al-Lubnaniyah, 1966), 400.
16. al-Balādhurī, *Kitāb futūḥ al-buldān*, 1956, 2:478; *The Origins of the Islamic State*, 2:130–1.
17. al-Mas'ūdī, *Murūj al-dhahab wa-ma'ādin al-jawhar*, 2:399; *Les prairies d'or*, ed. Abel Pavet de Courteille, vol. 2 (Paris: Société asiatique, 1962), 540.
18. Aḥmad ibn Muḥammad Ibn al-Faqīh al-Hamadhānī, *Mukhtaṣar kitāb al-buldān*, ed. M. J. de Goeje (Leiden: Brill, 1967), 246.
19. al-Jāḥiẓ, *al-Ḥayawān*, 4:480–81.
20. Anonymous, *Tarikh-i Sistan*, 92; al-Balādhurī, *Kitāb futūḥ al-buldān*, 1956, 2:478.
21. *Tarikh-i Sistan*, 92.
22. Savant, *New Muslims of Post-Conquest Iran*, 123.

23. See, for example, Natalie Zemon Davis, 'The Rites of Violence: Religious Riot in Sixteenth-Century France', *Past & Present*, no. 59 (1973): 51–91.
24. Jamsheed K. Choksy, 'Altars, Precincts, and Temples: Medieval and Modern Zoroastrian Praxis', *Iran* 44 (2006): 330; *EI2*, s.v. 'Madjus'; Frye, *Golden Age of Persia*, 145; Nariman, *Persia & Parsis*, 81.
25. This name varies in the sources. It is actually Barun al-Turk in *Kitab al-Buldan* and Birun-i Turk in *Tarikh-i Qom*, but I have favoured al-Tabari's spelling, Abrun. It is Bayram-i Turk in Michael M. J. Fischer, *Iran: From Religious Dispute to Revolution* (Cambridge, MA: Harvard University Press, 1980), 106.
26. Ibn al-Faqīh al-Hamadhānī, *Mukhtaṣar kitāb al-buldān*, 247.
27. Nirenberg, *Communities of Violence*, Chapter 1.
28. Nirenberg, Chapter 2.
29. al-Qomi, *Kitab-i Tarikh-i Qomi*, 67, 89.
30. Abū Ja'far Muḥammad ibn Jarīr al-Ṭabarī, *The Return of the Caliphate to Baghdad*, trans. Franz Rosenthal, vol. 38, History of Al-Tabari (Albany, NY: State University of New York Press, 1985), 104; al-Ṭabarī, *Tārīkh al-rusul wa-l-mulūk*, III, 2208–9.
31. Matthew Gordon, *The Breaking of a Thousand Swords: A History of the Turkish Military of Samarra, a.h. 200–275/815–889 c.e.* (Albany, NY: State University of New York Press, 2001), 128.
32. Louis Massignon, *The Passion of al-Hallaj: Mystic and Martyr of Islam*, vol. 1 (Princeton, NJ: Princeton University Press, 1982), 163; al-Ṭabarī, *Tārīkh al-rusul wa-l-mulūk*, III, 4 and 1936.
33. al-Ṭabarī, *The Return of the Caliphate to Baghdad*, 38:104; al-Ṭabarī, *Tārīkh al-rusul wa-l-mulūk*, III, 2208–9.
34. Roy Mottahedeh, 'The 'Abbasid Caliphate in Iran', in *Cambridge History of Iran*, vol. 4: From the Arab Invasion to the Saljuqs (Cambridge: Cambridge University Press, 1975), 79.
35. Massignon, *The Passion of al-Hallaj*, 1:167.
36. Abū Ja'far Muḥammad ibn Jarīr al-Ṭabarī, *The 'Abbasid Recovery*, trans. Philip Fields, vol. 37, History of Al-Tabari (Albany, NY: State University of New York Press, 1985), 169; al-Ṭabarī, *Tārīkh al-rusul wa-l-mulūk*, III, 2124.
37. al-Ṭabarī, *The Return of the Caliphate to Baghdad*, 38:13; al-Ṭabarī, *Tārīkh al-rusul wa-l-mulūk*, III, 2140.
38. al-Ṭabarī, *The Return of the Caliphate to Baghdad*, 38:13–14; al-Ṭabarī, *Tārīkh al-rusul wa-l-mulūk*, III, 2140.

39. Fischer, *Iran*, 107; Hossein Modarressi Tabataba'i, *Qum dar qarn-i nuhum-i Hijri, 801–900* (Qum: Chapkhana-yi Hikmat, 1971), 94–97.
40. A. K. S. Lambton, 'An Account of the "Tarikhi Qumm"', *Bulletin of the School of Oriental and African Studies* 12 (1948): 592.
41. Lambton, 592.
42. al-Ṭabarī, *The Return of the Caliphate to Baghdad*, 38:14; al-Ṭabarī, *Tārīkh al-rusul wa-l-mulūk*, III, 2140.
43. al-Qummi, *Kitāb-i tārīkh-i Qum*, 89.
44. al-Qummi, 242.
45. al-Qummi, 245, 262; Lambton, 'Account of the "Tarikhi Qumm"', 596.
46. A. K. S. Lambton, 'Persian Local Histories: The Tradition behind Them and the Assumptions of Their Authors', in Alessandro Bausani and Lucia Rostagno (eds), *Yad-Nama: In memoria di Alessandro Bausani* (Roma: Bardi editore, 1991), 235.
47. Mottahedeh, 'The 'Abbasid Caliphate in Iran', 79–80.
48. Richard Eaton, 'Temple Desecration and Indo-Muslim States', in David Gilmartin and Bruce Lawrence (eds), *Beyond Turk and Hindu: Rethinking Religious Identities in Islamicate South Asia* (Gainesville: University Press of Florida, 2002), 247, 257.
49. Barbara Metcalf, 'Too Little and Too Much: Reflections on Muslims in the History of India', *The Journal of Asian Studies* 54, no. 4 (1995): 958.
50. Cynthia Talbot, 'Inscribing the Other, Inscribing the Self: Hindu-Muslim Identities in Pre-Colonial India', *Comparative Studies in Society and History* 37, no. 4 (1995): 717–18.
51. Metcalf, 'Too Little and Too Much', 963; Asghar Ali Engineer, 'Muslim Views of Hindus since 1950', in Jacques Waardenburg (ed.), *Muslim Perceptions of Other Religions: A Historical Survey* (New York: Oxford University Press, 1999), 269.
52. Choksy, 'Altars, Precincts, and Temples', 331; Mehrdad Shokoohy, 'Two Fire Temples Converted to Mosques in Central Iran', *Acta Iranica* 11 (1985): 545.
53. Percy M. Sykes, *A History of Persia*, vol. 2 (London: Macmillan and Co, 1951), 16; Aḥmad 'Alī Vazīrī Kirmānī, *Tārīkh-i Kirmān*, ed. Muhammad Ibrahim Bastani Parizi (Tehran: Kitabha-yi Iran, 1961), 3.
54. Vazīrī Kirmānī, *Tārīkh-i Kirmān*, 31.
55. Vazīrī Kirmānī, 29–31.
56. C. E. Bosworth, *Sistan under the Arabs: From the Islamic Conquest to the Rise of the Saffarids (30–250/651–864)* (Rome: IsMEO, 1968), 24.

57. Mimi Hanaoka, *Authority and Identity in Medieval Islamic Historiography: Persian Histories from the Peripheries* (Cambridge: Cambridge University Press, 2016), Chapter 2.
58. Kitab Ahval-i Nishapur, folio 61b in Richard N. Frye, *The Histories of Nishapur* (London: Mouton, 1965).
59. al-Ṭabarī, *Tārīkh al-rusul wa-l-mulūk*, III, 2885–86; Abū Ja'far Muḥammad ibn Jarīr al-Ṭabarī, *The Crisis of the Early Caliphate*, trans. R. Stephen Humphreys, vol. 15, History of Al-Tabari (Albany, NY: State University of New York Press, 1990), 90.
60. al-Balādhurī, *Kitāb futūḥ al-buldān*, 2014, 315, 391; al-Balādhurī, *The Origins of the Islamic State*, I, 490; II, 136–37; Anonymous, *Tārikh-e Sistān*, 63.
61. Vazīrī Kirmānī, *Tārīkh-i Kirmān*, 31; *EI2*, s.v. 'Abd Allah b. Amir'.
62. Q 48:14.
63. Abū Ja'far Muḥammad ibn Jarīr al-Ṭabarī, *Biographies of the Prophet's Companions and Their Successors*, trans. Ella Landau-Tasseron, vol. 39, History of Al-Tabari (Albany, NY: State University of New York Press, 1998), 76; al-Ṭabarī, *Tārīkh al-rusul wa-l-mulūk*, III, 2353.
64. Jane Dammen McAuliffe (ed.), *Encyclopaedia of the Quran* (Leiden: Brill, 2001), s.vv. 'Tree' and 'Hudaybiyya'.
65. For information on the Zoroastrians of Kerman and Yazd in the nineteenth and twentieth centuries, see Ringer, *Pious Citizens*; Choksy, 'Despite Shāhs and Mollās'; Nile Green, 'The Survival of Zoroastrianism in Yazd', *Iran* 38 (2000): 115–22; Boyce, *A Persian Stronghold of Zoroastrianism.*
66. Boyce, 'Zoroastrianism in Iran after the Arab Conquest', 230; Choksy, *Conflict and Cooperation*, 104; *EI2*, s.v. 'Madjus'.
67. Frye, *The Histories of Nishapur*, 66b; Bulliet, *The Patricians of Nishapur: A Study in Medieval Islamic Social History*, 15.
68. Abū Bakr Muḥammad ibn Ja'far Narshakhī, *Tārīkh-i Bukhārā* (Tihran: Intisharat-i Tus, 1984), 67.
69. W. Barthold, *Turkestan Down to the Mongol Invasion*, 4th ed. (London: Luzac, 1977), 108–9; see also Narshakhī, *Tārīkh-i Bukhārā*, 29 where a place of idols and a fire temple are distinct.
70. Rose, *Zoroastrianism: An Introduction*, 158; Choksy, *Conflict and Cooperation*, 104–5.
71. Narshakhī, *Tārīkh-i Bukhārā*, 42–43.
72. Narshakhī, 43.

73. Richard N. Frye, *Bukhara: The Medieval Achievement* (Norman: University of Oklahoma Press, 1965), 74, 91–92.
74. Narshakhī, *Tārīkh-i Bukhārā*, 67; Barthold, *Turkestan Down to the Mongol Invasion*, 108. Although the pilfering of the gate appears in the text immediately after an episode of violence between Muslims and Zoroastrians in the seventh century, al-Narshakhi clearly states that the gate was not displayed at the mosque until the tenth century.
75. Narshakhī, *Tārīkh-i Bukhārā*, 67.
76. Narshakhī, 43–44.
77. Frye, *Bukhara: The Medieval Achievement*, 7; this must be the mosque of Makh-Attar, as it is the only one mentioned in the primary source. There was also a mosque of Makh-Turpi in the city, althought I have been unable to independently corroborate the assertion that it too was built on the site of a fire temple. See Jamsheed K. Choksy, 'Conflict, Coexistence, and Cooperation: Muslims and Zoroastrians in Eastern Iran during the Medieval Period', *Muslim World* 80, no. 3–4 (1990): 225–26; compare Abū Bakr Muḥammad ibn Jaʿfar Narshakhī, *The History of Bukhara*, trans. Richard N. Frye (Cambridge, MA: Mediaeval Academy of America, 1954), 120, ff. 102.
78. Narshakhī, *Tārīkh-i Bukhārā*, 29–30.
79. Narshakhī, *History of Bukhara*, xii; *EI2*, s.v. "Narshakhi."
80. ʿAbd al-Karīm ibn Muḥammad al-Samʿānī, *Kitāb al-ansāb*, ed. D.S. Margoliouth (Leiden: Brill, 1912), folio 499a; compare Yāqūt ibn ʿAbd Allāh al-Ḥamawī, *Muʿjam al-buldān*, ed. Ferdinand Wüstenfeld (Leipzig: F. A. Brockhaus, 1866), 4:380.
81. al-Samʿānī, *Kitāb al-ansāb*, 2.
82. *EI2*, s.v. 'al-Samʿani'; Narshakhī, *History of Bukhara*, xii.
83. Narshakhī, *History of Bukhara*, 120.
84. For a longer, more detailed study of such tales, see Magnusson, 'Muslim-Zoroastrian Relations and Religious Violence', 144–81.
85. See, for example, Shokoohy, 'Two Fire Temples Converted to Mosques in Central Iran'; Maxime Siroux, 'L'évolution des antiques mosquées rurales de la région d'Ispahan', *Arts Asiatiques* 26 (1973): 65–112; Klaus Schippmann, *Die iranischen Feuerheiligtümer*, Religionsgeschichtliche Versuche und Vorarbeiten 31 (Berlin: Walter de Gruyter, 1971).

6

Rhetorical Zoroastrians in Early Islamic Discourse

The Arabic term 'Zoroastrians' (*majūs*) frequently features in early Islamic discourse as a synonym for 'Other'. Muslims used it to describe groups they perceived as pagan, heretical or deviant. Hence the following report about 'Zoroastrian' Berbers occasionally appears in Islamic taxation literature:

> As for the Zoroastrians, the Messenger of God, may God bless him, accepted *jizya* from the Zoroastrians of Hajar on the condition that the meat slaughtered by them is impermissible, as is marrying their women. When Khālid ibn al-Walīd was the agent (*'āmil*) of Abū Bakr, he demanded [jizya] from the people of Iraq, who were Zoroastrians, in his letter to their Sasanian governors (*marāzibatihim*). 'Umar ibn al-Khaṭṭāb accepted [jizya] from them thereafter, and after him 'Uthmān ibn 'Affān also accepted it from them and from the Berbers, who were Zoroastrians (*al-barbar wa-kānū majūsan*).[1]

Who were these Zoroastrian Berbers that Uthman taxed? Abu Ubayd ibn Sallam (d. 224/838) identifies them as the Lawata people of Barqa and the Pentapolis of Cyrenaica, in what is now Libya.[2] That location places them beyond the plausible reach of Sasanian Zoroastrianism. Why, then, did early Muslims call these Berbers 'Zoroastrians'? In what ways were they like Zoroastrians?

Previous scholars have asserted that Muslims used this descriptor to justify accepting jizya from People without a Book – that is, adherents of neither Judaism nor Christianity – since Umar had set that precedent with

Zoroastrians (see Chapter Two).[3] From a legal perspective, it relieved them of the theoretical obligation to fight these groups because Muhammad had taxed them. Yet it is likely that in this case the Berbers' association with Zoroastrianism was the result of a simple error in transmission. The following version of the same report appears far more frequently in the early Islamic taxation literature:

> Yaḥyā ibn Ayyūb told me on the authority of Yūnus ibn Yazīd al-Aylī on the authority of Ibn Shihāb that the Messenger of God, may God bless him, collected *jizya* from the Zoroastrians of Hajar and that 'Umar collected *jizya* from the Zoroastrians of Persia, and that 'Uthmān collected *jizya* from the Berbers.[4]

In other words, the first caliphs accepted tax from Zoroastrians *and* Berbers – not from Zoroastrian Berbers.

Berbers were akin to Zoroastrians in that Muslims felt the need retrospectively to justify taxing them. Chapter Two dealt extensively with early jurists' ambivalence about accepting jizya from Zoroastrians because of their alleged lack of divinely revealed scripture. Apparently there was a similar concern about Berbers, who supposedly denied the idea of prophecy.[5] Although Muslims eventually incorporated them into the caliphal tax regime, there was evidently enough lingering doubt about their religious beliefs that a corrupted report about 'Zoroastrian' Berbers could circulate in respected legal manuals, such as Sahnun ibn Sa'id's (d. 240/854) *al-Mudawwana al-Kubra*.[6] Therefore, scholars of Islam are correct to interpret the term 'Zoroastrians' as a legal designation for People without a Book because that is what it later became, in part based on this corrupted report.

While some transmitters of hadith may have mistakenly labelled Berbers as Zoroastrians, other Muslims deliberately applied this term to religious and ethnic groups that they perceived as pagan, heretical or deviant. For example, the Syrian jurist Abu Amr Abd al-Rahman ibn Amr al-Awza'i (d. 157/774) applied it to Khazars and the people of Azerbaijan.[7] Centuries later, Izz al-Din Abu l-Hasan Ali ibn al-Athir (555–630/1160–1233) mentioned Zoroastrians among the Shi'i communities of Greater Syria during the Crusades.[8] With the possible exception of Azerbaijan, which was once part of the Sasanian Empire, the correlation between these groups and actual

Zoroastrians is doubtful. Rather, Muslims used the description rhetorically. The enduring salience of this label across the centuries betrays a lingering ambivalence about the exceptional status of Zoroastrians in early Islamic society. As noted in Chapter Three, Muslims could generally accept jizya from Zoroastrians but not marry them or consume meat slaughtered by them. Prophetic hadith instructed Muslims to treat Zoroastrians like People of the Book despite some uncertainty about the existence or legitimacy of Zoroastrian scripture. It is perhaps not surprising, then, that some Muslim authors applied the Zoroastrians' name to other liminal groups. The label thereby acquired a pejorative connotation, emphasising early Muslims' misgivings about Zoroastrianism.

This chapter will consider three examples of rhetorical uses of the term 'Zoroastrians' in early Islamic discourse. Muslim authors applied it to Vikings, Qadarites and a group of converts in South Asia. None of these groups likely had a genuine connection to Zoroastrianism, so the designation was rhetorical. It was also polemical because the beliefs of these groups were considered pagan, heretical or deviant. This label belonged to an internal Muslim discourse of identity construction. Only Muslims living far from Iran, without much direct experience with Zoroastrians, tended to use it. The invocation of this terminology in many places and across genres of literature demonstrates that medieval Muslims remained ambivalent about the exceptional status of Zoroastrians even as they used it to understand other marginalised peoples and mediate interactions with them.

Rhetorical Identities in the Qur'an

At the outset, it is important to acknowledge that identities are constructed. Religious groups often create oppositional identities in pursuit of communal solidarity against external threats (real and perceived). The same is true of ethnicities, nations and a host of other political and social associations.[9] One can choose a religious identity or acquire it at birth, like an ethnicity, regardless of personal belief or self-identification. Rhetorical labelling of one's opponents is a common tactic of identity formation that promotes group adhesion. Such labels assist the group in navigating interactions with outsiders who are perceived as suspicious, rival or aberrant.[10] Such labelling ultimately facilitates the construction of one's own group identity.

There are numerous examples of rhetorical labelling in early Islamic history. Scholars have recently emphasised the ways in which the Qur'an constructed rhetorical identities for its audience. The Qur'an distinguishes between believers (Ar., *mu'minūn*) who accepted Muhammad's message, and polytheists – or more accurately, 'associators' (*mushrikūn*) – who rejected it. These polytheists supposedly associated (*ashraka*) lesser beings or objects with God. Yet Patricia Crone has argued that the belief most commonly condemned in the Qur'an is *dahr*, the notion that human life is fleeting and death is the end thereof. The polytheists of the Qur'an, in other words, did not necessarily believe in multiple gods or worship idols; they may have simply rejected the idea of Resurrection and eternal recompense for the deeds of this short life.[11] Noting that accusations of polytheism are often the product of theological debates between monotheists, Gerald Hawting posits that the polytheists of the Qur'an were actually monotheists, probably heterodox Jews or Christians. By the time the sources of Islamic tradition were composed a century and a half after the death of the Prophet Muhammad, Muslims had forgotten the original context of Qur'anic debates and took its labels literally.[12] Angelika Neuwirth likewise concludes that Muhammad's audience must have been Christian, or at least familiar enough with Christianity to appreciate the frequent allusions to Jesus in the earliest chapters of the Qur'an. For example, the so-called polytheists knew enough about Christian doctrine to invoke Jesus' claim to be the divine Son of God against the Qur'anic claim that God is One.[13]

Whether the 'associators' mentioned in the Qur'an were *dahriyya*, Christians, or something else entirely, it is likely that Prophet Muhammad had to contend with a more religiously diverse lot of Meccans than the word 'polytheists' connotes in its strictest sense. According to Hawting, that was a polemical term, intended to delegitimise those who rejected Muhammad's message. Such exclusionary rhetoric also would have assisted Muslims in defining themselves against their antagonists. Fred Donner has argued that the early Islamic community used inclusionary rhetoric to create alliances with like-minded monotheists. The first Muslims identified themselves and their supporters as 'believers' (*mu'minūn*), a Qur'anic term with an unambiguously positive connotation.[14] It, too, helped early Muslims to forge an oppositional identity vis-à-vis polytheists. These examples demonstrate that authors constructed rhetorical identities for a number of groups in the early Islamicate era, and that such labels need not be taken literally.

Rhetorical Zoroastrians in Qur'an Commentaries

Although the term 'Zoroastrians' features just once in the Qur'an, rhetorical Zoroastrians abound in early Qur'an commentaries. Exegesis of the opening verses of *Sūrat al-Rūm* is a case in point. These verses foretell the Byzantines' miraculous triumph over the (unnamed) Sasanians in what must be the Perso–Roman War of 602–628. According to the exegetes, the Muslims favoured the Byzantines in this conflict because they were both People of the Book. The Meccans, on the other hand, supported the Sasanians. (Although certainly a convenient literary device in this context, the purported Sasanian–Meccan alliance might also reflect actual Persian influence in Arabia before the rise of Islam, as noted in Chapter Two.[15]) The Meccans taunted the Muslims after the Sasanians' early victories, which included the conquest of Jerusalem in 614. In response, God revealed the first five verses of *Sūrat al-Rūm*, prophesying that the Byzantines would be victorious after a few years. These verses comforted and eventually vindicated Muhammad's followers, as the Byzantines' fortunes miraculously reversed after 622 and Heraclius triumphed over the Sasanians.[16]

In the course of their exegesis, Qur'an commentators alternately described the Sasanians as Zoroastrians, illiterates or idol worshippers, depending on their exegetical needs. When merely seeking to identify the Persians' religion, the commentators called them 'Zoroastrians' (*majūs*).[17] However, when the intent was to highlight the affinity between Muslims and Byzantines as People of the Book, Zoroastrians became 'illiterates' (*ummiyyūn*) – People without a Book.[18] Finally, if the commentator wished to emphasise the fact that the 'infidel' Meccans (*kuffār*) were allied with the Persians, Sasanians were 'idol worshippers' (*'abadat al-awthān*) or 'polytheists' (*mushrikūn*).[19] It was not that the exegetes were unsure about the nature of the Persians' religion; their diction was deliberate. Qur'an commentators consciously chose words to fit their exegetical objectives. That much is obvious in their attempt to connect the Byzantines' victory over the Sasanians to the Muslims' triumph over the Meccans. Most commentators insisted that both events occurred simultaneously, but they could not agree whether it was on the day of Badr or Hudaybiyya.[20] The precise date of the victories was less important than their synchronisation. Likewise, rhetorical Persians could be anything from illiterates to idolaters. The fact that such disparaging terms could be synonyms for 'Zoroastrians' reveals the extent of early Muslim ambivalence about Zoroastrianism.

Qur'an commentators invented other rhetorical Zoroastrians. Sarah Bowen Savant has described the process by which early Muslim exegetes transformed Cain, the infamous son of Adam and Eve, into a proto-Zoroastrian.[21] Islamic tradition, like Jewish and Christian traditions, remembers Cain (*Qābīl*) as the first murderer. Cain killed his brother Abel (*Hābīl*) out of jealousy after God accepted Abel's sacrificial offerings but not Cain's. According to a report in Abu Ja'far Muhammad ibn Jarir al-Tabari's (d. 310/923) *Ta'rīkh al-rusul wa-l-mulūk*, Satan (*Iblīs*) deceived Cain, telling him that God had consumed Abel's sacrifice with fire because Abel had tended the fire. Satan urged Cain to do likewise. Thus, Cain built a fire temple and became the first human to worship fire. Savant notes that Muslims obviously had some familiarity with the importance of fire in Zoroastrianism, but 'their general ignorance made it possible for them to entertain such a damning tradition, which inserted a Zoroastrian practice into prophetic history and washed out earlier Iranian ideas about fire.'[22] Cain's proto-Zoroastrian innovations reportedly extended beyond fire worship. He refused to bury Abel's body, leaving it exposed to the elements – hence the Zoroastrians' practice of exposing corpses. Cain also preferred to marry his twin sister rather than Abel's sister, an allusion to the Late Antique Zoroastrian practice of consanguineous marriage.[23] Through clever exegesis and subtle insinuation, the world's first murderer became the inspiration behind Zoroastrianism.

'Zoroastrian' Vikings in Early Islamic Iberia

Vikings, or Norsemen, were rhetorical Zoroastrians in early Islamic Iberia. In 230/844, Vikings raided the Iberian Peninsula. Sailing from Scandinavia, they plundered the Umayyad emirate of al-Andalus. After fighting three battles in the Tagus River estuary with forces dispatched by the Muslim governor of Lisbon, Vikings sailed up the Guadalquivir River. They pillaged Seville for several days. The Umayyad ruler, Abd al-Rahman II (r. 206–238/822–852), sent troops against them, killing 1,000 Scandinavians and imprisoning

400 more. The remainder fled. Fourteen years later, however, they returned to Iberia. The Vikings sacked Algeciras, torching its congregational mosque. For three years they harried the coasts of the Iberian Peninsula, including Pamplona, where they captured the Basque *amīr* in 245/859. (He subsequently ransomed himself for a hefty sum.) A century later, in 355/966, Norsemen attacked Lisbon again. Muslim forces, dispatched from Seville, met them on land and at sea. Both sides suffered heavy casualties before the Vikings retreated. In 360/971, the Umayyad navy repelled the last Scandinavian raid on the west coast of Iberia, and Muslim forces deterred their final landing a year later.[24]

Almost without exception, Andalusi Arabic sources call these Vikings 'Zoroastrians'. Why? What was the significance of this term? According to Arne Melvinger, it meant something akin to 'pagans', people who are neither Jews nor Christians.[25] The Andalusi author Ibn Hayyan (377–469/987–1076) describes as 'Norman Zoroastrians' (*al-majūs al-urdumāniyyūn*) the perpetrators of the final assault on Iberia in 360–361/971–972.[26] They launched it from Normandy, where the Treaty of St Clair had ceded them territory in 911. Although Scandinavians initially held indigenous Nordic beliefs, many of them became Christians. A thirteenth-century Arabic source claims that Abd al-Rahman II dispatched an ambassador to the Vikings after their first raid in 230/844. This envoy reported that Norsemen used to be Zoroastrians but now mostly professed Christianity. A few still held to their original beliefs, which supposedly included fire worship and consanguineous marriage. Melvinger admits that the mention of consanguineous marriage is suspicious, but attributes it to 'a misunderstanding on the Arabic side' because Norse religion 'reminded the Arabs of that of the Persian Zoroastrians'.[27] It seems more likely, however, that Muslims attributed genuine Zoroastrian doctrines to rhetorical Zoroastrians. For instance, they claimed that the Berbers who established Fez built a fire temple there because they were Zoroastrians.[28]

Twelfth-, thirteenth- and fourteenth-century Muslims ascribed fire worship and the burning of corpses to northern Europeans. Muslims called them Zoroastrians because 'the Arabic authors were thinking about the religion in which fire in some form played a prominent part'.[29] It was a false association. Fire is a pure element in the Good Religion, representative of the divine presence, but Zoroastrians did not worship it. Although fire has some resonance in Nordic mythology, Vikings did not venerate it either.[30] Muslim authors may have ascribed fire worship to Scandinavians simply because the latter hailed from the frozen climes of the north. For example, the tenth-century Muslim geographer Ibn al-Faqih (fl. 290/903) alleges that the bitter cold of Central Asia prompted Zoroaster to venerate fire.[31] The funerary practices of many northern and eastern Europeans did involve cremation, at least according to several Muslim geographers.[32] But the corpse is a source of pollution in the Good Religion, and priests endeavoured not to contaminate the sacred flame. Therefore, it is erroneous to associate cremation with Zoroastrianism in the medieval period.

By contrast, authors from the eastern Islamic world seldom called Norsemen 'Zoroastrians'. Muslim geographers tended to use ethnonyms when describing northern European fire worshippers who cremated their dead.[33] The Abbasid ambassador, Ahmad ibn Fadlan, for instance, does not describe Vikings as Zoroastrians even though he witnessed their burning of a funeral pyre.[34] Abu Hamid al-Gharnati (d. 565/1169), who was raised in Iberia but spent considerable time in the eastern Islamic world before travelling throughout northern Europe, also does not use the term *majūs*.[35] It seems that only Muslims who had little or no direct experience with Persian Zoroastrians did so.

Nevertheless, some eastern geographers were aware of the rhetorical label. Abu al-Hasan Ali ibn al-Husayn al-Mas'udi (d. 345/956) noted that Andalusi Muslims called the Vikings 'Zoroastrians', but he identified them as *Rūs*.[36] The early Muslim geographer Abu al-Abbas Ahmad al-Ya'qubi (d. *c.* 292/905), who never made it further west than Egypt, utilised both terms.

> To the west of the city that is called al-Jazīra [Algeciras] is a city called Ishbiliyya [Seville] on the great river. It is the river of Qurṭuba [Cordoba] through which the Zoroastrians – who are called *Rūs* – entered in the year 229[/843]. They enslaved and plundered and burned and killed.[37]

The ethnic descriptor *Rūs* was more commonly used in the eastern Islamic world to describe Vikings. The term 'Zoroastrians' must have had a rhetorical value for Andalusi Muslims that *Rūs* lacked because Ann Christys has documented its regular use in the Maghrib to denote Vikings specifically and pagan outsiders generically.[38]

Robert Brunschvig argued decades ago that 'Zoroastrians' was a legal designation. He asserted that Andalusi Muslims labelled Vikings so because the jurist al-Awza'i (d. 157/774) deemed all heathens to be Zoroastrians legally. Since al-Awza'i's short-lived school of law established itself in al-Andalus after the Islamic conquest of the early eighth century, Brunschvig posited that Muslims used the term to justify their peace treaty with pagan Vikings.[39] However, it is unlikely that they had such a treaty. A single thirteenth-century source contains the second-hand testimony of an ambassador sent by Abd al-Rahman II to the Vikings after their first raid on Iberia in the ninth century.[40] Melvinger rejected Brunschvig's hypothesis on the grounds that Malik ibn Anas' disciples had arrived in Iberia by the early ninth century and had begun to supplant al-Awza'i's legal school (*madhhab*). Melvinger fails to note, however, that Malik also considered all non-Arabs without a Book to be 'Zoroastrians'.[41]

Míkel de Epalza has attempted to revive Brunschvig's legal explanation on the grounds that Andalusi Muslims sometimes referred to Basques as Zoroastrians. For example, Badr, the Muslim governor of Zaragosa, led an expedition up the Ebro Valley to the frontier (*thaghr*) of Castile in 150/767. After he conquered the city of Álava, its inhabitants paid jizya. Thereafter, Badr 'ordered all the men from that area to be examined and the most intelligent to be selected, and those in the *thaghr* in whom bad intentions were found, he took with him'.[42] Since the pagan population of Álava had no Christian clergy to represent them, de Epalza believes that Badr had to test their beliefs in order to determine their tax status. Later Andalusi Muslims called them 'Zoroastrians' on account of their unknown religion.[43] However, that term does not appear in this source, and Badr reportedly imposed jizya on the inhabitants of the city *before* testing them. Furthermore, the explicit purpose of the test was to select the most capable people – perhaps to serve in the administration – and to identify potential troublemakers on the frontier. While the Arabic word 'Zoroastrians' was used at times to identify people and places in the Basque country, it usually described people who remained beyond the borders of al-Andalus and, by extension, beyond the reach of Islamic law.[44] Therefore, it cannot be a strictly legal designation.

All of these theories have some merit, but none fully explains Andalusi Muslims' penchant for labelling outsiders as 'Zoroastrians'. A more comprehensive explanation is that *majūs* was a rhetorical term for pagan or unfamiliar 'Others'. Caroline Stone and Paul Lunde stress that ninth-century Muslims did not know who the Norsemen were, nor whence they came.[45] Later, even as they gained deeper understanding, authors writing in Arabic 'continued to place Vikings just beyond the limits of the familiar world'.[46] Eastern Muslim authors, who would have been most acquainted with Persian Zoroastrians, tended not to use this rhetorical label. They preferred more precise ethnonyms, such as *Rūs*. Although the word 'Zoroastrians' may have had a legal connotation in certain contexts, Scandinavians and Basques were generally not subject to Islamic law, so that cannot be its sole significance. It is more accurate to state that Andalusi Muslims applied this term to groups that were perceived as unfamiliar or pagan. In medieval Iberia, 'Zoroastrians' was a rhetorical description of the early Islamic Other.

'Zoroastrian' Qadarites in Early Islamic Theology

The *Sunan* of Abu Da'ud contains two reports that use the term 'Zoroastrians' rhetorically to describe Qadarites (*qadariyya*), or Muslims who believed in free will.

> 'Abd al-'Azīz ibn Abī Ḥāzim told us saying: I was told about fate (*manan*) by my father on the authority of Ibn 'Umar on the authority of the Prophet, may God bless him. He said: The Qadarites are the Zoroastrians of this community (*umma*). If they are ill, do not visit them, and if they die, do not attend their funerals.[47]

The polemical intent of this comparison is more apparent in a related report:

> The Messenger of God, may God bless him, said: Every community (*umma*) has Zoroastrians. The Zoroastrians of this community are those who say, 'There is no predestination' (*lā qadara*). Whoever among them dies, do not attend his funeral. Whoever among them becomes ill, do not visit them. They are the sect of the Antichrist (*shī'at al-dajjāl*), and verily God will link them with the Antichrist (*yulḥiqu bi-l-dajjāl*).[48]

Not only were Qadarites rhetorical Zoroastrians, but also partisans of the Antichrist, the sinister foe of the Believers whom the Rightly Guided One (*al-Mahdī*) will vanquish at the Last Day.[49] The Sunni hadith collections are replete with similar condemnations of Qadarites and their doctrines.

Such reports reflect a significant theological debate in the later Umayyad period about the limits of human agency. To what extent does God determine (*qadara*) an individual's behaviour? For piety-minded Muslim theologians, the implications of the answer were potentially profound. Qadarites, who believed that humans had free will, argued that if God dictates human behaviour then He is the author of sin. Instead, they believed that humans were responsible for their own deeds. The Qadarites' rivals, whom they deemed Jabrites (*Mujbira* or *Jabriyya*), held that God predetermined human behaviour. If humans could act independently of the divine will, Jabrites claimed, then He is not sovereign. They rejected the notion that humans are co-creators with Him. The Jabrites labelled their opponents 'Qadarites' because they arrogated to themselves the power of self-determination (*qadar*). According to Josef van Ess, the leading scholar in this field, that term was 'always derogatory, never applied to oneself'.[50] It had rhetorical resonance.

Although the contest between the Qadarites and the Jabrites was 'the first proper theological dispute in Islamic history', it also had a political dimension.[51] Leading members of the Umayyad dynasty were frequently accused of questionable behaviour, and politically minded Qadarites argued that impious rulers might be rightfully deposed.[52] The Umayyad caliphs, for their part, believed that God had appointed them to govern the Muslim community. Although imperfect, they were His deputies on earth.[53] Muslims therefore ought not to overthrow the caliph, even for reprehensible behaviour. The Umayyads found in the doctrine of *qadar* (that is, divine determination of acts) sufficient reason to ignore the grievances of their numerous critics. Khalid Yahya Blankinship notes that the Umayyads' theology, though self-serving, may not have been entirely disingenuous. In addition to justifying the political status quo, predestinarian arguments piously affirmed God's absolute sovereignty.[54]

Opponents of the dynasty naturally gravitated towards the Qadarites, promoting free will as an implicit critique of Umayyad abuses of power. The two centres of Qadarite thought were Basra and Damascus. The Umayyad caliphs Abd al-Malik (r. 65–86/685–705) and his son, Hisham

(r. 105–125/724–743), attempted to suppress the movement by executing Qadarite leaders in both places.[55] Steven Judd emphasises that the caliphs did not target Qadarites like Ghaylan al-Dimashqi for political crimes; they were tried and executed for heresy.[56] As a result of their harsh tactics, free will became a rallying cry in the revolt that toppled Hisham's chosen successor, al-Walid II. The new caliph, Yazid III, embraced the Qadarites who had brought him to power but died shortly thereafter. Most Qadarites fled to Basra when Marwan II defeated Yazid's chosen successor and became caliph.[57] The Abbasid Revolution toppled Marwan II and put an end to the Umayyad dynasty of Damascus in 132/750.

Since the debate over free will and predestination began in the Umayyad period, the previously cited reports, in which the Prophet Muhammad compares Qadarites to Zoroastrians, are anachronistic. Jabrites often articulated their theological positions in prophetic sayings, whose *isnads* (chains of transmission) van Ess traces to second-/eighth-century Medina.[58] Why might Jabrites have called Qadarites 'Zoroastrians'? What was the implication?

Qadarites as Heretics

Mohsen Zakeri, a scholar who has written about the persistence of Sasanian institutions in early Islamic Iran, takes this comparison as evidence of Zoroastrian influence on the Qadarite movement. He contends that Abu Yunus Sinawayh al-Uswari, a Persian convert to Islam from Zoroastrianism, taught the doctrine of free will to Ma'bad ibn Abd Allah al-Juhani. Ma'bad was later executed by the Umayyad caliph Abd al-Malik for heresy, thereby becoming the first Qadarite martyr.[59] For Zakeri, the hadith reports reveal the Zoroastrian inspiration behind Qadarite theology.[60] Yet Zakeri's interpretation disregards the obvious polemical intent of these prophetic sayings. Van Ess argues that the comparison was originally rhetorical, and later Muslims took it literally by mistake.[61]

Other scholars have understood these reports to mean that Qadarites, like Zoroastrians, were dualists because both attributed evil to a source other than God.[62] According to this logic, Qadarites believed that humans or Satan bore responsibility for sin in the same manner that Zoroastrians blamed Ahriman, the deity of chaos, darkness and deceit. That is certainly how Abu Da'ud understood the comparison.[63] This interpretation is problematic, however, because medieval Muslim philosophers of religion generally did not classify Zoroastrians as dualists.[64] Additionally, this argument only explains the first half of each report, which likens Qadarites to Zoroastrians. If the term 'Zoroastrians' in this context is simply a synonym for 'dualists', then what of the Prophet's injunction in the second half of each report about not attending their funerals or visiting their sick?

According to the heresiographer Abd al-Qahir ibn Tahir al-Baghdadi (d. 429/1037), several Companions of the Prophet sought to ostracise the Qadarites on account of their beliefs.

> In the time of the later Companions there arose the divergent views of the Qadarites (*Qadariyya*) as to predestination and free will . . . Among the later Companions who differed from [the Qadarites] was 'Abd Allāh ibn 'Umar, Jābir ibn 'Abd Allāh, Abū Hurayra, Ibn 'Abbās, Anas ibn Mālik, 'Abd Allāh ibn Abī Awfī, and 'Uqbah ibn 'Amir al-Juhani and their contemporaries. These enjoined their successors not to greet the Qadariyya, nor to pray over their bodies, and not to visit their sick.[65]

In other words, certain Companions restricted contact with the Qadarites because of the latter's deviant theology. Like the restrictions on interacting with Zoroastrians discussed in Chapter Three, these legal disabilities became embedded in prophetic sayings.

By the Abbasid era, the word 'Qadarites' came to mean 'heretics'. Mu'tazilites (*Mu'tazila*) were the theological heirs of the Qadarites. They shared some Qadarite views, including the individual's responsibility for his or her actions, although they were more concerned about defending the notion of a created Qur'an. Early Abbasid caliphs, particularly al-Ma'mun, patronised Mu'tazili theology but it slowly fell out of favour during and after the reign of al-Mutawakkil. In that brief interval, Mu'tazilites supported a theological litmus test (*miḥna*) among scholars to suppress the idea that the Qur'an existed co-eternally with God. Partisans of Hadith (*ahl al-ḥadīth*), such as the influential jurist Ahmad ibn Hanbal, furiously resisted this inquisition. They eventually triumphed and discredited Mu'tazilites by comparing them to Qadarites. Partisans of Hadith accused Mu'tazilites of making every person the creator of his or her own actions (*khāliq al-af'āl*), whereas God was the only true Creator. To subscribe to the doctrine of free will became heresy. Thus, Mu'tazilites were keen to avoid the accusation that they were Qadarites.[66]

Like Zoroastrians, Mu'tazilites and Qadarites were perceived as theologically deviant. As noted in Chapter Three, most jurists prohibited Muslims from marrying Zoroastrians or eating meat slaughtered by them because these privileges were reserved for People of the Book. Muslims were not to interact with Zoroastrians on the same basis as they did with Jews and Christians. In the case of Mu'tazilites, the prohibitions were different but the exclusionary intent was the same. Partisans of Hadith should not care for sick Mu'tazilites or mourn their dead because these condolences were reserved for orthodox Muslims. While heterodox Muslims could not be excluded entirely from society, they warranted ostracism on account of their beliefs. Every community has groups that do not truly belong, the Prophet reportedly said. Qadarites and Mu'tazilites were the rhetorical Zoroastrians of the Muslim community. Thus, Jabrites could not enjoy unbridled association with them.

'Zoroastrian' Converts in Early Islamic India

A final example, from South Asia, exemplifies three potential meanings of the polyvalent term 'Zoroastrians' – pagan, heretical and deviant. In the tenth century, the Fatimid chief judge al-Nu'man ibn Muhammad described a group of Sindi converts to Islam as Zoroastrians. Sind was at that time the easternmost province of the Islamic world, encompassing the upper Indus River Valley.[67] Although Muslims had conquered Sind in the eighth century, Isma'ili missionaries were the first to make a concerted effort to proselytise there.[68]

The first missionary (*dā'ī*) arrived in Sind from Yemen in 270/883. The Isma'ili mission then disappears from the sources until 341/953, when news reached the Fatimid caliph al-Mu'izz (r. 341–365/953–975) in Cairo that the mission leader was allowing converts in the city of Multan to maintain some of their previous practices, which were supposedly incompatible with Islam. The accusation against him appears in al-Nu'man's *Book of Audiences and Proceedings* (*Kitāb al-majālis wa-l-musāyarāt*):

> One of the missionaries (*du'āt*) was in a remote location in a distant region proselytizing on behalf of the Friends of God [i.e., the Shi'i Imams] . . .

> Most of its people are Zoroastrians but Islam had spread among them previously. The Commander of the Faithful, al-Mu'izz li-Dīn Allāh, heard that this last missionary had caused mischief among them. Specifically, [the missionary] proselytized many of the Zoroastrian people (*'ālaman kathīran min al-majūs*) who kept their religion and did not convert to Islam.[69]

Apparently the mission leader did not require these new Muslims to entirely abandon their old lifestyles. The source complains about several specific acts that he tolerated.

> He let them continue doing things forbidden by God, which they deem lawful; they used to deem lawful that which God prohibited. They practiced consanguineous marriage and consumed that which is unlawful to drink and eat, transgressing thereby the limits of God (*Tarakahum 'alā mā hum 'alayhi yastaḥillūna min maḥārim Allāh mā kānū yastaḥillūna mimmā nahā Allāhu 'anhu mā kāna ya'malūna min nikāḥ dhawāt al-maḥārim wa-l-tanāwul mā lā yaḥullu min al-mashārib wa-l-maṭā'im ta'addiyyan minhu bi-ḥudūd Allāh*).[70]

Al-Mu'izz determined to remove the mission leader from his post, but the man died before the caliph could act.

Scholars have debated the meaning of 'Zoroastrians' in this context. Abbas Hamdani reads it literally, asserting that Buddhists and Zoroastrians inhabited Multan.[71] However, the rhetorical intent is obvious from the fact that these putative Zoroastrians are called 'polytheists' (*mushrikūn*) elsewhere in the text.[72] While not excluding the possibility that there may have been actual Zoroastrians in Sind, Samuel Stern contends that the term must be 'a vague denomination for Hindus'.[73] Derryl Maclean concurs but notes that the sun cult at Multan had Zoroastrian roots. Therefore, he speculates that perhaps Muslims 'applied [the term] to the Hindus of Upper Sind due to the prominence of the Multān sun-temple'.[74] These interpretations do not seem to fully appreciate the polemical significance of this label.

Al-Nu'man was a Cairene judge who may have known very little about South Asian religions. Therefore, it is possible that the term 'Zoroastrians' is a rhetorical descriptor for pagans – people whose beliefs are unrecognised by the author. In that sense, both Hindus and Buddhists could be 'Zoroastrians', as were Vikings and Basques. Two sources related to the Umayyad conquest of Sind (89–92/708–711) state that the commander, Muhammad ibn al-Qasim al-Thaqafi, taxed the population at al-Rur after comparing their temple (Ar., *budd*) to houses of worship built by Christians, Jews and Zoroastrians.[75] Of these three groups, surely Zoroastrians were the all-important precedent for extending *dhimma* to the adherents of a religion not sanctioned by the Qur'an. After all, the Good Religion was the original exception. Even if such reports project later legal opinion into the past, as Yohanan Friedmann has argued, they demonstrate that early Muslims in Sind compared People without a Book to Zoroastrians.[76]

The meaning of 'Zoroastrians' in this context need not be limited to paganism. The term also connotes unorthodox belief, as it did when applied to the *qadariyya*. Maclean has argued that it was the spread of heresy in Sind, rather than the disregard for Islamic norms, that most worried the authorities in Cairo. The mission leader had apparently taught his converts that the Fatimids were not Imams in their own right but mere caliphs, successors to the Imams, and that the seventh Imam would return as a messianic figure (*al-Qā'im*) to inaugurate the end of the world during al-Mu'izz's reign.[77] The spread of this subversive doctrine undoubtedly troubled the Fatimids as much as the marital customs and dietary practices of recent converts.

There are other interpretive possibilities here. Considering the source's emphasis on the improper practice of Islam among proseltyes, the word *al-majūs* implies deviancy. Al-Nu'man accused them of consanguineous marriage and the consumption of unlawful food and beverage. As noted in Chapter Three, Muslims extensively debated whether they could marry Zoroastrians or eat meat slaughtered by them. Most jurists prohibited it. The Fatimid authorities were keen to discredit and replace the missionary but hesitated because of his popularity in Sind. Accusations of permissiveness with regard to these issues in particular may have justified his removal. Or, as with Vikings, this source may have falsely attributed actual Zoroastrian practices to rhetorical Zoroastrians. Consanguineous marriage, the Late Antique practice of marrying close kin, was odious to some Muslims because it violated the degrees of familial separation between marriage partners enjoined by the Qur'an (4:23).[78] The behaviour of these converts, whatever their identity, was deviant by Islamic standards.

It seems unlikely that the 'Zoroastrians' in this case married close kin. The *Chachnama*, a thirteenth-century chronicle about the conquest of Sind, hints that consanguineous marriage was unacceptable in that region before the advent of Islam. It reports an incident prior to Muhammad ibn al-Qasim's arrival in which a local ruler lost the support of his subjects after marrying his sister.[79] The king had wed her reluctantly, in order to avoid the fulfilment of a dire prophecy, so the text does not appear to sanction the practice. (This story resonates in some ways with the hadith about the Zoroastrians' lost book, narrated by Ali in Chapter Two.) The *Chachnama* is a later source that may reflect inaccurate or anachronistic views of South Asia in an attempt to justify the Umayyad conquest. But the sober, near-contemporary Muslim observer of Indian religions, Abu Rayhan Muhammad ibn Ahmad al-Biruni (362–442/973–1050), also notes that Hindus did not condone consanguineous marriage.[80] Therefore, it may be that al-Nu'man was imposing on these 'Zoroastrians' the contemptible practices of their Persian namesakes for rhetorical reasons.

Conclusion

As these three examples attest, medieval Muslims used the term 'Zoroastrians' to describe Others – groups perceived as pagan, heretical or deviant. This nomenclature facilitated the construction of an oppositional identity. It allowed Muslims to define themselves against outsiders – Vikings, Qadariyya and Sindi converts – while expressing ambivalence about the status of Zoroastrians in early Islamic society. Zoroastrians were People without a Book who should be treated like People of the Book in some ways (taxation) but not in others (marriage and meat). Thus, it was logical for Muslims to compare other suspicious, threatening or marginal groups to them. Scholars must consider the obvious rhetorical and pejorative significance of the term 'Zoroastrians' in these contexts. The Muslim authors making the comparison often had little direct knowledge of the Good Religion. Indeed, each example in this chapter emanates from a time and place in which there were few, if any, actual Zoroastrians: Umayyad Spain, eighth-century Medina and Fatimid Cairo. The fact that Muslims living far from Iran recognised Zoroastrians as quintessentially Other meant that they could include or exclude additional groups by extending the metaphor. Thus, the Umayyad conqueror of Sind invoked Zoroastrians to protect South Asian places of worship while a Cairene judge did so to dissociate the Fatimids from deviant converts in the same region.

Comparisons of this sort were often unflattering but rhetorical. Early Muslims produced and consumed them as part of an internal discourse of identity formation and maintenance. While the polemical connotations of the term 'Zoroastrians' certainly betray a lingering ambivalence about the Good Religion and its adherents, Muslims were ambivalent because their progenitors had taxed Zoroastrians without recognising them as People of the Book. Thus, Zoroastrians enjoyed the status of protected people despite their lack of – at least according to Islamic standards – a divinely inspired scripture. Therefore, the disparaging rhetoric of early Islamic discourse demonstrates a simultaneous recognition of and discomfort with the exceptional place of Zoroastrians in early Islamic society.

Notes

1. Qudāmah ibn Ja'far, *Kitāb al-Kharāj wa-ṣinā'at al-kitābah*, ed. Fuat Sezgin, vol. 42, Veröffentlichungen des Institutes für Geschichte der Arabisch-Islamischen Wissenschaften, Series C (Frankfurt: Johann Wolfgang Goethe University, 1986), 180; compare Qudāmah ibn Ja'far, *Kitāb al-kharāj*, 2:42–43.
2. Abū 'Ubayd al-Qāsim ibn Sallām, *Kitāb al-amwāl*, 239; Abū 'Ubayd al-Qāsim ibn Sallām, *The Book of Revenue*, 184; on the Lawata Berbers, see Robert Brunschvig, 'Ibn 'Abdalhakam et la conquête de l'Afrique du Nord par les Arabes', *Annales de l'Institut d'études Orientales (University of Algiers)* 6 (1942): 108–55; translated and republished as 'Ibn Abdelḥakam and the Conquest of North Africa', in Fred Donner (ed.), *The Expansion of the Early Islamic State*, Formation of the Classical Islamic World 5 (Aldershot: Ashgate, 2008), 189–228.
3. H. A. R. Gibb and J. H. Kramers (eds), *Shorter Encyclopaedia of Islam* (Leiden: Brill, 1953), s.v. 'Madjus'.
4. Abū 'Ubayd al-Qāsim ibn Sallām, *Kitāb al-amwāl*, 106; compare Abū 'Ubayd al-Qāsim ibn Sallām, *The Book of Revenue*, 30; see also al-Balādhurī, *The Origins of the Islamic State*, 123.
5. Yohanan Friedmann, 'The Classification of Unbelievers in Sunni Muslim Law and Tradition', *Jerusalem Studies in Arabic and Islam* 22 (1998): 190.
6. Mālik ibn Anas and 'Abd al-Salām ibn Sa'īd Saḥnūn, *Al-Mudawwana al-Kubrā*, vol. 2 (Baghdad: Maktabat al-Muthanna, 1970), 46.

7. Friedmann, 'The Classification of Unbelievers in Sunni Muslim Law and Tradition', 166.
8. Joshua Prawer, '"Minorities" in the Crusader States', in Norman Zacour and Harry Hazard (eds), *Impact of the Crusades on the Near East*, vol. 5, A History of the Crusades (Madison: University of Wisconsin Press, 1985), 63.
9. The literature on identity formation is vast but often Eurocentric and preoccupied with modern nationalism. On group identity in the pre-modern period, see Edith Hall, *Inventing the Barbarian: Greek Self-Definition through Tragedy* (Oxford: Clarendon Press, 1989); Walter Pohl, 'Conceptions of Ethnicity in Early Medieval Studies', in Barbara H. Rosenwein and Lester Little (eds), *Debating the Middle Ages: Issues and Readings* (Malden, Mass.: Blackwell Publishers, 1998), 13–24; Anthony Smith, *The Nation in History: Historiographical Debates about Ethnicity and Nationalism* (Hanover, NH: University Press of New England, 2000); and Patrick Geary, *The Myth of Nations: The Medieval Origins of Europe* (Princeton, NJ: Princeton University Press, 2002).
10. Amin Maalouf, *In the Name of Identity: Violence and the Need to Belong* (New York: Arcade, 2001).
11. Patricia Crone, 'The Quranic Mushrikūn and the Resurrection (Part I)', *Bulletin of the School of Oriental and African Studies* 75, no. 3 (2012): 445–72; and 'The Quranic Mushrikūn and the Resurrection (Part II)', *Bulletin of the School of Oriental and African Studies* 76, no. 1 (2013): 1–20.
12. G. R Hawting, *The Idea of Idolatry and the Emergence of Islam: From Polemic to History* (Cambridge: Cambridge University Press, 1999).
13. Angelika Neuwirth, 'Imagining Mary – Disputing Jesus: Reading Surat Maryam and Related Meccan Texts within the Qur'anic Communication Process', in Benjamin Jokisch, Ulrich Rebstock and Lawrence Conrad (eds), *Fremde, Feinde und Kurioses: innen- und aussenansichten unseres muslimischen Nachbarn* (Berlin: Walter de Gruyter, 2009), 383–416.
14. Donner, *Muhammad and the Believers*.
15. Lecker, 'The Levying of Taxes for the Sassanians in Pre-Islamic Medina (Yathrib)'; M. J. Kister, 'Al-Ḥīra, Some Notes on Its Relations with Arabia', *Arabica* 15 (1968): 144–49.
16. For an extended study of the relevant verses, see Nadia Maria el Cheikh, 'Sūrat Al-Rūm: A Study of the Exegetical Literature', *Journal of the American Oriental Society* 118, no. 3 (1998): 356–64; the historical context can be found in James Howard-Johnston, *Witnesses to a World Crisis: Historians and Histories*

of the Middle East in the Seventh Century (Oxford: Oxford University Press, 2010).

17. Rāzī, *Mafātīḥ al-ghayb*, 6:545.
18. Ibn Kathīr, *Tafsīr al-Qur'ān al-'aẓīm*, 3:408–411; Bayḍāwī, *Beidhawii Commentarius in Coranum*, 2:102; al-Baghawī, *Tafsīr al-Baghawī*, 6:259–262; Zamakhsharī, *al-Kashshāf*, 3:466; Vāḥidī Nīshābūrī, *Al-Wāḥidī's Asbāb al-Nuzūl*, 179.
19. al-Ṭabarī, *Jāmi' al-bayān fī tafsīr al-Qur'ān*, 20/23:11–14; al-Qurṭubī, *al-Jāmi' li-aḥkām al-Qur'ān*, 14:1–6; Maḥallī and Suyūṭī, *Tafsīr al-Jalālayn*, 383.
20. Ibn Kathīr, *Tafsīr al-Qur'ān al-'aẓīm*, 3:411; Fīrūzābādī, *Tafsir Ibn Abbas*, 525; Maḥmūd ibn 'Umar Zamakhsharī, *Tafsīr al-Qur'ān al-kashshāf* (Bayrūt: Dār al-Kitāb al-'Arabī, 1966), 3:466; al-Baghawī, *Tafsīr al-Baghawī*, 6:260; al-Qurṭubī, *al-Jāmi' li-aḥkām al-Qur'ān*, 14:4.
21. Savant, *New Muslims of Post-Conquest Iran*, 165–67.
22. Ibid., 166.
23. On this topic, see Touraj Daryaee, 'Marriage, Property, and Conversion among the Zoroastrians: From Late Sasanian to Islamic Iran', *Journal of Persianate Studies* 6, no. 1–2 (2013): 91–100; and Brian Spooner, 'Iranian Kinship and Marriage', *Iran: Journal of the British Institute of Persian Studies* 4 (1966): 1–9.
24. This summary adapted from *EI2*, s.v. 'al-Madjus' (Arne Melvinger).
25. Arne Melvinger, *Les premières incursions des Vikings en Occident d'après les sources arabes* (Uppsala, Sweden: Almqvist & Wiksells, 1955), 44–63.
26. Aḥmad Ibn Faḍlān, *Ibn Fadlan and the Land of Darkness: Arab Travelers in the Far North*, trans. Paul Lunde and Caroline Stone (London: Penguin, 2012), 105; *EI2*, s.v. 'al-Madjus' (Melvinger).
27. *EI2*, s.v. 'al-Madjus' (Melvinger).
28. Melvinger, *Les premières incursions des Vikings en Occident*, 76.
29. *EI2*, s.v. 'al-Madjus'; Aḥmad Ibn Faḍlān, *Ibn Fadlan's Journey to Russia: A Tenth-Century Traveler from Baghdad to the Volga River*, trans. Richard Frye (Princeton, NJ: Markus Wiener Publishers, 2005), 99–100; Ghrab, 'Islam and Non-Scriptural Spirituality', 67.
30. For information on Norse religion, see Thomas A. DuBois, *Nordic Religions in the Viking Age* (Philadelphia: University of Pennsylvania Press, 1999). My thanks to Phyllis Jestice for this reference.
31. Ibn al-Faqīh al-Hamadhānī, *Mukhtaṣar kitāb al-buldān*, 247.
32. Ibn Faḍlān, *Ibn Fadlan and the Land of Darkness*, 118, 122, 124, 132, 141, 186.

33. The relevant sections of Ibn Khuradadhbih, Ibn Rusta, Ibn Hayyan, Ibn al-Faqih, Miskawayh, al-Istakhri, al-Marwazi, al-Muqaddasi, Ibn Hawqal, al-Mas'udi and Ibn Batuta are translated in *Ibn Fadlan and the Land of Darkness*, 93–200.
34. James Montgomery, 'Ibn Fadlan and the Rusiyyah', *Journal of Arabic and Islamic Studies* 3 (2000): 12–15.
35. I cannot find evidence to support Frye's assertion that al-Gharnati used the term. See *Ibn Fadlan's Journey to Russia*, 100; compare César E. Dubler, *Abū Ḥāmid el Granadino y su relación de viaje por tierras eurasiáticas* (Madrid: Maestre, 1953); and Muḥammad ibn 'Abd al-Raḥīm Ibn Abī al-Rabī', *Al-Mu'rib 'an ba'ḍ 'aŷā'ib al-Magrib (Elogio de algunas maravillas del Magrib)*, ed. Ingrid Bejarano, Fuentes arábico-hispanas 9 (Madrid: Consejo Superior de Investigaciones Científicas, Instituto de Cooperación con el Mundo Árabe, 1991).
36. Ibn Faḍlān, *Ibn Fadlan and the Land of Darkness*, 143; *EI2*, s.v. 'al-Madjus' (Melvinger).
37. Aḥmad ibn Abī Ya'qūb al-Ya'qūbī, *Kitāb al-buldān*, ed. M. J. de Goeje, 2nd ed., Bibliotheca geographorum Arabicorum 7 (Leiden: Brill, 1967), 354.
38. Ann Christys, *Vikings in the South: Voyages to Iberia and the Mediterranean* (London: Bloomsbury Academic, 2015), 15–20.
39. Brunschvig, 'Ibn Abdelḥakam and the Conquest of North Africa', 4–5.
40. Christys, *Vikings in the South*, 25; *EI2*, s.v. 'al-Madjus' (Arne Melvinger).
41. Friedmann, *Tolerance and Coercion in Islam*, 78.
42. Quoted in Míkel de Epalza, 'A Note about the Muslim Conquest of the 7th–8th Centuries: The Basque, Berber, Norse Viking, Norman, and British "Magicians"', *Imago Temporis. Medium Aevum* 1 (2007): 63. My thanks to Debra Blumenthal for this citation.
43. See also Míkel de Epalza, 'Los Maŷūs (<<Magos>>): un hápax coránico (XXII, 17), entre lo étnico y lo jurídico, hasta su utilización en al-Andalus', in Miguel Hernando de Larramendi and Salvador Peña Martín (eds), *El Corán ayer y hoy: perspectivas actuales sobre el islam: estudios en honor al profesor Julio Cortés* (Córdoba: Editorial Berenice, 2008), 399–414.
44. Christys, *Vikings in the South*, 17–19.
45. *Ibn Fadlan and the Land of Darkness*, 204.
46. Christys, *Vikings in the South*, 27.
47. Abū Dā'ūd Sulaymān ibn al-Ash'ath al-Sijistānī, *Sunan Abī Dā'ūd* (Cairo: Sharikat maktabat wa-maṭba'at Muṣṭafā al-Bābī al-Ḥalabi wa-awlādihi fī Miṣr, 1952), 2:524.
48. Abū Dā'ūd Sulaymān ibn al-Ash'ath al-Sijistānī, 2:525.

49. *EI2*, s.v. 'Dadjdjal' (A. Abel).
50. s.v. 'Kadariyya'.
51. Khalid Yahya Blankinship, 'The Early Creed', in Tim Winter (ed.), *The Cambridge Companion to Classical Islamic Theology* (Cambridge: Cambridge University Press, 2008), 38.
52. Steven Judd, 'The Early Qadariyya', in Sabine Schmidtke (ed.), *Oxford Handbook of Islamic Theology* (Oxford: Oxford University Press, 2016), 51–52.
53. Patricia Crone and Martin Hinds, *God's Caliph: Religious Authority in the First Centuries of Islam* (Cambridge: Cambridge University Press, 1986).
54. Blankinship, 'The Early Creed', 88–89.
55. Steven Judd, 'Muslim Persecution of Heretics during the Marwānid Period (64–132/684–750)', *Al-Masāq: Islam and the Medieval Mediterranean* 23, no. 1 (2011): 1–14.
56. EI3, s.v. 'Ghaylan al-Dimashqi' (Steven Judd).
57. Gyorgy Fodor, 'Some Aspects of the Qadar Controversy in Early Islam', *The Arabist: Budapest Studies in Arabic* 1 (1988): 62.
58. Josef van Ess, *Zwischen Ḥadīṯ und Theologie: Studien zum Entstehen prädestinatianischer Überlieferung* (Berlin: De Gruyter, 1975), 137–48.
59. Judd, 'Muslim Persecution of Heretics during the Marwānid Period (64–132/684–750)', 5–6.
60. Mohsen Zakeri, *Sāsānid Soldiers in Early Muslim Society: The Origins of ʿAyyārān and Futuwwa* (Wiesbaden: Harrassowitz Verlag, 1995), 325–26.
61. Van Ess, *Zwischen Ḥadīṯ und Theologie*, 139.
62. Fazlur Rahman, *Islam*, 2nd ed. (Chicago: University of Chicago Press, 1979), 241–42; *EI2*, s.v. 'Kadariyya' (van Ess).
63. Abū Dā'ūd Sulaymān ibn al-Ashʿath al-Sijistānī, *al-Sunan* (Beirut: Dār al-Kitāb al-ʿArabī, 1967), 4:357.
64. *EI2*, s.v. 'Thanawiyya' (Guy Monnot).
65. Ibn Ṭāhir al-Baghdādī, *al-Farq bayn al-firaq (Moslem Schisms and Sects)*, 1966, 1:33; ʿAbd al-Qāhir Ibn Ṭāhir al-Baghdādī, *Mukhtaṣar kitāb al-farq bayna al-firaq*, ed. Philip Hitti (Misr: Matba'at al-Hilal, 1924), 21, where the last lines and phrases do not appear.
66. *Shorter Encyclopaedia of Islam*, s.v. 'Kadariyya'.
67. For the history of the Fatimids in Sind, see Wink, *Al-Hind: The Making of the Indo-Islamic World*, 1, Early Medieval India and the Expansion of Islam, 7th–11th Centuries: 212–18.
68. Derryl N. Maclean, *Religion and Society in Arab Sind* (Leiden: Brill, 1989), 148.

69. Arabic text in S. M. Stern, 'Isma'ili Propaganda and Fatimid Rule in Sind', *Islamic Culture* 23 (1949): 70; compare to the English translation in S. M. Stern, 'Heterodox Ismā'īlism at the Time of Al-Mu'izz', *Bulletin of the School of Oriental and African Studies* 17, no. 1 (1955): 15.
70. Emended Arabic text in Stern, 'Isma'ili Propaganda and Fatimid Rule in Sind', 304; compare to Stern's English translation in 'Heterodox Ismā'īlism at the Time of Al-Mu'izz', 15.
71. 'Abbas Hamdani, 'The Fatimid-'Abbasid Conflict in India', *Islamic Culture* 41 (1967): 186.
72. Stern, 'Heterodox Ismā'īlism at the Time of Al-Mu'izz', 30.
73. Stern, 'Isma'ili Propaganda and Fatimid Rule in Sind', 299.
74. Maclean, *Religion and Society in Arab Sind*, 132; on the sun cult, see pp. 18–20.
75. al-Balādhurī, *Kitāb futūḥ al-buldān*, 2014, 439; al-Balādhurī, *The Origins of the Islamic State*, 2:221; 'Alī ibn Ḥāmid al-Kūfī, *The Chachnamah: An Ancient History of Sind*, trans. Mirza Kalichbeg Faridunbeg (Karachi: Commissioner's Press, 1900), 1:169.
76. Yohanan Friedmann, 'The Temple of Multan: A Note on Early Muslim Attitudes to Idolatry', *Israel Oriental Studies* 2 (1972): 181.
77. Maclean, *Religion and Society in Arab Sind*, 133.
78. For Arab attitudes toward consanguinity in this period, see Geert Jan Van Gelder, *Close Relationships: Incest and Inbreeding in Classical Arabic Literature* (London: I. B. Tauris, 2005).
79. al-Kūfī, *The Chachnamah: An Ancient History of Sind*, 1:43–47.
80. Muḥammad ibn Aḥmad Bīrūnī, *Taḥqīq Mā li-l-Hind: min muqawwilat maqbūla fī l-'aql aw mardhūla* (Bayrūt: 'Ālam al-Kutub, 1983), 1:429; Muḥammad ibn Aḥmad Bīrūnī, *Alberuni's India. An Account of the Religion, Philosophy, Literature, Geography, Chronology, Astronomy, Customs, Laws and Astrology of India about A.D. 1030*, trans. Eduard Sachau (London: Trübner, 1910), 2:155.

Conclusion
An Ambivalent Accommodation

Just a decade ago, the contemporary relevance of some of the issues treated in this book – from the taxation of Zoroastrians to their legal status in medieval Islamdom – may not have been readily apparent to the non-specialist. However, their significance and, indeed, their urgency, became undeniable with the rise of the Islamic State of Iraq and Syria (ISIS) in 2014. ISIS emerged from the aftermath of the United States' invasion of Iraq in 2003 and the eruption of the Arab Spring in Syria in 2011. The organisation's complex history, including its evolution from al-Qaeda in Iraq to the Islamic State of Iraq and the latter's fraught relationship with the Nusra Front, a militia fighting in Syria's civil war, has been documented elsewhere and will not be repeated here.[1] Suffice it to say that Abu Bakr al-Baghdadi, previously leader of the Islamic State of Iraq, attempted to siphon fighters from the Nusra Front by declaring the creation of ISIS to coordinate attacks in both countries. He also opened a new front in the Islamic State's insurgency against the Iraqi government by ordering the invasion of northern Iraq from Syria.[2]

In June 2014, ISIS came roaring across the Syrian border into Iraq. Thus began a brutal campaign of conquest, rape and enslavement of the local population in the process of creating a caliphate. ISIS fighters descended on the Kurdish region of Sinjar (*Shingal* in Kurdish), massacring men and raping women. Survivors fled to the mountains for protection. Between August and September, the forces of the Islamic State displaced approximately 100,000 people, killing an estimated 5,000 men and enslaving 7,000 women in the process.[3] The Iraqi army, trained and equipped by the United States, fled in fear. The Obama Administration began airstrikes against ISIS in the name of humanitarian intervention, which quickly expanded beyond their stated purpose of protecting Kurds into a full-scale war against ISIS to prevent it from toppling the Iraqi government.

ISIS justified the violence against the Kurds of Sinjar in religious terms.[4] Its fighters claimed that Yazidi Kurds lacked a divinely revealed religion and were therefore undeserving of the protection that Muslims have historically afforded to Jews and Christians. Yazidis, who call themselves Ezedi, are monotheistic. They claim to be proselytes of a twelfth-century Sufi Muslim from Lebanon, Adi ibn Musafir al-Umawi. Their beliefs also include ideas that are akin to but distinct from Persian Zoroastrianism.[5] Yazidis, in other words, practice an indigenous religion that incorporates elements of many traditions and is consequently difficult to categorise. Nevertheless, ISIS deemed Yazidis to be devil worshippers who could be legitimately killed and enslaved.

Scholars of Islamic law had more or less universally disavowed slavery by the early twentieth century, often under pressure from European imperialists.[6] Nevertheless, an issue of *Dabiq*, ISIS's monthly magazine, justified the group's revival of slavery as a precondition for the apocalyptic return of the Mahdi and the end of the world.[7] To refute ISIS' tendentious claims, experts in Islamic law from around the world – whether trained in religious seminaries or holding doctorates from secular universities – signed an open letter to Abu Bakr al-Baghdadi, which appeared on the Internet in September 2014. Posted in Arabic and English, it is a point-by-point indictment of the Islamic State's behaviour and a rebuttal of its attempt to speak on behalf of all Muslims.[8] More than 100 Muslim scholars from the Middle East and North Africa, South and Central Asia, North America and Europe signed it, including the highest-ranking religious authorities in countries as diverse as Egypt, Uzbekistan and Malaysia.

In his declaration of the caliphate on 1 July 2014, al-Baghdadi proclaimed that he was open to correction if he erred as caliph. Thus, the Open Letter begins with an invitation to him and his followers to repent and trust in God's mercy. It then outlines the many ways that the Islamic State had deviated from Islamic norms, quoting the Qur'an, hadith and legal precedents as evidence. It addresses twenty-four points of error, such as the killing of non-combatants, mistreatment of Jews and Christians, denial of women's rights, revival of slavery and mutilation of corpses. These scholars further criticised followers of the Islamic State for their limited understanding of Arabic, penchant for oversimplifying complex legal issues, and application of doctrine without regard to circumstance. At seventy-six pages in the English translation, the Open Letter is a fairly comprehensive critique.

Section 11 of the Open Letter decries ISIS's treatment of Yazidis. It does so by comparing Yazidis to Zoroastrians. The section is quoted here in its entirety, divided into sections with the most pertinent passages underlined for easier analysis.

> You fought the Yazidis under the laws of jihad but they neither fought you nor Muslims. You accused them of worshipping Satan and gave them the choice to either be killed or forcibly convert to Islam. You killed hundreds of them and buried them in mass graves. You were the reason for the death and suffering of hundreds of others, and had it not been for Americans' and Kurds' intervention tens of thousands of their women, men, elders, and children would have been killed. These are all abominable crimes.
>
> From the legal perspective of Islamic law (*sharīʿa*) they are Zoroastrians based on the saying of the Prophet, peace be upon him: 'Follow the custom of the People of the Book with them.'[9] Thus they are People of the Book. The Most High God says: 'Truly those who believe, and those who are Jewish, and the Sabi'ans, and the Christians, and the Zoroastrians and the polytheists—God will indeed judge between them on the Day of Resurrection. Assuredly God is witness of all things.' (Al-Hajj, 22:17). On the basis of the previous hadith, many of the scholars among the pious forebearers (*ʿulamāʾ al-salaf al-ṣāliḥ*) regarded them [Yazidis] as Zoroastrians for legal purposes.
>
> The Umayyads even considered Hindus and Buddhists to be Protected People (*ahl al-dhimma*). Al-Qurtubi said: 'Al-Awzaʿi said: "*Jizya* is taken from the worshipper of an idol or of fire or the unbeliever or disbeliever". The school of Malik [does] likewise, for it was his opinion that *jizya* is taken from all types of polytheism (*shirk*) and unbelief, Arab or non-Arab . . . except the apostate (*al-murtadd*).'[10]

The Open Letter criticises the killing and displacement of Yazidis on the grounds that they are legally Zoroastrians. It urges the Islamic State to follow the custom of the People of the Book with Yazidis because that is what the first generations of Muslims determined to do with Zoroastrians.

The Open Letter endorses many of the conclusions reached in this book. Its authors cite the Qur'an when referring to Zoroastrians but emphasise that it is on the basis of hadith that followers of the Good Religion warranted the custom of the People of the Book. Chapter Two made the same argument, despite assertions in the secondary literature that the Qur'an or Avesta was the primary focus of early Muslim debates about Zoroastrians. The custom to follow with them was taxation, as identified by most of the jurists surveyed in Chapter Three. The authors of the Open Letter mention the historical protection (*dhimma*) afforded to Hindus and Buddhists by way of comparison. Chapter Six treated the tendency of authors to compare Zoroastrians to other liminal groups. The ideas of al-Awza'i and Malik, two jurists who deemed idolaters and pagans eligible to pay jizya, were also noted in Chapter Six. In sum, the Open Letter urges Muslims not to fight or enslave non-Muslims if they pay tax. It affirms the legal status of Zoroastrians – and Yazidis by extension – on the basis of their productive capacity. In doing so, the Open Letter vindicates the definition of accommodation given in the Introduction: *to extend a special dispensation to a non-normative group in order for society to benefit from its useful endeavours.*

Accommodation and Memory

This book has demonstrated that some early Muslims advocated for the accommodation of Zoroastrians. They did do so largely on their own terms. Most medieval jurists did not recognise Zoroastrians as People of the Book. They reserved that designation for Jews and Christians, normative believers with whom Muslims claimed some theological affinity. Nevertheless, Muslim administrators incorporated Zoroastrians into the fiscal regime of the caliphate. They did so seemingly without regard for the existence of a written Avesta. Collecting jizya from Zoroastrians was the practice perhaps from the time that the Prophet first dispatched deputies to Hajar. He may not have identified them specifically or set a recognisable precedent, though, because Umar allegedly did not know what to do with Zoroastrians when he became caliph. Abd al-Rahman ibn Awf reminded him that Muhammad had taxed them, and Umar followed suit.

The decision to accommodate Zoroastrians met with some opposition. A few Muslim administrators were reluctant to accept jizya from People without a Book, but statements attributed to the Prophet ultimately justified the practice. Members of the Banu Tamim, an Arab tribe that had been associated with the Sasanian Empire and Zoroastrianism, circulated these hadith. They may have been advocating for members of the tribe who had not converted to Islam. Regardless, it was to the advantage of the caliphs to tax Zoroastrians. Not only did jizya fill the imperial coffers, but collecting it from Zoroastrians relieved Muslims of the theoretical obligation to fight a population engaged in useful endeavours. Those endeavours, as defined by the empire, were undoubtedly first and foremost the generation of a taxable surplus. It was better to keep productive subjects serving the empire fiscally. Perhaps for that reason early Muslim jurists urged inquirers not to question the policy.

There were limits to this accommodation. Muslims were not to marry Zoroastrians or eat meat slaughtered by them. Hasan ibn Muhammad attributed this prohibition to the Prophet, although it may have been the ruling of early jurists. A nearly contemporaneous hadith narrated by Muhammad al-Baqir and Ja'far al-Sadiq urged Muslims to follow the custom of the People of the Book with Zoroastrians. Abu Thawr interpreted that statement to mean that Muslims could interact with Zoroastrians on the same basis as they did with Jews and Christians. Most jurists disagreed, arguing that the hadith meant nothing more than taxation. Members of Ali's family featured prominently in these debates because of their eminence in law and, as one hadith proclaimed, because Ali was the most knowledgeable person about Zoroastrians. Questions about the legal status of Zoroastrians were closely connected to juridical rulings about Sabi'ans, whose beliefs were unknown, and the Banu Taghlib, an Arab tribe against whom Ali railed frequently on account of their exceptional tax status. These rulings may have been the inspiration for the ban on marriage and meat that applied to Zoroastrians.

There were other limits to accommodation. Some Muslim jurists rendered Zoroastrians legally inferior to Jews and Christians. They granted followers of the Good Religion less blood money than the People of the Book. Not all schools of law agreed, including the Hanafi school that was prominent in Iran. Therefore, the practical effect of such rulings is difficult to gauge. Without surviving case law, historians are left to contend with the abstractions of jurists who were keen on boundary marking and the regulation of religious hierarchies. Yet the judicial archive of memory preserves the judgments of Hanafis and Hanbalis in Iraq who authorised the consumption of 'Zoroastrian' cheese (made by Persians with rennet) despite the general prohibition on meat slaughtered by Zoroastrians. These schools of law were influential in a region where Zoroastrians likely lived, which is suggestive of the emerging consensus among scholars of Late Antiquity that Muslims and non-Muslims found ways to interact across communal boundaries.

The ahd-nama suggests that Zoroastrians resented some aspects of Islamic law. This charter, supposedly issued by the Prophet Muhammad, sought to liberate the Zoroastrian family of Salman al-Farisi from jizya and the differentiating regulations advocated by Muslim jurists. It also entitled Salman's family to a stipend from the imperial treasury. The ahd-nama is almost certainly a forgery. It was modelled on the Treaties of Najran and Khaybar, texts mobilised by Christian and Jewish communities, respectively, to claim financial relief from Muslim rulers. The ahd-nama seems to have become a site of memory, where Muslims remembered Salman's virtues and his relationship with the Prophet. A Seljuk ruler, a Sufi master and an Ilkhanid scribe all took an interest in it. The charter eventually arrived in Mughal India where Parsis copied it. The ahd-nama has become a site of memory in that community, too, a place for modern Parsis to reflect on the difficulties faced by followers of the Good Religion in earlier eras and to imagine a better future.

Medieval Persian historians chose to remember events differently. They wrote triumphal narratives of religious supersession. Local histories presented Islam as dominant in Iran from the seventh century. Muslims had allegedly looted fire temples, appropriated sacred space and extinguished holy fires. There is some archaeological evidence for the transformation of Zoroastrian temples into mosques, but Muslim historians invented other stories to enhance the prestige of their pious progenitors or peripheral home towns. The most credible accounts of violence expose the cross-confessional fault lines in particular localities at specific times, underscoring the contingent nature of that violence. In the medieval period, when the desecration of another's shrine seemingly validated one's own claims to truth, local histories accentuated the destructive aspects of interreligious encounter.

If some Muslim authors chose to ignore the history of accommodation, others could not forget it. They simultaneously registered their recognition of and discomfort with the integration of Zoroastrians into the imperial hierarchy through rhetorical uses of the term *majūs*. Muslims outside of Iran applied it to liminal groups from Iberia to India. Vikings, Qadariyya or Sindi converts, perceived as pagan, heretical and deviant, were putative Zoroastrians. These unflattering comparisons reveal a lingering ambivalence about the accommodation of Zoroastrians. Later Muslims remembered that the early Islamic community had taxed adherents of the Good Religion even though they were People without a Book, so their name became synonymous with alterity.

While some of these examples challenge dismal conceptions of Zoroastrian history, others are important counterpoints to the notion that a blissful intercommunal harmony prevailed in the early caliphates. Non-Muslims were legally subordinate to Muslims, and Zoroastrians occupied a rung in the theological and social hierarchy below Jews and Christians. At the same time, non-Muslims who paid jizya were generally protected people in early Islamicate society, and – if an emerging consensus in the field is correct – they may have constituted a majority of the population in some places for centuries. Caliphal administrators extended protection to Zoroastrians on the basis of taxation, although most jurists could not countenance intimate forms of familiarity with them. Following an imperial logic of accommodation, the first Muslims had incorporated adherents of the Good Religion into their fiscal regime but subsequent generations remained ambivalent about that decision even as they benefited from Zoroastrians' useful endeavours.

Notes

1. See, for example, Fawaz Gerges, *ISIS: A History* (Princeton, NJ: Princeton University Press, 2016); and James Gelvin, *The Arab Uprisings: What Everyone Needs to Know*, 2nd ed. (Oxford: Oxford University Press, 2015).
2. Jessica Stern and J.M. Berger, *ISIS: State of Terror* (New York: Ecco, 2015), 41–43.

3. Richard Foltz, 'The "Original" Kurdish Religion? Kurdish Nationalism and the False Conflation of the Yezidi and Zoroastrian Traditions', *Journal of Persianate Studies* 10 (2017): 87.
4. Rukmini Callimachi, 'ISIS Enshrines a Theology of Rape', *New York Times*, 14 August 2015.
5. Foltz, '"Original" Kurdish Religion?', 89.
6. See Jonathan A. C. Brown, *Slavery and Islam* (Oxford: Oneworld, 2019); Rudolph T. Ware III, 'Slavery in Islamic Africa, 1400–1800', in David Eltis and Stanley L. Engerman (eds), *The Cambridge World History of Slavery*, vol. 3: AD 1420–AD 1804 (Cambridge: Cambridge University Press, 2011), 47–80.
7. Graeme Wood, 'What ISIS Really Wants', *The Atlantic*, March 2015, https://www.theatlantic.com/magazine/archive/2015/03/what-isis-really-wants/384980/.
8. 'Open Letter to Baghdadi', accessed 14, January 2019, http://www.lettertobaghdadi.com/.
9. The authors of the Open Letter cite Malik ibn Anas and al-Shafi'i for this hadith.
10. 'Open Letter to Baghdadi', p. 17 in Arabic; p. 18 in English. Underline added; translation is mine.

Appendix A: Translation of an Iranian Recension of Salman's Charter[1]

In the name of God, the Merciful, the Compassionate

This is a piece of writing from Muhammad the Messenger of God. Salmān asked him for a testament (*waṣiyya*) regarding his brother, Māhbandādh Farrūkh, and the people of his house and his posterity after him, anyone they beget, whether they convert to Islam or stand steadfast in their religion.

I praise to you the God who commanded me to say, 'There is no god except God alone; He has no partner.' I say it, and I command the people to do so. Truly, mankind is the creation of God and every matter (*al-amr*) is God's. He created them and their languages, and rears them, and they return to Him. Truly, every matter ends and everything perishes and is annihilated and every soul tastes death. Whosoever believes in God and His Messenger has in the end the victors' ascent. Whosoever stands steadfast in his religion, we leave him alone for 'There is no compulsion in religion'.[2]

This is a piece of writing to the people of Salmān's house: verily they have the protection (*dhimma*) of God and my protection over their lives and wealth in the land on which they stand – its valleys and hills, its pastures and springs. They are not to be oppressed and there is no imposition on them. It is incumbent upon anyone among the believers, both male and female, to whom this writing of mine is read, to protect them and please them and not inflict injury or discomfort on them. I have relieved them of shaving the forelocks and the jizya and military conscription (*al-ḥashr*) and the tithe and the rest of the burdens and inconveniences. Therefore, if they ask of you, then give them. And if they seek your assistance, then assist them; and if they seek refuge with you, then protect them;[3] and if they err, then forgive them; and if they are mistreated, then prohibit it.

They [the Muslim authorities] should give [them] from the Muslims' treasury each year 200 *ḥulla* in the month of Rajab and 100 *ḥulla* in Dhū al-Ḥijja. Salmān deserves that from us since God prefers Salmān over many of the Muslims. It was revealed to me in the revelation that Paradise yearns for Salmān more than Salmān yearns for Paradise. He is a trustworthy and faithful person, devout and pure, an advisor to the Messenger of God, may God bless and grant him salvation, and to the believers. Salmān is one of us, the people of the household of the Prophet.

Let no one contravene any part of the testament (*waṣiyya*) that I gave you regarding the protection and kindness due to the people of Salmān's household and their descendants, whether they convert to Islam or stand steadfast in their religion. Whosoever contravenes this testament has contravened God and His Messenger and there is a curse upon him until Judgement Day. Whosoever honours them has honoured me and God has a reward for him. Whosoever harms them has harmed me and I will be his antagonist on the Day of Resurrection. His recompense is hellfire and I am free of my responsibility toward him. Peace be upon you.

ʿAlī ibn Abī Ṭālib wrote by command of the Messenger of God, may God bless and grant him salvation, in Rajab, year 9 of the *hijra*. Accompanying him were Abū Bakr, ʿUmar, ʿUthmān, Ṭalḥa, al-Zubayr, ʿAbd al-Raḥmān, Saʿd, Saʿīd, Salmān, Abū Dharr, ʿAmmār, ʿUyayna, Ṣuhayb, Bilāl, al-Miqdād and another group of believers.

Notes

1. al-Iṣfahānī, *Kitāb dhikr akhbār Iṣfahān*, 1:52–54; Sarah Bowen Savant has also published an English translation of this document, which I only discovered after my work on it was complete. See her *New Muslims*, 84–85. My translation is original and independent.
2. Qur'an 2: 256.
3. This phrase has been emended for clarity.

Appendix B: Translation of an Indian Recension of Salman's Charter[1]

In the name of God, the Merciful, the Compassionate

A copy of an edict in the handwriting of the Commander of the Faithful, 'Alī ibn Abī Ṭālib, may God be pleased with him. He wrote on red parchment. This is a piece of writing from the Messenger of God, may God bless him and grant him salvation, to Mahdī Farrūkh bin Shakhsān, the brother of Salmān al-Fārisī, may God be pleased with him, and the members of his household, and his posterity after him, anyone they beget, whether they convert to Islam or retain their religion.

The peace of God is [extended] to you. Truly God commanded me to say, 'There is no god but God alone; He has no partner.' I say it and they commanded the people. Mankind is the creation of God, and every matter is God's. He creates them and causes them to live and die and then resurrects them and they return to Him. Everything ends and is annihilated, and every soul tastes death. God's command cannot be averted and his authority is complete. There is no end to his majesty and no one shares His dominion. Praise to the King of heaven and earth who subverts things as He pleases and prospers mankind in whatever He wills! Praise to the One who cannot be even remotely defined by the description of orators even if they are philosophers; the One who prefaced His book with praise, giving it as a reminder of Himself, and is pleased with the gratitude of His servants. I praise Him!

It is impossible to calculate the number of those who praise God and testify that there is no god but God. It remains hidden in secret for safekeeping and protection. O people, fear your Lord and remember the coming day of the destruction of the earth, and the raging of hellfire, and the great terror and the remorse that awaits while standing in the presence of the Lord of Both Worlds!

I exhort you all, just as the messengers exhorted you, to ask about the good news and its tidings hereafter. Whoever believes in it, and accepts what came down in that which my Lord revealed to me, he has what we have and he obtains what we obtain. He has protection in this world and joy in the gardens of delight – with the ministering angels and the prophets and the messengers – and safety and deliverance from the torment of hell. This is what God promises the believers. He has mercy on whom He will. He is infinitely wise and all-knowing, severe in punishing anyone who defies Him; and He is the all-merciful Forgiver. 'If We had sent down this recitation (*qur'ān*) on a mountain, you would have seen it humble itself, trembling for fear of God.'[2] Whosoever does not believe in it, he is one of those who have gone astray. Whosoever believes in God and in His religion and His messengers, he is in the victors' path.

This is my writ: that he has the protection of God and it extends over his children and their lives and their wealth in the land on which they stand – its valleys and hills, its springs and pastures. They are not to be oppressed and there is no imposition on them. To whomsoever this writ of mine is read, it is incumbent upon him to protect them and please them and prohibit the mistreatment of them, and not to inflict injury or discomfort on them. I have relieved them of shaving the bangs, and the girdle (*al-zunnāra*) and the jizya, and the rest of the burdens and inconveniences until the Resurrection.

They have complete control over fire temples, including their domains and wealth. Do not prohibit them from wearing luxurious clothing, or riding, building estates and stables, or carrying biers or adopting whatever they adopt in their religion and their schools of interpretation (*madhāhibihim*). Favour them over the rest of the sects among the protected people (*ahl al-dhimma*).

Truly the right of Salmān, may God be pleased with him, is a duty incumbent upon all the believers, God rest their souls. It is in the revelation to me that 'Paradise yearns for Salmān more than Salmān yearns for Paradise'. He is my trustworthy and faithful one, an advisor to the Messenger of God, may God bless him and grant him salvation, and to the believers. Salmān is one of us. Do not contravene any part of the testament (*waṣiyya*) that I gave you regarding the preservation and kindness and protection (*dhimma*) due to the people of Salmān's house and their descendants, whether they convert to Islam or stand steadfast in their religion.

Whosoever accepts my instruction, he is in the good graces of the Most High God. Whosoever contravenes God and His messenger, there is a curse upon him until Judgement Day. Whosoever honours them has honoured me, and God has a blessing for him. Whosoever harms them has harmed me, and I will be his antagonist on the Day of Resurrection. His recompense is hellfire and I am free of my responsibility toward him. Peace be upon you. May your Lord grant longevity to you.

'Alī ibn Abī Ṭālib wrote by order of the Messenger of God, may God bless him and grant him salvation, in the presence of Abū Bakr, 'Umar, 'Uthmān, Ṭalḥa, Zubayr, 'Abd al-Raḥmān ibn 'Awf, Salmān, Abū Dharr, 'Ammār, Ṣuhayb, Bilāl, Miqdād ibn al-Aswad and another group of believers, may God be pleased with them and all of the Companions.

This is the seal. It was in the shoulder of the Arab prophet, Muḥammad al-Qurayshī, may God bless and grant him, his family, and his Companions an exceedingly peaceful salvation.

Notes

1. Jejeebhoy, *Tuqviuti-Din-i-Mazdiasna*, 1–11.
2. Qur'an 59: 21.

Bibliography

Abū Dā'ūd Sulaymān ibn al-Ash'ath al-Sijistānī. *Sunan Abu Dawud*. Translated by Ahmad Hasan. Lahore: Sh. M. Ashraf, 1984.

———. *al-Sunan*. Beirut: Dār al-Kitāb al-'Arabī, 1967.

———. *Sunan Abī Dā'ūd*. 2 vols. Cairo: Sharikat maktabat wa-maṭba'at Muṣṭafā al-Bābī al-Ḥalabi wa-awlādihi fī Miṣr, 1952.

Abū 'Ubayd al-Qāsim ibn Sallām. *The Book of Revenue*. Translated by Imran Ahsan Khan Nyazee. Reading: Garnet, 2002.

———. *Kitāb al-amwāl*. Beirut: Dar al-Shuruq, 1989.

Abū 'l-Fatḥ ibn Abī 'l-Ḥasan al-Sāmirī. *The Kitāb al-Tarīkh of Abu 'l-Fath*. Translated by Paul Stenhouse. Sydney: University of Sydney, 1985.

Abū Yūsuf Ya'qūb ibn Ibrāhīm al-Kūfī. *Kitāb al-kharāj*. Edited by Taha Abd al-Ra'uf Sa'd and Sa'd Hasan Muhammad. Cairo: al-Maktaba al-Azhariyya lil-Turath, 1999.

———. *Kitāb al-kharāj*. Edited by Mahmud Baji. Tunis: Dar Busalamah, 1984.

———. *Kitāb al-kharāj*. Translated by Adam Ben Shemesh. Vol. 3. Taxation in Islam. Leiden: Brill, 1969.

Afsaruddin, Asma. *Striving in the Path of God: Jihad and Martyrdom in Islamic Thought*. New York: Oxford University Press, 2013.

Aḥmad ibn Muḥammad Khallāl. *Aḥkām ahl al-milal min al-jāmi' li-masā'il al-Imām Aḥmad ibn Ḥanbal*. Beirut: Dār al-Kutub al-'Ilmīyah, 1994.

Anonymous. *Mujmal al-tawārīkh wa-'l-qiṣaṣ*. Edited by Iraj Afshar and Mahmoud Omidsalar. Tehran: Talayah, 2001.

———. *Mujmal al-tawārīkh wa-'l-qiṣaṣ*. Edited by Muhammad Taqi Bahar. Tehran: Khavar, 1939.

Anonymous. *Tārikh-e Sistān*. Translated by Milton Gold. Roma: Istituto Italiano per il Medio ed Estremo Oriente, 1976.

———. *Tārikh-e Sistān*. Edited by Muhammad Taqi Bahar. Tehran: Kitabkhanah-i Zavvar, 1935.

Ansari, Khizar Humayun. 'Kamal-Ud-Din, Khwaja (1870–1932), Islamic Scholar and Missionary'. In *Oxford Dictionary of National Biography*. Oxford University Press, 2013. https://www.oxforddnb.com/view/10.1093/ref:odnb/9780198614128.001.0001/odnb-9780198614128-e-94519.

Arjomand, Said. 'The Constitution of Medina: A Sociolegal Interpretation of Muhammad's Acts of Foundation of the Umma'. *International Journal of Middle East Studies* 41, no. 4 (2009): 555–75.

Axelrod, Paul. 'Cultural and Historical Factors in the Population Decline of the Parsis of India'. *Population Studies* 44, no. 3 (1990): 401–19.

'Aynī, Badr al-Dīn Maḥmūd ibn Aḥmad ibn Mūsā al-. *al-Bināya sharḥ al-hidāya*. Edited by Amin Salih Sha'ban. Beirut: Dār al-Kutub al-'Ilmīyah, 2000.

Baghawī, al-Ḥusayn ibn Mas'ūd al-. *al-Tahdhīb fī fiqh al-Imām al-Shāfi'ī*. Edited by Adil Ahmad Abd al-Mawjud. Beirut: Dār al-Kutub al-'Ilmīyah, 1997.

———. *Ma'ālim al-tanzīl*. Edited by Muḥammad 'Abd Allāh Nimr, 'Uthmān Jum'ah Ḍumayrīyah and Sulaymān Muslim Ḥarash. Riyadh, Saudi Arabia: Dār al-Ṭībah, 1993.

Baghdādī, Abū Bakr Aḥmad ibn 'Alī al-Khaṭīb al-. *Tārīkh Baghdād aw madīnat al-salām*. Edited by Muḥammad Sa'īd 'Urfī. Beirut: Dar al-Kitab al-'Arabi, 1966.

Balādhurī, Aḥmad ibn Yaḥyá al-. *Kitāb futūḥ al-buldān*. Edited by M. J. de Goeje. Leiden: Brill, 2014.

———. *The Origins of the Islamic State*. Translated by Philip Hitti. 2 vols. Beirut: Khayats, 1966.

Balādhurī, Aḥmad ibn Yaḥyá al-. *Ansāb al-ashrāf*. Edited by Muhammad Hamidullah. Vol. 1. Cairo: Dar al-Ma'arif, 1959.

Balādhurī, Aḥmad ibn Yaḥyá al-. *Kitāb futūḥ al-buldān*. Edited by Salah al-Din Munajjid. Cairo: Maktabat al-Nahdah al-Misriyah, 1956.

Barthold, W. *Turkestan Down to the Mongol Invasion*. 4th ed. London: Luzac, 1977.

Bayḍāwī, 'Abd Allāh ibn 'Umar. *Beidhawii Commentarius in Coranum*. Edited by Heinrich Leberecht Fleischer. Osnabrück: Biblio, 1968.

Beaman, Lori G. *Reasonable Accommodation: Managing Religious Diversity*. Vancouver: University of British Columbia Press, 2010.

Beinin, Joel. *The Dispersion of Egyptian Jewry: Culture, Politics, and the Formation of the Modern Diaspora*. Contraversions 11. Berkeley: University of California Press, 1998.

Bekhradnia, Shahin. 'The Decline of the Zoroastrian Priesthood and its Effect on the Iranian Zoroastrian Community in the Twentieth Century. *Journal of the Anthropological Society of Oxford* 23, no. 1 (1992): 37–47.

Berkey, Jonathan. 'Circumcision Circumscribed: Female Excision and Cultural Accommodation in the Medieval Near East'. *International Journal of Middle East Studies* 28 (1996): 19–38.

Bīrūnī, Muḥammad ibn Aḥmad. *Alberuni's India. An Account of the Religion, Philosophy, Literature, Geography, Chronology, Astronomy, Customs, Laws and Astrology of India about ad 1030*. Translated by Eduard Sachau. 2 vols. London: Trübner, 1910.

———. *Taḥqīq Mā li-l-Hind: min muqawwilat maqbūla fī l-ʿaql aw mardhūla*. Beirut: ʿĀlam al-Kutub, 1983.

Blankinship, Khalid Yahya. 'The Early Creed'. In *The Cambridge Companion to Classical Islamic Theology*, edited by Tim Winter, 33–54. Cambridge: Cambridge University Press, 2008.

Blois, François de. 'The "Sabians" (Sabi'un) in Pre-Islamic Arabia'. *Acta Orientalia* 56 (1995): 39–61.

Borrut, Antoine. 'Remembering Karbalā: The Construction of an Early Islamic Site of Memory'. *Jerusalem Studies in Arabic and Islam* 42 (2015): 249–82.

Bosworth, C. E. *Sistan under the Arabs: From the Islamic Conquest to the Rise of the Saffarids (30–250/651–864)*. Rome: IsMEO, 1968.

———. 'Al-Khwārazmī on Various Faiths and Sects, Chiefly Iranian'. In *Iranica Varia: Papers in Honor of Professor Ehsan Yarshater*, edited by D. Amin, M. Kasheff and A. Sh. Shabbazi, 30:10–19. Acta Iranica. Leiden: Brill, 1990.

Boyce, Mary. *Zoroastrianism: Its Antiquity and Constant Vigour*. Costa Mesa, CA: Mazda Publishers, 1992.

———. *Zoroastrians, Their Religious Beliefs and Practices*. London: Routledge & Kegan Paul, 1979.

———. *A Persian Stronghold of Zoroastrianism*. Oxford: Clarendon Press, 1977.

———. 'Zoroastrianism in Iran after the Arab Conquest'. In *A Zoroastrian Tapestry: Art, Religion & Culture*, edited by Pheroza Godrej and Firoza Mistree. Usmanpura: Mapin, 2002.

———. 'On the Zoroastrian Temple Cult of Fire'. *Journal of the American Oriental Society* 95, no. 3 (1975): 454–65.

Bravmann, Meïr. 'The Ancient Arab Background of the Qur'ānic Concept al-Ǧizyatu an Yadin'. *Arabica* 13 (1966): 307–14.

Brown, Jonathan A. C. *Slavery and Islam*. Oxford: Oneworld, 2019.

Brown, Wendy. *Regulating Aversion: Tolerance in the Age of Identity and Empire.* Princeton: Princeton University Press, 2006.

Brunschvig, Robert. 'Ibn Abdelḥakam and the Conquest of North Africa'. In *The Expansion of the Early Islamic State*, edited by Fred Donner, 189–228. Formation of the Classical Islamic World 5. Aldershot: Ashgate, 2008.

———. 'Ibn 'Abdalhakam et la conquête de l'Afrique du Nord par les Arabes'. *Annales de l'Institut d'études Orientales (University of Algiers)* 6 (1942): 108–55.

Buck, Christopher. 'The Identity of the Sābi'ūn: An Historical Quest'. *Muslim World* 74, no. 3–4 (1984): 172–86.

Bulliet, Richard W. *Cotton, Climate, and Camels in Early Islamic Iran: A Moment in World History.* New York: Columbia University Press, 2009.

———. *Conversion to Islam in the Medieval Period: An Essay in Quantitative History.* Cambridge, MA: Harvard University Press, 1979.

———. *The Patricians of Nishapur: A Study in Medieval Islamic Social History.* Cambridge, MA: Harvard University Press, 1972.

Bürgel, J. Christoph. 'Zoroastrians as Viewed in Medieval Islamic Sources'. In *Muslim Perceptions of Other Religions: A Historical Survey*, edited by Jacques Waardenburg, 202–12. New York: Oxford University Press, 1999.

Calder, Norman. 'Legitimacy and Accommodation in Safavid Iran: The Linguistic Theory of Muhammad Baqir al-Sabzavari (1090/1679)'. *Iran* 25 (1987): 91–105.

Callimachi, Rukmini. 'ISIS Enshrines a Theology of Rape'. *New York Times*, 14 August 2015.

Cantera, Alberto. *Studien zur Pahlavi-Übersetzung des Avesta.* Iranica 7. Wiesbaden: Harrassowitz, 2004.

——— (ed.). *The Transmission of the Avesta.* Wiesbaden, Germany: Harrassowitz, 2012.

Carlson, Thomas A. *Christianity in Fifteenth-Century Iraq.* Cambridge: Cambridge University Press, 2018.

———. 'When Did the Middle East Become Muslim? Trends in the Study of Islam's "Age of Conversions"'. *History Compass* 16 (2018): 1–10.

Chaumont, M.-L. 'Recherches sur le clerge zoroastrien: le herbad (deuxieme article)'. *Revue de l'histoire des religions* 158, no. 2 (1960): 161–79.

Cheikh, Nadia Maria el. 'Sūrat Al-Rūm: A Study of the Exegetical Literature'. *Journal of the American Oriental Society* 118, no. 3 (1998): 356–64.

Choksy, Jamsheed K. *Conflict and Cooperation: Zoroastrian Subalterns and Muslim Elites in Medieval Iranian Society.* New York: Columbia University Press, 1997.

———. *Purity and Pollution in Zoroastrianism: Triumph over Evil.* Austin: University of Texas Press, 1989.

———. 'How Iran Persecutes Its Oldest Religion'. *CNN.* Accessed 26 April 2014. http://www.cnn.com/2011/11/14/opinion/choksy-iran-zoroastrian/index.html?iref=allsearch.

———. 'Reassessing the Material Contexts of Ritual Fires in Ancient Iran'. *Iranica Antiqua* 42 (2007): 229–69.

———. 'Altars, Precincts, and Temples: Medieval and Modern Zoroastrian Praxis'. *Iran* 44 (2006): 327–46.

———. 'Despite Shāhs and Mollās: Minority Sociopolitics in Premodern and Modern Iran'. *Journal of Asian History* 40, no. 2 (2006): 129–84.

———. 'Conflict, Coexistence, and Cooperation: Muslims and Zoroastrians in Eastern Iran during the Medieval Period'. *Muslim World* 80, no. 3–4 (1990): 213–33.

———. 'Zoroastrians in Muslim Iran: Selected Problems of Coexistence and Interaction during the Early Medieval Period'. *Iranian Studies* 20, no. 1 (1987): 17–30.

Christys, Ann. *Vikings in the South: Voyages to Iberia and the Mediterranean.* London: Bloomsbury Academic, 2015.

Cohen, Mark R. *Under Crescent and Cross: The Jews in the Middle Ages.* Princeton, NJ: Princeton University Press, 1994.

Cook, Michael. 'Magian Cheese: An Archaic Problem in Islamic Law'. *Bulletin of the School of Oriental and African Studies* 47 (1984): 449–67.

Coorlawala, Mithoo. *Ahd-Namaha: Covenants of Faith.* Bombay: K. R. Cama Oriental Institute, 1995.

Crone, Patricia. *Pre-Industrial Societies: Anatomy of the Pre-Modern World.* London: Oneworld, 2015.

———. *The Nativist Prophets of Early Islamic Iran: Rural Revolt and Local Zoroastrianism.* Cambridge: Cambridge University Press, 2012.

———. 'The Quranic Mushrikūn and the Resurrection (Part I)'. *Bulletin of the School of Oriental and African Studies* 75, no. 3 (2012): 445–72.

———. 'The Quranic Mushrikūn and the Resurrection (Part II)'. *Bulletin of the School of Oriental and African Studies* 76, no. 1 (2013): 1–20.

Crone, Patricia and Martin Hinds. *God's Caliph: Religious Authority in the First Centuries of Islam.* Cambridge: Cambridge University Press, 1986.

Darukhanawala, H. D. *Parsi Lustre on Indian Soil.* Vol. 1. Bombay: G. Claridge, 1939.

Daryaee, Touraj. 'Marriage, Property, and Conversion among the Zoroastrians: From Late Sasanian to Islamic Iran'. *Journal of Persianate Studies* 6, no. 1–2 (2013): 91–100.

———. 'Apocalypse Now: Zoroastrian Reflections on the Early Islamic Centuries'. *Medieval Encounters* 4, no. 3 (1998): 188–202.

Das, Debabrata. *Essays on Islam and Zoroastrianism.* Kolkata: Sanskrit Pustak Bhandar, 2007.

Davis, Natalie Zemon. 'The Rites of Violence: Religious Riot in Sixteenth-Century France'. *Past & Present*, no. 59 (1973): 51–91.

Davis, Richard H. *The Lives of Indian Images.* Princeton, NJ: Princeton University Press, 1997.

Day, Shelagh and Gwen Brodsky. 'The Duty to Accommodate: Who Will Benefit?'. *Canadian Bar Review* 75 (1996): 433–73.

Denny, Frederick Mathewson. *An Introduction to Islam.* Upper Saddle River, NJ: Pearson Prentice Hall, 2006.

Dewhurst, R. P. 'Review: Ahad Nameh'. *Journal of the Royal Asiatic Society of Great Britain and Ireland*, no. 4 (1925): 785–87.

Dhabhara, Bamanaji (ed.). *The Persian Rivayats of Hormazyar Framarz and Others: Their Version with Introduction and Notes.* Reprint of the 1932 edition. Bombay: K. R. Cama Oriental Institute, 1999.

Donner, Fred M. *Muhammad and the Believers: At the Origins of Islam.* Cambridge, MA: Harvard University Press, 2010.

Dubler, César E. *Abū Ḥāmid el Granadino y su relación de viaje por tierras eurasiáticas.* Madrid: Maestre, 1953.

DuBois, Thomas A. *Nordic Religions in the Viking Age.* Philadelphia: University of Pennsylvania Press, 1999.

Duby, Georges. 'Ideologies in Social History'. In *Constructing the Past: Essays in Historical Methodology*, edited by Jacques Le Goff and Pierre Nora, 151–65. Cambridge: Cambridge University Press, 1985.

Eaton, Richard. 'Temple Desecration and Indo-Muslim States'. In *Beyond Turk and Hindu: Rethinking Religious Identities in Islamicate South Asia*, edited by David Gilmartin and Bruce Lawrence, 246–81. Gainesville: University Press of Florida, 2002.

Elverskog, Johan. *Buddhism and Islam on the Silk Road.* Encounters with Asia. Philadelphia: University of Pennsylvania Press, 2010.

Emon, Anver M. *Religious Pluralism and Islamic Law: 'Dhimmis' and Others in the Empire of Law.* Oxford: Oxford University Press, 2012.

Engineer, Asghar Ali. 'Muslim Views of Hindus since 1950'. In *Muslim Perceptions of Other Religions: A Historical Survey*, edited by Jacques Waardenburg, 263–69. New York: Oxford University Press, 1999.

Epalza, Míkel de. 'Los Maŷūs (<<Magos>>): un hápax coránico (XXII, 17), entre lo étnico y lo jurídico, hasta su utilización en al-Andalus'. In *El Corán ayer y hoy: perspectivas actuales sobre el islam: estudios en honor al profesor Julio Cortés*, edited by Miguel Hernando de Larramendi and Salvador Peña Martín, 399–414. Córdoba: Editorial Berenice, 2008.

———. 'A Note about the Muslim Conquest of the 7th–8th Centuries: The Basque, Berber, Norse Viking, Norman, and British "Magicians"'. *Imago Temporis. Medium Aevum* 1 (2007): 61–69.

Fasā'ī, Ḥasan Ḥusainī. *Fārsnāma-i Nāṣirī*. Edited by Mansur Rastgar Fasa'i. Vol. 2. Tehran: Mu'assasa-i Intisharat-i Amir Kabir, 1988.

Fattal, Antoine. *Le Statut légal des non-musulmans en pays d'Islam*. Beyrouth: Impremiere catholique, 1958.

———. 'How Dhimmis Were Judged in the Islamic World'. In *Muslim Perceptions of Other Religions: A Historical Survey*, edited by Jacques Waardenburg, 83–102. New York: Oxford University Press, 1999.

Fīrūzābādī, Muḥammad ibn Ya'qūb. *Tanwīr al-miqbās min Tafsīr Ibn 'Abbās*. Translated by Mokrane Guezzou. Great Commentaries on the Holy Qur'an 2. Louisville, KY: Fons Vitae; and Amman, Jordan: Royal Aal al-Bayt Institute for Islamic Thought, 2008.

Fischer, Michael M. J. *Iran: From Religious Dispute to Revolution*. Cambridge, MA: Harvard University Press, 1980.

Flood, Finbarr Barry. *Objects of Translation: Material Culture and Medieval Hindu-Muslim Encounter*. Princeton, NJ: Princeton University Press, 2009.

Fodor, Gyorgy. 'Some Aspects of the Qadar Controversy in Early Islam'. *The Arabist: Budapest Studies in Arabic* 1 (1988): 57–66.

Foltz, Richard. 'The "Original" Kurdish Religion? Kurdish Nationalism and the False Conflation of the Yezidi and Zoroastrian Traditions'. *Journal of Persianate Studies* 10 (2017): 87–106.

———. 'Zoroastrians in Iran: What Future in the Homeland?'. *Middle East Journal* 65, no. 1 (2011): 73–84.

Fozi, Navid. *Reclaiming the Faravahar: Zoroastrian Survival in Contemporary Iran*. Leiden: Leiden University Press, 2014.

Freidenreich, David. *Foreigners and Their Food: Constructing Otherness in Jewish, Christian, and Islamic Law*. Berkeley: University of California Press, 2011.

Friedmann, Yohanan. *Tolerance and Coercion in Islam: Interfaith Relations in the Muslim Tradition*. New York: Cambridge University Press, 2003.

———. 'The Classification of Unbelievers in Sunni Muslim Law and Tradition'. *Jerusalem Studies in Arabic and Islam* 22 (1998): 163–95.

———. 'The Temple of Multan: A Note on Early Muslim Attitudes to Idolatry'. *Israel Oriental Studies* 2 (1972): 176–82.

Frye, Richard N. *The Golden Age of Persia: The Arabs in the East*. London: Weidenfeld and Nicolson, 1975.

———. *Bukhara: The Medieval Achievement*. Norman: University of Oklahoma Press, 1965.

———. *The Histories of Nishapur*. London: Mouton, 1965.

———. 'The Fate of Zoroastrians in Eastern Iran'. In *Au carrefour des religions: mélanges offerts à Philippe Gignoux*, edited by Rika Gyselen. Leuven, Belgium: Peeters, 1995.Frye, Richard N. 'City Chronicles of Central Asia and Khurasan: The Ta'rix-i Nisapur'. In *Islamic Iran and Central Asia (7th–12th Centuries)*, 405–20. London: Variorum Reprints, 1979.

———. 'Islamic Book Forgeries from Iran'. In *Islamwissentschaftliche Abhandlungen: Fritz Meier zum sechzigsten Geburtstag*, edited by Richard Gramlich, 106–9. Wiesbaden: F. Steiner, 1974.

Geary, Patrick. *The Myth of Nations: The Medieval Origins of Europe*. Princeton, NJ: Princeton University Press, 2002.

Gelvin, James. *The Arab Uprisings: What Everyone Needs to Know*. 2nd ed. Oxford: Oxford University Press, 2015.

Gerges, Fawaz. *ISIS: A History*. Princeton, NJ: Princeton University Press, 2016.

Ghrab, Saâd. 'Islam and Non-Scriptural Spirituality'. *Islamochristiana* 14 (1988): 51–70.

Gibb, H. A. R. (ed.). *Encyclopaedia of Islam*. 2nd ed. Leiden: Brill, 1960.

Gibb, H. A. R. and J. H. Kramers (eds). *Shorter Encyclopaedia of Islam*. Leiden: Brill, 1953.

Gil, Moshe. *A History of Palestine, 634–1099*. Cambridge: Cambridge University Press, 1992.

Goitein, S. D. *A Mediterranean Society: The Jewish Communities of the Arab World as Portrayed in the Documents of the Cairo Geniza*. Vol. 2. Berkeley: University of California Press, 1967.

Goldziher, Ignaz. *Introduction to Islamic Theology and Law*. Translated by Andras and Ruth Hamori. Princeton, NJ: Princeton University Press, 1981.

———. *Muslim Studies*. Translated by S. M. Stern. Chicago: Aldine, 1968.

Gordon, Matthew. *The Breaking of a Thousand Swords: A History of the Turkish Military of Samarra, AH 200–275/815–889 CE*. Albany, NY: State University of New York Press, 2001.

Green, Nile. 'The Survival of Zoroastrianism in Yazd'. *Iran* 38 (2000): 115–22.

Halbwachs, Maurice. *On Collective Memory*. Edited by Lewis Coser. Chicago: University of Chicago Press, 1992.

Halevi, Leor. *Muhammad's Grave: Death Rites and the Making of Islamic Society*. New York: Columbia University Press, 2007.

Hall, Edith. *Inventing the Barbarian: Greek Self-Definition through Tragedy*. Oxford: Clarendon Press, 1989.

Ḥamawī, Yāqūt ibn 'Abd Allāh al-. *Mu'jam al-buldān*. Edited by Ferdinand Wüstenfeld. 4 vols. Leipzig: F. A. Brockhaus, 1866.

Hambly, Gavin. 'From Baghdad to Bukhara, From Ghazna to Delhi: The Khil'a Ceremony in the Transmission of Kingly Pomp and Circumstance'. In *Robes and Honor: The Medieval World of Investiture*, edited by Stewart Gordon, 193–222. New York: Palgrave, 2001.

Hamdani, 'Abbas. 'The Fatimid-'Abbasid Conflict in India'. *Islamic Culture* 41 (1967): 185–91.

Hanaoka, Mimi. *Authority and Identity in Medieval Islamic Historiography: Persian Histories from the Peripheries*. Cambridge: Cambridge University Press, 2016.

Haug, Robert. *The Eastern Frontier: Limits of Empire in Late Antique and Early Medieval Central Asia*. London: I. B. Tauris, 2019.

Hawting, G. R. *The Idea of Idolatry and the Emergence of Islam: From Polemic to History*. Cambridge: Cambridge University Press, 1999.

Hinds, Martin. 'The First Arab Conquests in Fars'. In *Studies in Early Islamic History*, edited by Jere Bacharach, Lawrence Conrad and Patricia Crone, 199–231. Princeton, NJ: Darwin Press, 1996.

Hinnells, John R. *Zoroastrians in Britain: The Ratanbai Katrak Lectures, University of Oxford, 1985*. Oxford: Clarendon Press, 1996.

———. *Persian Mythology*. London: Hamlyn, 1973.

Hirschfeld, Hartwig. 'The Arabic Portion of the Cairo Genizah at Cambridge'. *Jewish Quarterly Review* 15, no. 2 (1903): 167–81.

Hodgson, Marshall G. S. *Venture of Islam*. Chicago: University of Chicago Press, 1974.

Howard-Johnston, James. *Witnesses to a World Crisis: Historians and Histories of the Middle East in the Seventh Century*. Oxford: Oxford University Press, 2010.

Hoyland, Robert G. *In God's Path: The Arab Conquests and the Creation of an Islamic Empire*. New York: Oxford University Press, 2015.

———. *Muslims and Others in Early Islamic Society*. Burlington, VT: Ashgate, 2004.

———. *Seeing Islam as Others Saw It: A Survey and Evaluation of Christian, Jewish and Zoroastrian Writings on Early Islam*. Studies in Late Antiquity and Early Islam 13. Princeton, NJ: Darwin Press, 1997.

Huart, Clément. 'Selman du Fars'. In Gaston Mesparo (ed.), *Mélanges Hartwig Derenbourg, 1844–1908*, 297–310. Paris: E. Leroux, 1909.

Huff, Dietrich. 'Formation and Ideology of the Sasanian State in the Context of Archaeological Evidence'. In *The Sasanian Era*, edited by Vesta Sarkhosh Curtis and Sarah Stewart, 3:31–59. The Idea of Iran. London: I. B. Tauris, 2008.

Humphreys, R. Stephen. *Islamic History: A Framework for Inquiry*. Revised edition. Princeton, NJ: Princeton University Press, 1991.

Huyse, Philip. 'Late Sasanian Society between Orality and Literacy'. In *The Sasanian Era*, edited by Vesta Sarkhosh Curtis and Sarah Stewart, 3:140–55. The Idea of Iran. London: I. B. Tauris, 2008.

Ibn Abī al-Rabī', Muḥammad ibn 'Abd al-Raḥīm. *Al-Mu'rib 'an ba'ḍ 'aŷā'ib al-Magrib (Elogio de algunas maravillas del Magrib)*. Edited by Ingrid Bejarano. Fuentes arábico-hispanas 9. Madrid: Consejo Superior de Investigaciones Científicas, Instituto de Cooperación con el Mundo Árabe, 1991.

Ibn Abī Shaybah, 'Abd Allāh ibn Muḥammad. *al-Kitāb al-Muṣannaf fī l-aḥādīth wa-l-āthār*. Edited by Kamāl Yūsuf al-Ḥūt. Beirut: Dar al-Taj, 1989.

Ibn Abī Ṭālib, Makkī. *Al-Hidāya ilā Bulūgh al-Nihāya*. Shariqa: Kulliyyat al-Dirāsāt al-'Ulyā wa-l-Baḥth al-'Ilmī, Jāmi'at Shāriqa, 1429. https://al-mak taba.org/book/31728.

Ibn al-Faqīh al-Hamadhānī, Aḥmad ibn Muḥammad. *Mukhtaṣar kitāb al-buldān*. Edited by M. J. de Goeje. Leiden: Brill, 1967.

Ibn Faḍlān, Aḥmad. *Ibn Fadlan and the Land of Darkness: Arab Travelers in the Far North*. Translated by Paul Lunde and Caroline Stone. London: Penguin, 2012.

———. *Ibn Fadlan's Journey to Russia: A Tenth-Century Traveler from Baghdad to the Volga River*. Translated by Richard Frye. Princeton, NJ: Markus Wiener Publishers, 2005.

Ibn Ḥamdūn, Bahā' al-Dīn Muḥammad ibn al-Ḥasan. *al-Tadhkirah al-Ḥamdūnīyah*. Edited by Iḥsān 'Abbās. Vol. 2. Beirut: Ma'had al-Inma al-'Arabi, 1983.

Ibn Hishām, 'Abd al-Malik and Muḥammad Ibn Isḥāq. *The Life of Muhammad: A Translation of Ishāq's Sīrat rasūl Allāh.* Translated by Alfred Guillaume. London: Oxford University Press, 1955.

Ibn Kathīr, Ismā'īl ibn 'Umar. *al-Bidāya wa 'l-Nihāya.* Vol. 14. Beirut: Dar al-Kutub al-'Ilmiya, 2001.

Ibn Kathīr, Ismā'īl ibn 'Umar. *Tuḥfat al-ṭālib bi-ma'rifat aḥādīth-Mukhtaṣar Ibn al-Ḥājib.* Edited by Abd al-Ghani ibn Humayd ibn Mahmud Kubaysi. Beirut: Ibn Hazm, 1996.

Ibn Kathīr, Ismā'īl ibn 'Umar. *Tafsīr al-Qur'ān al-'aẓīm.* Beirut: Dār al-Jīl, 1988.

Ibn Qudāmah, 'Abd al-Raḥmān ibn Muḥammad. *al-Mughnī wa-l-Sharḥ al-kabīr 'alá matn al-Muqni'.* Edited by Muḥammad Rashīd Riḍá. Reprint of 1922 Cairo edition. Beirut: Dār al-Kitāb al-'Arabī, 1972.

Ibn Sa'd, Muḥammad. *Al-Ṭabaqāt al-Kubrá.* Al-Ṭab'ah 1. Beirut: Dār al-Kutub al-'Ilmīyah, 1990.

Ibn Ṭāhir al-Baghdādī, 'Abd al-Qāhir. *al-Farq bayn al-firaq (Moslem Schisms and Sects).* Translated by Kate Chambers Seelye. Reprint of 1920 edition. Vol. 1. New York: AMS Press, 1966.

Ibn Ṭāhir al-Baghdādī, 'Abd al-Qāhir. *al-Farq bayn al-firaq (Moslem Schisms and Sects).* Translated by Abraham Halkin. Vol. 2. Tel-Aviv: Palestine Publishing Co., 1935.

Ibn Ṭāhir al-Baghdādī, 'Abd al-Qāhir. *Mukhtaṣar kitāb al-farq bayna al-firaq.* Edited by Philip Hitti. Misr: Matba'at al-Hilal, 1924.

Ibn Zanjawayh, Ḥamīd ibn Mukhlid. *Kitāb al-amwāl.* Edited by Shakir Dhib Fayyad. Riyadh, Saudi Arabia: Markaz al-Malik Faysal lil-Buhuth wa-al-Dirasat al-Islamiyya, 1986.

I.O. Islamic Ms. 2556/7, 14 November 1802. India Office, British Library.

Iṣfahānī, Abū l-Shaykh 'Abd Allāh ibn Muḥammad. *Ṭabaqāt al-muḥaddithīn bi-Iṣbahān.* Edited by 'Abd al-Ghafur 'Abd al-Haqq Husayn Balushi. Beirut: Mu'assasat al-Risālah, 1987.

Iṣfahānī, Abū Nu'aym Aḥmad ibn 'Abd Allāh al-. *Kitāb dhikr akhbār Iṣfahān.* Edited by Sven Dedering. Vol. 1. Leiden: Brill, 1931.

Jackson, Peter. 'World Conquest and Local Accommodation: Threat and Blandishment in Mongol Diplomacy'. In Judith Pfeiffer and Sholeh Quinn (eds), *History and Historiography of Post-Mongol Central Asia and the Middle East: Studies in Honor of John E. Woods*, 3–22. Wiesbaden, Germany: Harrassowitz, 2008.

Jāḥiẓ, 'Amr ibn Baḥr al-. *al-Ḥayawān.* Edited by Abd al-Salam Muhammad Harun. Vol. 4. Cairo: Maktabat Mustafa al-Babi al-Halabi wa-Awladuh, 1938.

Jaṣṣāṣ, Aḥmad ibn ʻAlī al-. *Kitāb Aḥkām al-Qur'ān*. Edited by Muhammad Sadiq al-Qamhawi. Beirut: Dar al-Ihya al-Turath al-Arabi, 1984.

Jejeebhoy, Sorabjee Jamsetjee. *Tuqviuti-Din-i-Mazdiasna*. Bombay: Jam-i-Jamsheed Press, 1851.

Judd, Steven. 'The Early Qadariyya'. In *Oxford Handbook of Islamic Theology*, edited by Sabine Schmidtke, 44–54. Oxford: Oxford University Press, 2016.

———. 'Muslim Persecution of Heretics during the Marwānid Period (64–132/684–750)'. *Al-Masāq: Islam and the Medieval Mediterranean* 23, no. 1 (2011): 1–14.

Kamal-ud-Din, Khwajah. *Islam and Zoroastrianism*. Woking: Basheer Muslim Library, 1925.

Kennedy, Hugh. *The Great Arab Conquests: How the Spread of Islam Changed the World We Live In*. Philadelphia: Da Capo, 2007.

Kestenberg Amighi, Janet. *The Zoroastrians of Iran: Conversion, Assimilation, or Persistence*. New York: AMS Press, 1990.

Khadduri, Majid. *War and Peace in the Law of Islam*. Baltimore: Johns Hopkins Press, 1955.

Khanbaghi, Aptin. *The Fire, the Star and the Cross: Minority Religions in Medieval and Early Modern Iran*. London: I. B. Tauris, 2006.

Kister, M. J. 'Social and Religious Concepts of Authority in Islam'. *Jerusalem Studies in Arabic and Islam* 18 (1994): 85–127.

———. 'Al-Ḥīra, Some Notes on Its Relations with Arabia'. *Arabica* 15 (1968): 143–69.

Kotwal, Dastur Firoze M. 'A Brief History of the Parsi Priesthood'. *Indo-Iranian Journal* 33, no. 3 (1990): 165–75.

Kremer, Alfred. *Culturgeschichte des Orients unter den Chalifen*. Vol. 2. Wien: W. Braumuller, 1875.

Kreyenbroek, Philip G. 'How Pious Was Shapur? Religion, Church, and Propaganda under the Early Sasanians'. In *The Sasanian Era*, edited by Vesta Sarkhosh Curtis and Sarah Stewart, 3:7–16. The Idea of Iran. London: I. B. Tauris, 2008.

———. 'Millennialism and Eschatology in the Zoroastrian Tradition'. In *Imagining the End: Visions of Apocalypse from the Ancient Middle East to Modern America*, edited by Abbas Amanat and Magnus T. Bernhardsson, 33–55. London: I. B. Tauris, 2001.

———. 'The Zoroastrian Priesthood after the Fall of the Sasanian Empire'. In *Transition Periods in Iranian History: Actes Du Symposium de Fribourg-En-Brisgau (22–24 Mai 1985)*, 151–66. Leuven, Belgium: Peeters, 1987.

Kūfī, ʻAlī ibn Ḥāmid al-. *The Chachnamah: An Ancient History of Sind.* Translated by Mirza Kalichbeg Faridunbeg. Karachi: Commissioner's Press, 1900.

Lalani, Arzina. *Early Shi'i Thought: The Teachings of Imam Muhammad al-Baqir.* London: I. B. Tauris, 2000.

Lambton, A. K. S. 'Persian Local Histories: The Tradition behind Them and the Assumptions of Their Authors'. In *Yad-Nama: In memoria di Alessandro Bausani*, edited by Alessandro Bausani and Lucia Rostagno. Roma: Bardi editore, 1991.

———. 'An Account of the "Tarikhi Qumm"'. *Bulletin of the School of Oriental and African Studies* 12 (1948): 586–96.

Lane, Edward William. *An Arabic-English Lexicon.* London: Williams and Norgate, 1863.

Lecker, Michael. *People, Tribes, and Society in Arabia around the Time of Muḥammad.* Variorum Collected Studies Series. Burlington, VT: Ashgate, 2005.

———. 'The Preservation of Muhammad's Letters'. In *People, Tribes, and Society in Arabia around the Time of Muhammad.* Aldershot: Ashgate, 2005.

———. 'The Levying of Taxes for the Sassanians in Pre-Islamic Medina (Yathrib)'. *Jerusalem Studies in Arabic and Islam* 27 (2002): 109–26.

Levy-Rubin, Milka. *Non-Muslims in the Early Islamic Empire: From Surrender to Coexistence.* New York: Cambridge University Press, 2011.

Lewis, Bernard. *The Jews of Islam.* Princeton, NJ: Princeton University Press, 1984.

Lucas, Scott. 'Where Are the Legal Hadith? A Study of the Musannaf of Ibn Abi Shayba'. *Islamic Law & Society* 15 (2008): 283–314.

Luhrmann, Tanya. *The Good Parsi: The Fate of a Colonial Elite in a Postcolonial Society.* Cambridge, MA: Harvard University Press, 1996.

Maalouf, Amin. *In the Name of Identity: Violence and the Need to Belong.* New York: Arcade, 2001.

McAuliffe, Jane Dammen (ed.). *Encyclopaedia of the Quran.* Leiden: Brill, 2001.

MacEvitt, Christopher. *The Crusades and the Christian World of the East: Rough Tolerance.* The Middle Ages Series. Philadelphia: University of Pennsylvania Press, 2008.

Mackenzie, John. 'Empires in World History: Characteristics, Concepts, and Consequences'. In John Mackenzie (ed.), *Encyclopedia of Empire.* Malden, MA: Wiley, 2016.

Maclean, Derryl N. *Religion and Society in Arab Sind.* Leiden: Brill, 1989.

Madelung, Wilferd. *Religious Trends in Early Islamic Iran.* Bibliotheca Persica, no. 4. Albany, NY: Persian Heritage Foundation, 1988.

Magnusson, Andrew D. 'A History of Violence? Islam, British Orientalism, and the Bombay Riot of 1851'. In *Britain in the Islamic World: Imperial and Post-Imperial Connections*, edited by Justin Quinn Olmstead, 3–26. London: Palgrave Macmillan, 2019.

———. 'Muslim-Zoroastrian Relations and Religious Violence in Early Islamic Discourse, 600–1100 CE'. Ph.D. Dissertation, University of California at Santa Barbara, 2014.

Maḥallī, Jalāl al-Dīn Muḥammad ibn Aḥmad and Jalāl al-Dīn 'Abd al-Raḥmān ibn Abī Bakr Suyūṭī. *Tafsīr al-Jalālayn*. Translated by Feras Hamza. Louisville, KY: Fons Vitae, 2008.

Mahmood, Saba. *Religious Difference in a Secular Age: A Minority Report*. Princeton, NJ: Princeton University Press, 2016.

Maḥmūd ibn 'Us̱mān. *Kitāb-i Firdaws al-murshidīyah fī asrār al-ṣamadiyah (Die Vita des Scheich Abu Ishaq al-Kazaruni in der persischen Bearbeitung)*. Edited by Friedrich Max Meier. Leipzig: Kommissionsverlag F. A. Brockhaus, 1948.

Mālik ibn Anas and 'Abd al-Salām ibn Sa'īd Saḥnūn. *al-Mudawwana al-kubrā*. Beirut: Dār al-kutub al-'ilmiyya, 1994.

———. *al-Mudawwana al-kubrā*. Vol. 2. Baghdad: Maktabat al-Muthanna, 1970.

Marashi, Afshin. *Exile and the Nation: The Parsi Community of India and the Making of Modern Iran*. Austin: University of Texas Press, 2020.

Mas'ūdī, Abū l-Ḥasan ibn 'Ali b. al-Husayn al-. *Murūj al-dhahab wa-ma'ādin al-jawhar*. Edited by Abel Pavet de Courteille, Charles Barbier de Meynard and Charles Pellat. Vol. 2. Beirut: al-Jami'ah al-Lubnaniyah, 1966.

———. *Les prairies d'or*. Edited by Abel Pavet de Courteille. Vol. 2. Paris: Société asiatique, 1962.

Massignon, Louis. *The Passion of al-Hallaj: Mystic and Martyr of Islam*. Vol. 1. Princeton, NJ: Princeton University Press, 1982.

———. 'La politique islamo-chrétienne des scribes nestoriens de deir qunna à la cour de bagdad au IXe de notre ère'. In Youakim Moubarac (ed.), *Opera minora: Textes recueillis, classés et présentés avec une bibliographie*, 250–57. Beirut: Dar-el-Maaref, 1963.

Massignon, Louis and Jamshedji Maneckji Unvala. *Salman Pak and the Spiritual Beginnings of Iranian Islam*. Bombay: Bombay University Press, 1955.

Matar, Nabil. 'Islam in Britain, 1689–1750'. *Journal of British Studies* 47, no. 2 (2008): 284–300.

Meddeb, Abdelwahab and Benjamin Stora (eds). *A History of Jewish-Muslim Relations: From the Origins to the Present Day*. Princeton, NJ: Princeton University Press, 2013.

Melvinger, Arne. *Les premières incursions des Vikings en Occident d'après les sources arabes*. Uppsala, Sweden: Almqvist & Wiksells, 1955.

Menasce, J. P. de. 'Questions Concerning the Mazdaeans of Muslim Iran'. In *Muslims and Others in Early Islamic Society*, edited by Robert G. Hoyland, 331–41. Aldershot: Ashgate, 2002.

———. 'Zoroastrian Literature after the Muslim Conquest'. In *Cambridge History of Iran*, edited by Richard N. Frye, 4:543–65. Cambridge: Cambridge University Press, 1975.

Metcalf, Barbara. 'Too Little and Too Much: Reflections on Muslims in the History of India'. *The Journal of Asian Studies* 54, no. 4 (1995): 951–67.

Modarressi Tabataba'i, Hossein. *Qum dar qarn-i nuhum-i Hijri, 801–900*. Qum: Chapkhana-yi Hikmat, 1971.

Moin, Azfar. 'Temple Destruction in India and Shrine Desecration in Iran and Central Asia'. *Comparative Studies in Society and History* 57, no. 2 (2015): 467–96.

Monnot, Guy. 'Les religions dans le miroir de l'islam'. In *Islam et religions*, 97–125. Paris: Masionneuve et Larose, 1986.

———. 'Sabéens et idolâtres selon 'Abd al-Jabbār'. In *Islam et religions*, 207–38. Paris: Masionneuve et Larose, 1986.

———. 'L'echo musulman aux religions d'Iran'. *Islamochristiana* 3 (1977): 85–98.

Montgomery, James. 'Ibn Fadlan and the Rusiyyah'. *Journal of Arabic and Islamic Studies* 3 (2000): 1–25.

Moritz, B. *Beiträge zur geschichte der Sinaiklosters im mittelalter nach arabischen quellen*. Berlin: Verlag der Königlich-Preussische Akademie der Wissenschaften, 1918.

Morony, Michael. *Iraq after the Muslim Conquest*. Princeton, NJ: Princeton University Press, 1984.

———. 'Conquerors and Conquered: Iran'. In *Studies on the First Century of Islamic Society*, edited by G. H. A. Juynboll, 73–88. Carbondale: Southern Illinois University Press, 1982.

Mottahedeh, Roy. 'The 'Abbasid Caliphate in Iran'. In *Cambridge History of Iran*, 4: From the Arab Invasion to the Saljuqs: 57–89. Cambridge: Cambridge University Press, 1975.

Motzki, Harald. *The Origins of Islamic Jurisprudence: Meccan Fiqh before the Classical Schools*. Translated by Marion H. Katz. Leiden: Brill, 2002.

———. 'Dating Muslim Traditions: A Survey'. *Arabica* 52, no. 2 (2005): 204–53.

———. 'The Muṣannaf of 'Abd Al-Razzāq al-Ṣan'ānī as a Source of Authentic Aḥādīth of the First Century AH'. *Journal of Near Eastern Studies* 50, no. 1 (1991): 1–71.

Mouton, Jean-Michel. *Le Sinaï médiéval: Un espace stratégique de l'Islam*. Paris: Presses Universitaires de France, 2000.

———. 'Les Musulmans à Sainte-Catherine au Moyen Âge'. In *Le Sinaï durant l'antiquité et le Moyen-Âge: 4000 ans d'histoire pour un désert*, edited by Dominique Valbelle and Charles Bonnet, 177–82. Paris: Éditions Errance, 1998.

MS Or. 885 Qissat Salman wa Islamihi, n.d. University of Leiden.

Muqaddasī, Muḥammad ibn Aḥmad. *Aḥsan at-taqāsīm fī ma'rifat al-aqālīm (The Best Divisions for Knowledge of the Regions)*. Translated by Basil Anthony Collins. Reading: Garnet, 1994.

Mustawfī Qazvīnī, Ḥamd Allāh. *Ta'ríkh-i-Guzída*. Edited by E. G. Browne. Leiden: Brill, 1910.

Nakhjavānī, Muḥammad ibn Hindūshāh. *Dastūr al-kātib fī ta'yīn al-marātib*. Edited by Ăbdülğärim Ăli oghlü Ălizadă. Moscow: Danish, 1964.

Nariman, G. K. *The Ahad Nameh*. Bombay: Iran League, 1925.

———. *Persia & Parsis*. Bombay: Iran League, 1925.

———. 'Was It Religious Persecution Which Compelled the Parsis to Migrate from Persia to India?'. *Islamic Culture* 7 (1933): 277–80.

———. 'Islam and Parsis'. *Islamic Culture* 1 (1927): 632–39.

Narshakhī, Abū Bakr Muḥammad ibn Ja'far. *Tārīkh-i Bukhārā*. Tehran: Intisharat-i Tus, 1984.

———. *The History of Bukhara*. Translated by Richard N. Frye. Cambridge, MA: Mediaeval Academy of America, 1954.

Neale, Harry. *Jihad in Premodern Sufi Writings*. New York: Palgrave Macmillan, 2017.

Neuwirth, Angelika. 'Imagining Mary – Disputing Jesus: Reading Surat Maryam and Related Meccan Texts within the Qur'anic Communication Process'. In *Fremde, Feinde und Kurioses: innen- und aussenansichten unseres muslimischen Nachbarn*, edited by Benjamin Jokisch, Ulrich Rebstock and Lawrence Conrad, 383–416. Berlin: Walter de Gruyter, 2009.

Nirenberg, David. *Communities of Violence: Persecution of Minorities in the Middle Ages*. Princeton, NJ: Princeton University Press, 1996.

Nora, Pierre. 'Between Memory and History: Les Lieux de Mémoire'. *Representations*, no. 26 (1989): 7–24.

'Open Letter to Baghdadi'. Accessed 14 January 2019. http://www.lettertobaghdadi.com/.

Palsetia, Jesse S. *Jamsetjee Jejeebhoy of Bombay: Partnership and Public Culture in Empire*. New Delhi: Oxford University Press, 2015.

Patel, Dinyar. 'Gustaspshah Kaikhusroo Nariman: Improving Ties between Zoroastrianism and Islam'. *FEZANA: The Federation of Zoroastrian Associations of North America* 15 (2009): 43–45.

Paul, Jürgen. 'The Histories of Isfahan: Mafarrukhi's Kitab Mahasin Isfahan'. *Iranian Studies* 33, no. 2 (2000): 117–32.

Payne, Richard E. *A State of Mixture: Christians, Zoroastrians, and Iranian Political Culture in Late Antiquity*. Transformation of the Classical Heritage 56. Oakland, California: University of California Press, 2015.

Penn, Michael Philip. *Envisioning Islam: Syriac Christians and the Early Muslim World*. Philadelphia: University of Pennsylvania Press, 2015.

Pohl, Walter. 'Conceptions of Ethnicity in Early Medieval Studies'. In *Debating the Middle Ages: Issues and Readings*, edited by Barbara H. Rosenwein and Lester Little, 13–24. Malden, MA: Blackwell Publishers, 1998.

Pourshariati, Parvaneh. *Decline and Fall of the Sasanian Empire: The Sasanian-Parthian Confederacy and the Arab Conquest of Iran*. London: I. B. Tauris, 2008.

Prawer, Joshua. '"Minorities" in the Crusader States'. In *Impact of the Crusades on the Near East*, edited by Norman Zacour and Harry Hazard, 5:59–115. A History of the Crusades. Madison: University of Wisconsin Press, 1985.

Qudāmah ibn Ja'far. *Kitāb al-Kharāj wa-ṣinā'at al-kitābah*. Edited by Fuat Sezgin. Vol. 42. Veröffentlichungen des Institutes für Geschichte der Arabisch-Islamischen Wissenschaften, Series C. Frankfurt: Johann Wolfgang Goethe University, 1986.

———. *Kitāb al-kharāj*. Translated by Adam Ben Shemesh. Vol. 2. Taxation in Islam. Leiden: Brill, 1965.

Qummi, Hasan ibn Muhammad b. Hasan al-. *Kitāb-i tārīkh-i Qum*. Edited by Jalal al-Din Tehrani. Translated by Ḥasan ibn 'Alī Qummī. Tehran: Majlis, 1934.

Qurṭubī, Muḥammad ibn Aḥmad al-. *al-Jāmi' li-aḥkām al-Qur'ān*. Edited by Aḥmad 'Abd al-'Alīm Baraddūnī. Beirut: Iḥyā' al-Turāth al-'Arabī, 1985.

Rahman, Fazlur. *Islam*. 2nd ed. Chicago: University of Chicago Press, 1979.

Rāzī, Fakhr al-Dīn Muḥammad ibn 'Umar. *Mafātīḥ al-ghayb wa-bi-hāmishih Tafsīr Abī al-Sa'ūd*. Cairo: al-Matba'ah al-Amirah al-Sharafiyah, 1890.

Rezakhani, Khodadad. *ReOrienting the Sasanians: East Iran in Late Antiquity*. Edinburgh: Edinburgh University Press, 2017.

Rezania, Kianoosh. 'The Dēnkard against Its Islamic Discourse'. *Der Islam* 94, no. 2 (2017): 336–62.

Rezwi, S. M. Taher. *Parsis, A People of the Book: Being a Brief Survey of Zoroastrian Religion in the Light of Biblical & Quranic Teachings*. Calcutta: D. B. Taraporewala & Sons, 1928.

Ringer, Monica. *Pious Citizens: Reforming Zoroastrianism in India and Iran*. Syracuse, NY: Syracuse University Press, 2011.

Robinson, Chase F. *Empire and Elites after the Muslim Conquest: The Transformation of Northern Mesopotamia*. New York: Cambridge University Press, 2000.

———. 'Neck-Sealing in Early Islam'. *Journal of the Economic and Social History of the Orient* 48, no. 3 (2005): 401–41.

Rose, Jenny. *Zoroastrianism: An Introduction*. London: I. B. Tauris, 2011.

Sahner, Christian. *Christian Martyrs under Islam: Religious Violence and the Making of the Muslim World*. Princeton, NJ: Princeton University Press, 2018.

Saklatwalla, Jamshedji Edulji. *A Contribution on the Life, Time, Identity & Career of Salman-al-Faresi, Alias Dasturan Dastur Dinyar*. Bombay: Central Printing Works, 1938.

Samʿānī, ʿAbd al-Karīm ibn Muḥammad al-. *Kitāb al-ansāb*. Edited by D.S. Margoliouth. Leiden: Brill, 1912.

Ṣanʿānī, ʿAbd al-Razzāq ibn Hammām al-Ḥimyarī al-. *al-Muṣannaf*. Edited by Ḥabīburraḥmān Aʿẓamī. Beirut: Tawzīʿ al-Maktab al-Islāmī, 1983.

Sanasarian, Eliz. *Religious Minorities in Iran*. Cambridge: Cambridge University Press, 2000.

Savant, Sarah Bowen. *New Muslims of Post-Conquest Iran*. Cambridge: Cambridge University Press, 2013.

Scher, Addai (ed.). *Histoire nestorienne (Chronique de Séert) Deuxieme Partie (II)*. Vol. 13, no. 4. Patrologia Orientalis. Paris: Firmin-Didot, 1919.

Schimmel, Annemarie. 'The Ornament of the Saints: The Religious Situation in Iran in Pre-Safavid Times'. *Iranian Studies* 7, no. 1–2 (1974): 88–111.

Schippmann, Klaus. *Die iranischen Feuerheiligtümer*. Religionsgeschichtliche Versuche und Vorarbeiten 31. Berlin: Walter de Gruyter, 1971.

Serjeant, R. B. 'The Sunnah Jami'ah, Pacts with the Yathrib Jews and the Tahram of Yathrib: Analysis and Translation of the Documents Comprised in the So-Called "Constitution of Medina"'. *Bulletin of the School of Oriental and African Studies* 41 (1978): 1–42.

Sethna, Ervad Darius. 'Reader's Forum'. *Parsiana* 13, no. 10 (1991): 3–4.

Shahrazūrī, ʿUthmān ibn ʿAbd al-Raḥmān Ibn al-Ṣalāḥ al-. *An Introduction to the*

Science of the Hadith (Kitab Ma'rifat Anwā' 'ilm al-Ḥadīth). Translated by Eerik Dickinson. Reading: Garnet, 2006.

Shaked, Shaul. 'Religion in the Late Sasanian Period: Eran, Aneran, and Other Religious Designations'. In *The Sasanian Era*, edited by Vesta Sarkhosh Curtis and Sarah Stewart, 3:103–17. The Idea of Iran. London: I. B. Tauris, 2008.

———. 'Some Islamic Reports Concerning Zoroastrianism'. *Jerusalem Studies in Arabic and Islam* 17 (1994): 43–84.

Shāshī, al-Haytham ibn Kulayb al-. *Musnad al-Shāshī*. Edited by Mahfuz al-Rahman Zayn Allah. Medina: Maktabat al-Ulum wa-l-Hikam, 1989.

Shaybānī, Muḥammad ibn al-Ḥasan. *Siyar*. Edited by Majid Khadduri. Beirut: al-Dar al-Muttahida Li-l-Nashr, 1975.

———. *The Islamic Law of Nations: Shaybānī's Siyar*. Translated by Majid Khadduri. Baltimore: Johns Hopkins Press, 1966.

Sheffield, Daniel J. 'In the Path of the Prophet: Medieval and Early Modern Narratives of the Life of Zarathustra in Islamic Iran and Western India'. Ph.D. Dissertation, Harvard University, 2012.

Shokoohy, Mehrdad. 'Two Fire Temples Converted to Mosques in Central Iran'. *Acta Iranica* 11 (1985): 545–72.

Simonsohn, Uriel. *A Common Justice: The Legal Allegiances of Christians and Jews under Early Islam*. Philadelphia: University of Pennsylvania Press, 2011.

———. 'Communal Boundaries Reconsidered: Jews and Christians Appealing to Muslim Authorities in the Medieval Near East'. *Jewish Studies Quarterly* 14, no. 4 (2007): 328–63.

Siroux, Maxime. 'L'évolution des antiques mosquées rurales de la région d'Ispahan'. *Arts Asiatiques* 26 (1973): 65–112.

Sizgorich, Thomas. *Violence and Belief in Late Antiquity: Militant Devotion in Christianity and Islam*. Divinations. Philadelphia: University of Pennsylvania Press, 2009.

Skrobucha, Heinz. *Sinai*. London: Oxford University Press, 1966.

Smith, Anthony. *The Nation in History: Historiographical Debates about Ethnicity and Nationalism*. Hanover, NH: University Press of New England, 2000.

Sourdel, Dominique. 'Robes of Honor in Abbasid Baghdad during the Eighth to Eleventh Centuries'. In *Robes and Honor: The Medieval World of Investiture*, edited by Stewart Gordon, 137–47. New York: Palgrave, 2001.

Spellberg, Denise A. *Thomas Jefferson's Qur'an: Islam and the Founders*. New York: Alfred A. Knopf, 2013.

Spooner, Brian. 'Iranian Kinship and Marriage'. *Iran: Journal of the British Institute of Persian Studies* 4 (1966): 1–9.

Stausberg, Michael. 'From Power to Powerlessness: Zoroastrianism in Iranian History'. In *Religious Minorities in the Middle East: Domination, Self-Empowerment, Accommodation*, edited by Anh Nga Longva and Anne Sofie Roald. Social, Economic, and Political Studies of the Middle East and Asia, v. 108. Leiden: Brill, 2012.

———. 'The Invention of a Canon: The Case of Zoroastrianism'. In *Canonization and Decanonization: Papers Presented to the International Conference of the Leiden Institute for the Study of Religions*, edited by A. van der Kooij and K. van der Toorn, 257–78. Leiden: Brill, 1998.

Stepaniants, Marietta. 'The Encounter of Zoroastrianism with Islam'. *Philosophy East and West* 52, no. 2 (2002): 159–72.

Stern, Jessica, and J.M. Berger. *ISIS: State of Terror*. New York: Ecco, 2015.

Stern, S. M. 'Heterodox Ismāʿīlism at the Time of Al-Muʿizz'. *Bulletin of the School of Oriental and African Studies* 17, no. 1 (1955): 10–33.

———. 'Ismaʿili Propaganda and Fatimid Rule in Sind'. *Islamic Culture* 23 (1949): 298–307.

Stewart, Sarah. 'The Politics of Zoroastrian Philanthropy and the Case of Qasr-e Firuzeh'. *Iranian Studies* 45, no. 1 (2012): 59–80.

Sykes, Percy M. *A History of Persia*. Vol. 2. London: Macmillan and Co, 1951.

Ṭabarī, Abū Jaʿfar Muḥammad ibn Jarīr al-. *Biographies of the Prophet's Companions and Their Successors*. Translated by Ella Landau-Tasseron. Vol. 39. History of Al-Tabari. Albany, NY: State University of New York Press, 1998.

———. *The Crisis of the Early Caliphate*. Translated by R. Stephen Humphreys. Vol. 15. History of Al-Tabari. Albany, NY: State University of New York Press, 1990.

———. *The End of Expansion*. Translated by Khalid Yahya Blankinship. Vol. 25. History of Al-Tabari. Albany, NY: State University of New York Press, 1989.

———. *Jāmiʿ al-bayān fī tafsīr al-Qurʾān*. Edited by al-Ḥasan ibn Muḥammad Nīsābūrī. 30 vols. Beirut: Dār al-Maʿrifah, 1989.

———. *The Victory of Islam*. Translated by Michael Fishbein. Vol. 8. History of Al-Tabari. Albany, NY: State University of New York Press, 1989.

———. *The ʿAbbasid Recovery*. Translated by Philip Fields. Vol. 37. History of Al-Tabari. Albany, NY: State University of New York Press, 1985.

———. *The Return of the Caliphate to Baghdad*. Translated by Franz Rosenthal.

Vol. 38. History of Al-Tabari. Albany, NY: State University of New York Press, 1985.

———. *Tārīkh al-rusul wa-l-mulūk*. Edited by M. J. de Goeje. 15 vols. Leiden: Brill, 1964.

Ṭabarsī, Ḥusayn Taqī l-Nūrī. *Nafas al-Raḥmān fī faḍā'il Salmān*. Edited by Jawad Qayyumi al-Jazah'i al-Isfahani. Iran: Muassasat al-Afaq, 1990.

Talbot, Cynthia. 'Inscribing the Other, Inscribing the Self: Hindu-Muslim Identities in Pre-Colonial India'. *Comparative Studies in Society and History* 37, no. 4 (1995): 692–722.

Tannous, Jack. *The Making of the Medieval Middle East: Religion, Society, and Simple Believers*. Princeton, NJ: Princeton University Press, 2020.

Thapar, Romila. *Somanatha: The Many Voices of a History*. London: Verso, 2005.

Torkī, Moḥammad Rezā. *Pārsā-yi Pārsī: Salmān Fārsī beh Revāyat-i Motūn-i Fārsī*. Tehrān: Sherkat-i Inteshārāt-i 'Ilmī va Farhangī, 2008.

Tremblay, Xavier. 'Ibant Obscuri Uaria Sub Nocte: Les Textes Avestiques et Leurs Recensions Des Sassanides Aux XIIIe s. Ad En Particulier d'après l'alphabet Avestique. Notes de Lecture Avestiques VIII'. In *Transmission of the Avesta*, edited by Alberto Cantera, 98–135. Wiesbaden, Germany: Harrassowitz, 2012.

Tritton, Arthur. 'Islam and the Protected Religions'. *Journal of the Royal Asiatic Society of Great Britain and Ireland*, no. 3 (1927): 479–84.

Tsafrir, Nurit. 'The Attitude of Sunnī Islam toward Jews and Christians as Reflected in Some Legal Issues'. *Qanṭara: Revista de Estudios Arabes* 26, no. 2 (2005): 317–36.

Vāḥidī Nīshābūrī, Abū l-Ḥasan 'Alī. *Al-Wāḥidī's Asbāb al-Nuzūl*. Great Commentaries on the Holy Qur'an 3. Louisville, KY: Fons Vitae, 2008.

Van Ess, Josef. *Theology and Society in the Second and Third Century of the Hijra. Volume 1: A History of Religious Thought in Early Islam*. Translated by John O'Kane. Leiden: Brill, 2016.

———. *Zwischen Ḥadīṯ und Theologie: Studien zum Entstehen prädestinatianischer Überlieferung*. Berlin: De Gruyter, 1975.

Van Gelder, Geert Jan. *Close Relationships: Incest and Inbreeding in Classical Arabic Literature*. London: I. B. Tauris, 2005.

Vazīrī Kirmānī, Aḥmad 'Alī. *Tārīkh-i Kirmān*. Edited by Muhammad Ibrahim Bastani Parizi. Tehran: Kitabha-yi Iran, 1961.

Waardenburg, Jacques (ed.). *Muslim Perceptions of Other Religions: A Historical Survey*. New York: Oxford University Press, 1999.

Wadia, Jal H. *Sir Jamsetjee Jejeebhoy Parsee Benevolent Institution Centenary Volume.* Bombay: Mody Printing Press, 1950.

Waghmar, Burzine K. 'A Note on Parsi Islamology'. In *Third International Congress Proceedings: K. R. Cama Oriental Institute*, edited by H. N. Modi, 252–58. Bombay: K. R. Cama Oriental Institute, 2001.

Wakin, Jeanette A. *The Function of Documents in Islamic Law: The Chapters on Sales from Tahawi's Kitab al-Shurut al-Kabir.* Albany, NY: State University of New York Press, 1972.

Walker, Shaun. 'The Last of the Zoroastrians'. *The Guardian*, 6 August 2020. http://www.theguardian.com/world/2020/aug/06/last-of-the-zoroastrians-parsis-mumbai-india-ancient-religion.

Wāqidī, Muḥammad ibn 'Umar al-. *The Life of Muhammad: al-Wāqidī's Kitāb al-maghāzī.* Translated by Rizwi Faizer. New York: Routledge, 2011.

Ware III, Rudolph T. 'Slavery in Islamic Africa, 1400–1800'. In *The Cambridge World History of Slavery*, edited by David Eltis and Stanley L. Engerman, 3: AD 1420–AD 1804:47–80. Cambridge: Cambridge University Press, 2011.

Williams, Alan. *The Zoroastrian Myth of Migration from Iran and Settlement in the Indian Diaspora: Text, Translation and Analysis of the 16th century Qeṣṣe-ye Sanjān/The Story of Sanjan.* Leiden: Brill, 2009.

Wink, André. *Al-Hind: The Making of the Indo-Islamic World.* Vol. 1, Early Medieval India and the Expansion of Islam, 7th–11th Centuries. Leiden: Brill, 1990.

Wood, Graeme. 'What ISIS Really Wants'. *The Atlantic*, March 2015. https://www.theatlantic.com/magazine/archive/2015/03/what-isis-really-wants/384980/.

Ya'qūbī, Aḥmad ibn Abī Ya'qūb al-. *Kitāb al-buldān.* Edited by M. J. de Goeje. 2nd ed. Bibliotheca geographorum Arabicorum 7. Leiden: Brill, 1967.

Yaḥyā ibn Ādam. *Kitab al-Kharaj.* Translated by A. Ben Shemesh. Vol. 1. Taxation in Islam. Leiden: Brill, 1967.

———. *Kitāb al-kharāj.* Edited by Aḥmad Muḥammad Shākir. 2nd ed. Cairo: al-Maṭba'ah al-Salafīyah wa-Maktabatuhā, 1964.

Yarbrough, Luke. 'Origins of the Ghiyār'. *Journal of the American Oriental Society* 134, no. 1 (2014): 113–21.

———. 'Upholding God's Rule: Early Muslim Juristic Opposition to the State Employment of Non-Muslims'. *Islamic Law & Society* 19, no. 1/2 (2012): 11–85.

Yarshater, Ehsan (ed.). *Encyclopaedia Iranica.* London: Routledge, 1982.

Yavari, Neguin. 'Conversion Stories of Shaykh Abu Ishaq Kazaruni (963–1033)'. In

Christianizing Peoples and Converting Individuals, edited by Guyda Armstrong and Ian Woods, 225–46. Turnhout, Belgium: Brepols, 2000.

Zadeh, Travis. *The Vernacular Qur'an: Translation and the Rise of Persian Exegesis.* London: Institute of Ismaili Studies, 2012.

Zakeri, Mohsen. *Sāsānid Soldiers in Early Muslim Society: The Origins of 'Ayyārān and Futuwwa.* Wiesbaden: Harrassowitz Verlag, 1995.

Zamakhsharī, Maḥmūd ibn 'Umar. *al-Kashshāf 'an ḥaqā'iq ghawāmiḍ al-tanzīl.* Edited by Muhammad Alyan Marzuqi. Beirut: Dar al-Kitab al-Arabi, 1966.

———. *Tafsīr al-Qur'ān al-kashshāf.* Beirut: Dār al-Kitāb al-'Arabī, 1966.

Zaman, Muhammad Qasim. 'Death, Funeral Processions, and the Articulation of Religious Authority in Early Islam'. *Studia Islamica* 93 (2001): 27–58.

Zarrinkub, 'Abd al-Husayn. 'The Arab Conquest of Iran and Its Aftermath'. In *Cambridge History of Iran*, 4: From the Arab Invasion to the Saljuqs: 1–56. Cambridge: Cambridge University Press, 1975.

Zia-Ebrahimi, Reza. *The Emergence of Iranian Nationalism: Race and the Politics of Dislocation.* New York: Columbia University Press, 2016.

———. '"Arab Invasion" and Decline, or the Import of European Racial Thought by Iranian Nationalists'. *Ethnic and Racial Studies*, no. 3 (2012): 1–19.

Žižek, Slavoj. 'Tolerance as an Ideological Category'. *Critical Inquiry* 34, no. 4 (2008): 660–82.

Index

Abbasid Caliphate, 20, 22, 41, 43, 45, 61, 80–1, 83, 89, 93–4, 96, 101, 118–19, 143, 147–8
Abrun the Turk, 117–21, 130
Abd Allah ibn Amir, 123–6, 130
Abd al-Malik ibn Marwan, 120, 146–7
Abd al-Qadir, Hamid, 35
Abd al-Rahman II, 141–2, 144
Abd al-Rahman ibn Awf, 57, 85, 162
Abd al-Razzaq ibn Hammam al-San'ani, 44, 53, 189
Abu Bakr, 38, 41, 44–5, 85, 98, 136, 159–60, 168, 171
Abu Da'ud Sulayman ibn al-Ash'ath al-Sijistani, 39, 45, 145, 147
Abu Dharr al-Ghifari, 85, 168, 171
Abu Hanifa, 38, 61, 70; *see also* Islamic law
Abu Hashim ibn Muhammad ibn al-Hanafiyya, 57
Abu Musa al-Ash'ari, 46
Abu Thawr, 57, 65–6, 72, 172
Abu Ubayd al-Qasim ibn Sallam, 40–1, 43, 45, 48–9, 59, 61, 83, 91, 136
Abu Ubayda ibn al-Jarrah, 41
Abu Yusuf Ya'qub ibn Ibrahim, 39, 41, 43, 55–8, 63, 94
accommodation, 9–13, 27–8, 47, 50, 57, 71–2, 112, 130, 162–5
  definition of, 162
  limits of, 13, 28, 57, 72
  see also taxation
Achaemenian Empire, 21
Adam, 40, 141
Adurfarnbag i Farroxzadan, 38
Afghanistan, 113
ahd-nama, 13, 78–84, 86–102, 164
Ahmad ibn Fadlan, 143
Ahmad ibn Hanbal, 148; *see also* Islamic law
Ahriman, 2, 147
Ahura Mazda, 2–5
Ahwaz, 47
al-'Ala' al-Hadrami, 41–2
Algeciras, 142–3
Ali ibn Abi Talib, 39, 57, 61, 63, 101, 168–9, 171
Allah *see* God
ambivalence, 1, 12–14, 28, 137–8, 141, 152–3, 165
Amr ibn Dinar, 44
Amr ibn al-Harith, 48
Anahita, 3
Anatolia, 82, 102
al-Andalus, 141, 144
Andhra Pradesh, 122
angels, 42, 61, 170
animal *see* meat
Antichrist, 145
apocalypticism, 1, 3, 21, 160

Apostle, 84
Arabian Peninsula, 34, 41, 82
Arabic language, 4–5, 9, 33, 35, 47, 78, 92, 99–100, 121, 126, 129, 136, 142, 144–5, 160–1
Arabs, 1, 21, 25–6, 33, 40, 47–8, 59–60, 62, 99, 115, 127, 142, 144
Aragon, 7, 69, 117–18
Ardashir I, 1, 114
Aryans, 6, 26
Asbadhiyyin see *spahbed*
Ata ibn Abi Rabah, 61–2
Avesta, 2, 3, 5, 20–1, 33–4, 37–8, 49, 162
al-Awza'i, Abu Amr Abd al-Rahman ibn Amr, 137, 144, 161–2
Axelrod, Paul, 24
Ayodhya, 122–3
Azerbaijan, 3, 137

Babur, 122
Badr, Battle of, 141
Badr al-Din al-Ayni, 63, 65
Badr of Zaragosa, 144
al-Baghawi, Abu Muhammad al-Husayn ibn Mas'ud, 36, 65
Baghdad, 38, 83, 100, 118–19, 121
al-Baghdadi, Abd al-Qadir ibn Tahir, 38, 148
al-Baghdadi, Abu Bakr, 85, 98, 159–60
Bahrayn, 41–6, 48, 59
Bajala ibn Abda al-Tamimi, 45–6; *see also* Banu Tamim
al-Baladhuri, Ahmad ibn Yahya ibn Jabir, 41–2, 58–9, 62, 83, 89–92, 113, 115
Balkh, 33
Bam, 123–6, 130
Banu Makhlad, 83–4
Banu 'l-Nadir, 90–2
Banu Qurayza, 90–1
Banu Taghlib, 57, 61–2, 64, 163
Banu Tamim, 12, 46–7, 50, 59, 163
Bar Hebraeus, 83
Basques, 144–5, 151
Basra, 46, 66, 124, 146–7
Battle of the Trench, 90–2, 99
al-Baydawi, Abd Allah ibn Umar, 36
Beaman, Lori, 11
behavioural manuals, 56, 66, 72
believers, 3, 9, 35–7, 88, 124, 139, 145, 162, 167–8, 170–1
Berbers, 136–7, 142
biers, 95, 97–8, 170
Bihafaridh, 22
Bilal, 85, 168, 171
al-Biruni, Abu Rayhan Muhammad ibn Ahmad, 152
Bishtasif, 38
Blankinship, Khalid Yahya, 146
blood price, 69–72
Bombay Riot of 1851, 78, 102; *see also* Mumbai
Borrut, Antoine, 56
boundary marking, 13, 67–8, 164
Boyce, Mary, 21, 25
Brodsky, Gwen, 9
Brown, Wendy, 6–7
Brunschvig, Robert, 144
Buddhists, 9, 38, 150, 161–2
Bukhara, 4, 22, 97, 126–9
Bulliet, Richard, 8, 99
Bürgel, Christoph, 35–6
Byzantine Empire, 20
  Byzantines, 102, 140

Cahen, Claude, 34
Cain, 141
Cairo, 82, 92, 95–6, 149, 151–2
caliphs, 8, 20, 25–6, 40–1, 89, 97, 101, 118, 137, 146–8, 151, 163; *see also* Abbasid Caliphate; Umayyad Caliphate
Canada, 10
Cantera, Alberto, 37
Carlson, Thomas, 8
Central Asia, 4, 8, 18, 30, 108, 126, 130, 143, 160, 179–80, 182, 186
charter *see ahd-nama*

cheese, 66–7, 72, 164
children, 24–5, 57, 60–2, 68, 161, 170
Choksy, Jamsheed, 8, 21–2, 24, 34, 68
Christianity, 2–3, 5, 37, 62, 136, 139, 142
  Arab Christians, 62, 64
  Nestorian Christians, 83
Christys, Anne, 143
churches, 82, 97, 116
cloth(es), 42–3, 88, 94–5, 100, 170
Cohen, Mark, 19, 23
Companions of the Prophet Muhammad, 37, 44, 46, 64–7, 78, 85, 101, 134, 148, 171
conscription, 10, 83, 87, 94, 167
Constitution of Medina, 91
conversion, 8, 21–2, 62, 79, 84, 98–100, 129
Cook, Michael, 66
Coorlawala, Mithoo, 79
Crone, Patricia, 22
Crusades, 137
  First Crusade, 82
  Shepherds' Crusade, 117

dahr, 139
dakhma see Tower of Silence
Damascus, 93, 116, 146–7
Darabjird, 114, 116; *see also* Kariyan
date fruit (palms), 42–3, 60
Day, Shelagh, 9
defence pact *see* Banu Qurayza
Denkard, 38
Dezpul, 97
dhimma, 9, 59, 70, 87, 93, 151, 161–2, 167, 170–1; *see also* Protected People
differentiation *see ghiyar*
dinar, 42–4, 96
al-Dinawari, Abu Hanifa Ahmad ibn Dawud, 38
diplomacy, 40
dirham, 96, 113–15, 127
dissent, 47–8
Donner, Fred, 139
dualism, 25
Duby, Georges, 56, 66
Dulafids, 119

Eaton, Richard, 122
Egypt, 7, 35, 71, 82, 85, 143, 160
Emed i Ashawahishtan, 68
Emon, Anver, 7, 11
Enlightenment, 6
Epalza, Mikel de, 144
eschatology *see* apocalypticism

al-Farmadi, Abu Ali, 81, 89–91, 100
Fars, 3, 5, 69, 80–1, 101–2, 114, 119, 124
Farwa ibn Nawfal al-Ashja'i, 46
Fattal, Antoine, 83
Fatimid dynasty, 82, 93, 149, 151–3
Fez, 142
fire temples, 7, 20, 26, 28, 38, 60, 78, 95, 97, 112–21, 123–4, 127–30, 141–2, 164, 170; *see also* temple desecration
firman see St Catherine's Monastery
Firuzabad *see* Jur
forelocks, 87, 94, 96, 167
France, 104, 117–18, 132, 177
Freidenreich, David, 67–8
Friedmann, Yohanan, 70, 151
Frye, Richard, 4, 128–9
funerals, 98, 145, 148
Furdujan, 117–21

Gathas *see* Avesta
Gayomart, 40; *see also* Adam
Geniza *see* Cairo
al-Gharnati, Abu Hamid, 143
Ghassan ibn Zadhan ibn Shadhawayh ibn Mahbandad ibn Mahadhu Farrukh, 99–100
Ghaylan al-Dimashqi, 147
Ghazali, Abu Hamid Muhammad ibn Muhammad, 67
ghiyar, 13, 93–8, 102
Ghraab, Saad, 51, 155, 179

Gil, Moshe, 96, 119
God, 2, 35–9, 42, 44–5, 47–9, 58–60, 63, 66, 69, 84, 87–8, 90–1, 99–101, 120–2, 124–5, 136–7, 139–41, 145–50, 160–1, 167–71
Goldziher, Ignaz, 35
Good Religion *see* Zoroastrianism
Gospel, 34, 62, 69
Granada, 117
Guadalquivir River, 141
Gujarat, 78, 101

hadith, 12, 23, 33, 35, 39–46, 48–9, 56–9, 63–7, 86, 129, 137–8, 146–9, 152, 160–3
  collections of, 12, 39, 45, 56, 67, 146
  harmonisation of, 42–4
  transmitters of, 49, 137
  see also isnad; Partisans of Hadith
Hajar, 41–6, 48–9, 58–61, 136–7, 162; *see also* Bahrayn
Hajjaj ibn Yusuf, 120
al-Hakim (Fatimid caliph), 93
Halbwachs, Maurice, 56, 79
Halevi, Leor, 98
Hamdani, Abbas, 150
Hanaoka, Mimi, 124
Harun al-Rashid, 41, 61, 89
al-Hasan al-Basri, 49, 62
al-Hasan ibn Muhammad ibn al-Hanafiyya, 57
Haug, Michael, 22
Hawting, Gerald, 139
Hebrew Immigrant Aid Society, 23
Hebrew language, 66, 93
Herat, 33, 97
Herbad, 4, 115–16; *see also* priesthood
Hindus, 9, 38, 122–3, 150, 152, 161–2
Hirschfeld, Hartwig, 92
historiography, 12, 19–20, 23, 25
  lachrymose narratives of, 19, 23
  myths and countermyths in, 12, 20, 25
  see also supersession; triumphalism
Hodgson, Marshall G. S., 8
Holocaust, 19, 117
Hudaybiyya, 125, 141
Hudhayfa ibn al-Yaman, 65, 85
hulla, 88–9, 168
Humayd, 49, 58
Humphreys, R. Stephen, 11
hunting, 67, 71
Husayn ibn Ali ibn Abi Talib, 39, 57, 61, 63, 65, 101, 168–9, 171
Huyayy ibn Akhtab, 89–92
Huyse, Philip, 37
Hypocrites, 37, 47–8

Iberia, 13, 19, 117, 141–5, 152, 165; *see also* Andalus; Aragon
Iblis *see* Satan
Ibn Abbas, Abd Allah, 39, 61–2
Ibn Abi Shayba, Abd Allah ibn Muhammad, 58, 63
Ibn al-Athir, Izz al-Din Abu l-Hasan Ali, 137
Ibn al-Faqih, Ahmad ibn Muhammad, 115, 117, 120, 143
Ibn Hayyan, Abu Muhammad Abd Allah ibn Muhammad ibn Ja‘far, 81, 142
Ibn Hazm, Abu Muhammad Ali ibn Ahmad, 44
Ibn Kathir, Imad al-Din Isma‘il ibn Umar, 36
Ibn Maja, Abu Abd Allah Muhammad ibn Yazid, 67
Ibn Zanjawayh, Hamid ibn Mukhlid, 58
Ibrahim ibn Yazid al-Nakha‘i, 70
identity, 21, 60, 67, 99, 117, 138–9, 151–3
idolatry *see* polytheism
Ikrima, 62
Ilkhanid dynasty, 100, 102, 164
illiteracy, 81, 140–1
Imams, 49, 66, 149, 151; see *also* Ja‘far al-Sadiq; Muhammad al-Baqir
inclusion, 7, 9–10, 139

India, 13, 20–1, 24–5, 78–9, 98, 101–2, 122–3, 149, 164–5; see *also* South Asia
Iran, 1, 4–6, 8–9, 13–16, 18, 20–34, 37, 50–2, 54, 66, 70, 72, 74, 76–9, 81, 98, 100, 103–4, 106, 108–9, 111–13, 116–17, 121, 123, 125, 130–5, 138, 147, 152, 155, 163–5, 174–81, 183, 185–94
  Arab-Muslim conquest of, 13, 20, 26, 33–4, 37, 112
  Islamic Republic of, 6, 23
  Revolution of 1979, 6
Iran League, 26, 78
Iraq, 14, 20, 45–6, 61, 65–6, 71, 82, 89, 100, 110, 136, 159, 164
Isfahan, 86, 98–100, 102
al-Isfahani, Abu Nu'aym Ahmad ibn Abd Allah, 81
al-Isfahani, Hamza ibn al-Hasan, 81, 98, 100
Islam, 1–38, 40–8, 50–6, 58–62, 64, 66–80, 82, 84–6, 88–92, 94, 96–110, 112–14, 116, 118, 120–1, 123–6, 128–34, 136–94; *see also* Isma'ili Islam; Shi'i Islam; Sufi Islam
  Muslims, 1, 4, 6, 8–13, 16–17, 20–1, 23, 26–30, 33–43, 46–7, 49, 52, 54–5, 57–9, 61–72, 78–80, 82–4, 87–9, 93, 100, 102–4, 106, 108–10, 112–13, 115–17, 120–31, 133, 135–47, 149–53, 155, 160–5, 168, 176, 181, 184, 186, 189, 194
Islamdom, 11–12, 23, 80, 159; *see also* Middle East
Islamic law, 7, 13–14, 20, 22, 28, 34, 65, 69–70, 72, 116, 144–5, 160–1, 164
  jurists, 9, 12, 22, 28, 33, 35, 40, 48, 50, 56–7, 60–2, 65–72, 93–4, 98, 137, 149, 151, 162–5
  Hanafi school of, 38, 65–6, 70–2, 85, 94, 163–4
  Hanbali school of, 65–6, 70, 164
  Maliki school of, 59, 66, 70
  Shafi'i school of, 62, 65–6, 69–70, 94, 96
  see also judicial archive
Islamic State of Iraq and Syria (ISIS), 14, 159–61
Islamicate societies, 9, 14, 35, 56, 99, 165
Isma'ili Islam, 149
isnad, 59, 63–4, 66, 147; see also *hadith*
Israel
  State of, 23
  Tribes of, 62
Istakhr, 97

Jabrites, 146–7, 149
Ja'far al-Sadiq, 64, 163
Jafarey, Ali, 79
al-Jahiz, Amr ibn Bahr, 114–15
al-Jassas, Abu Bakr, 38, 65
Jaz ibn Mu'awiya, 47
Jejeebhoy, Sorabjee Jamsetjee, 78
Jerusalem, 19, 85
Jesus, 34, 62, 84, 139
jihad, 20, 122, 161
jizya, 10, 12, 20, 34, 40–50, 55–6, 58–62, 65, 70, 87, 92–4, 96, 101, 116, 136–8, 144, 161–7, 170
Judaism, 2, 35, 37, 117, 136
  Jews, 7, 9, 11, 13, 19, 21–3, 34–7, 42, 48, 59–60, 62–3, 69–71, 92–3, 96, 98, 102, 116–18, 139, 142, 149, 151, 160, 162–3, 165
Judd, Steven, 147
Judgment Day *see* Resurrection
judicial archive, 12, 56, 61, 164; *see also* Islamic law; memory
Jur, 114–15

Ka'ba, 120
Karbala, 57
Kariyan, 3, 114–16; *see also* Darabjird
Kashkathan, 127–8
Kayghalagh, 118
Kazarun, 101–2
al-Kazaruni, Abu Ishaq, 101–2

Khabar Salman see Salman al-Farisi
Khalid ibn al-Walid, 136
Khanbaghi, Aptin, 22, 35, 70
kharaj, 39, 41, 43, 55–6, 96, 120
al-Khatib al-Baghdadi, Abu Bakr Ahmad ibn Ali, 85, 98
Khaybar, 42, 86, 89–90, 92–3, 95–8, 102, 164
  Treaty of, 86, 89–90, 92–3, 95–8
Khurasan, 3, 33, 119, 123–5
Khusrau I Anushirvan, 37
Khuz, 38
Khuzistan, 119
Khwaja Kamal-ud-Din, 25
al-Khwarazmi, Muhammad ibn Ahmad, 38, 52, 174
Kirman, 123–6
Kreyenbroek, Philip, 21
Kufa, 23, 57, 66, 121
Kurds, 160–1

lachrymose narratives *see* historiography
Lambton, Anne, 120
Last Day *see* Resurrection
Late Antiquity, 1, 3–6, 8, 20, 47, 129, 164
Lawata *see* Berbers
Lecker, Michael, 47
Levy-Rubin, Milka, 87, 93–4
liberalism, 10, 19
Libya, 136
London, 21
Lucas, Scott, 64
Lunde, Paul, 145

Maʿafir, 43; *see also* cloth; Yemen
Maʿbad ibn Abd Allah al-Juhani, 147
McLachlin, Beverley, 10
Maclean, Derryl, 150–1
Mada'in, 65, 99
Magi *see* priesthood
Magians, 5, 38, 76, 127–8, 176; *see also* Bukhara; Zoroastrians
Mahadhar Farrukh, 99
Mahdi, 146, 160, 169
Mahmood, Saba, 7, 16, 185
Mahmud ibn Muhammad ibn Malik Shah, 100
al-majus see Berbers; Qadarites; Sind; Vikings; Zoroastrians
majlis, 23, 44, 101
Makh, 128–9
Makki ibn Abi Talib, 65
Malik ibn Anas, 144; *see also* Islamic law
al-Ma'mun, 148
Manichaeism, 2–3, 27
Mansur al-Din ibn Jaradin, 123
manumission *see* Salman al-Farisi
al-Maqdisi, Abd al-Rahman ibn Muhammad ibn Qudama, 65
Maqna *see* Treaty of Khaybar
Markwart, Josef, 25
marriage, 24, 57
  consanguineous, 27, 39, 49, 141–2, 150–2
  prohibition of Muslim-Zoroastrian, 12, 27, 40, 55, 58–60, 66, 68, 72, 149, 152, 163–4
marzuban, 59, 136; *see also* Sasanian Empire
Massignon, Louis, 83–4, 86
al-Mawardi, Abu l-Hasan, 39
Mazdakites, 27
Mazdeans *see* Zoroastrians
meat, 12, 28, 55, 57–62, 64–9, 71–2, 136, 138, 149, 151–2, 163–4
Mecca, 47, 66, 120, 125, 139–40
Medina, 47, 64, 82, 85, 90–2, 147, 152
Melvinger, Arne, 142, 144, 155–6, 186
memory, 12–13, 27–8, 56, 61, 79–81, 84, 86, 102, 121, 130, 164
  sites of, 13, 79–80, 102, 164
  see also Pierre Nora; Maurice Halbwachs; Georges Duby
Merv, 30
Mesopotamia *see* Iraq
Middle Ages, 7, 19

Middle East, 6–8, 12, 14, 19, 80–1, 84, 92–3, 160; *see also* Islamdom
Middle Persian language, 2, 5, 37–8
migration, 20
Mihrijan, 33
al-Miqdad ibn al-Aswad, 85, 168
Mithra, 3
mobed, 4; *see also* priesthood
Monnot, Guy, 35
Morony, Michael, 60
Mosul, 98
Moses, 34, 62
mosque, 25, 44, 71, 82, 98, 142
  tales of construction, 13, 28, 112–13, 122–30, 164
Motzki, Harald, 63–4
Mouton, Jean-Michel, 82
Mu'adh ibn Jabal, 43, 46
Mu'awiya ibn Abi Sufyan, 93
Mughal dynasty, 101–2, 122–3, 164
Muhammad the Prophet, 13, 27, 34, 37–8, 41–9, 60, 63–7, 70–1, 78–9, 81–92, 99, 100–2, 116, 124–5, 139, 145, 147–9, 161–4, 168, 170–1
  household of (*ahl al-bayt*), 99, 168
  seal of prophethood of, 85
  letters of, 38, 99
Muhammad al-Baqir, 57, 63–4, 67, 72, 163
Muhammad ibn Abi l-Saj, 119
Muhammad ibn al-Hanafiyya, 57
Muhammad ibn Malik Shah, 100
Muhammad ibn al-Qasim al-Thaqafi, 151–2
Muhammad ibn Zufar ibn Umar, 129
al-Muhtadi, 118
al-Mu'izz li-Din Allah, 150
Mujahid, 61
Mujashi' ibn Mas'ud, 123, 125
Mukhtar, 57
al-Muktafi, 119
Multan, 149–50
Mumbai, 24, 78; *see also* Bombay Riot of 1851
al-Mundhir ibn Sawa, 43, 48, 59
al-Muqaddasi, Muhammad ibn Ahmad, 38, 69–70, 95
Murji'ite movement, 57
al-Mustawrid ibn al-Ahnaf, 46–7
al-Mas'udi, Abu l-Hasan Ali ibn al-Husayn, 115, 143
al-Mu'tadid, 119
al-Mutawakkil, 84, 94, 148
Mu'tazilites, 148–9
myths *see* historiography

Najran, 82–4, 86–9, 93–4, 97, 102, 164
  Treaty of, 82–4, 86–9, 93–4, 97
Nakhjavani, Muhammad ibn Hindushah, 81, 89, 92–3, 100
Nanabhai Punjiya, 101
Nariman, G. K., 26
Narmashir, 123–4
al-Narshakhi, Muhammad ibn Ja'far, 126–7, 129
Neuwirth, Angelika, 139
New Persian language, 4–5, 38
Nile-to-Oxus region *see* Islamdom
Nirenberg, David, 7, 19, 69, 117–18
Nishapur, 3, 70, 97, 125–6
al-Nishapuri, Abu l-Hasan Abd al-Rahman ibn Muhammad, 129
non-Muslims *see* Protected People
non-normative groups, 9, 12,14, 162; *see also* People without a Book
Nora, Pierra, 56, 79, 84, 102
Norsemen *see* Vikings
al-Nu'man ibn Muhammad, 149–52

Ohrmazd *see* Ahura Mazda
Oman, 44, 59
Orientalism, 25–6, 35, 103

Pact of Umar, 94
pagans, 13, 28, 35, 142, 150, 162
Pahlavi script *see* Middle Persian language
Palestine, 82

paradise, 68, 168, 170
Parsis, 13, 20–1, 24–6, 78–80, 101–2, 164; *see also* Zoroastrians
Partisans of Hadith, 148–9
Payne, Richard, 3, 7, 20
Penn, Michael, 20, 47
People of the Book, 9, 11–13, 22, 26, 28, 33–40, 44, 46–9, 55, 57, 61–3, 65–72, 138, 140, 149, 152–3, 161–3; *see also* Christians; Jews
People without a Book, 11, 38, 45, 50, 56, 68–9, 136–7, 140, 151–2, 163, 165; *see also* non-normative groups
persecution, 19–21, 23, 26, 117, 121
Persia *see* Iran
Persian language *see* Middle Persian; New Persian
Pledge of Good Pleasure, 125
polytheism, 35–7, 49, 139, 161
prayer, 59–60, 85, 125
predestination, 145, 147–8
priesthood, 3, 4, 20, 25–6, 38
  priests, 3–4, 20–1, 25, 37, 39, 115, 143
  see also mobed; herbad
prohibition *see* marriage; meat
prophet(hood) *see* Muhammad; Zoroaster
Protected People, 8–13, 21, 23, 36, 40, 42–3, 69–71, 83–4, 87, 93–8, 100, 116, 153, 161–2, 164–5, 170; *see also dhimma*
Psalms, 61
purity, 3, 69, 71
Pyrenees, 117–18

Qadarites, 138, 145–9
Qajar dynasty, 123
al-Qasim al-Dimashqi, 38
al-Qasri, Asad ibn Abd Allah, 33
Qatada ibn Di'ama, 37, 62
Qays ibn al-Rabi' al-Asadi, 63
Qays ibn Muslim al-Jadali, 58
Qazwin, 118–19
Qom, 117–21, 130
Qubavi, Abu Nasr Ahmad, 128
Qur'an, 9, 34–6, 38, 40, 47–9, 55, 60–1, 65–6, 68, 70, 99, 124–5, 139–41, 148, 151, 160, 162, 170
  exegetes of, 12, 36–7, 49, 60–1, 140–1
al-Qurtubi, Abu Abd Allah Muhammad ibn Ahmad, 36, 161
Qutb Shahs, 122
Qutayba ibn Muslim, 22, 126–7

Rabi'a ibn Abi Abd al-Rahman, 48
Rajab, 78, 88–9, 168
Rayy, 38, 97, 118–20
Razi, Fakhr al-Din, 37, 65
Resurrection, 35–7, 87, 139, 146, 161, 168, 170–1
Reza Shah, 6, 26–7
Reza Shah, Mohammad, 27
Rezakhani, Khodadad, 6
Rezwi, Taher, 26–7
Rose, Jenny, 4–5, 33
Rus, 143, 145

Sabi'ans, 9, 34–8, 48, 57, 60–1, 63, 161, 163
sadaqa, 61, 101
saddles, 97
Saffarid dynasty, 119
Sahnun ibn Sa'id, 59, 137
Sa'id ibn Jubayr, 62
Sa'id ibn al-Musayyab, 62
St Catherine's Monastery, 81–3
Saklatwalla, Jamshedji, 78
salat see prayer
Salman al-Farisi, 13, 28, 78, 84–6, 102, 164, 169
  Khabar Salman, 84–6, 102
  Salmaniyya, 99
  see also ahd-nama
al-Sam'ani, Abd al-Karim ibn Muhammad, 129
Samanid dynasty, 119, 127
Samarra, 118

Sasanian Empire, 3–5, 7, 25, 46, 66, 99, 114, 137, 163
laws of the, 38, 68, 98
Sasanians 12, 33, 59, 140
see also marzuban; *spahbed*
Satan, 37, 39, 141, 147, 161
Savant, Sarah Bowen, 5, 45, 56, 141
Sawad *see* Iraq
Scandinavia *see* Vikings
scriptures *see* Gospel; Torah
secularism, 6–7
Seljuk dynasty, 100, 102, 164
Serjeant, R. B., 91
Sethna, Ervad Darius, 79
Seville, 141–3
sexual intercourse, 68–9
al-Shafi'i, Muhammad ibn Idris, 62, 65, 69–70, 94, 96; *see also* Islamic law
Shah Jahan, 101
al-Shahrastani, Muhammad ibn Abd al-Karim, 3, 39
Shaked, Shaul, 5
Shapur I, 5
al-Shaybani, Muhammad, 94
Shi'i Islam, 23, 27, 57, 64, 66, 137, 149
Shiraz, 95, 98–102
silver, 88
Simonsohn, Uriel, 71
Sinai Peninsula, 82
Sind, 149–53
Sinjar, 14, 159–60
Sistan, 114, 116
Sizgorich, Thomas, 9, 47
slaughter *see* meat
slavery, 160–1; *see also* manumission
South Asia, 4, 13, 80–1, 102, 122, 138, 149–50, 152–3; *see also* India
spahbed, 45, 59–60
Spain *see* Iberia
stables, 95, 97, 170
Stausberg, Michael, 27, 33–4
Stern, Samuel, 150
Stone, Caroline, 145
Sufi Islam, 81, 99–100, 102, 160, 164
Sufyan al-Thawri, 61, 63–4
supersession, 13, 112, 122, 126, 130
al-Suyuti, Abu l-Fadl Abd al-Rahman ibn Abi Bakr, 37
Syria, 14, 61, 82, 137, 159

al-Tabari, Abu Ja'far Muhammad ibn Jarir, 37, 59, 91, 118–20, 141
Tabaristan, 119
al-Tahawi, Abu Ja'far Ahmad ibn Muhammad, 85–6
Tahir al-Din ibn Shams al-Din, 38, 123, 126, 148
Tahirid dynasty, 119
tafsir see Qur'an
Tannous, Jack, 8, 47
taxation, 9, 40–1, 43, 46–7, 49, 55–7, 59, 65, 72, 81, 83, 96, 120–1, 136–7, 152, 159, 162–3, 165
tax collectors, 35, 43, 46
tax revolt, 119–20
see also jizya; kharaj; ushr
temple desecration, 13, 28, 112–14, 116–17, 120–3, 126, 129–30; *see also* fire temples
al-Tirmidhi, Abu Isa Muhammad ibn Isa, 67
tolerance, 6–7, 10, 22, 26, 79, 117
Torah, 34, 62, 69
Torki, Mohammad Reza, 80–1
Tower of Silence, 98
Transoxiana, 22, 71
Tremblay, Xavier, 37
triumphalism, 13, 112, 122, 164
Tsafrir, Nurit, 62

Ubayd al-Muktib, 86
Ubayd Allah ibn Abi Bakra, 113–16, 130
ulama see Islamic law
Umar ibn Abd al-Aziz, 49, 69, 89, 94
Umar ibn al-Khattab, 1, 44, 89, 94, 136; *see also* Pact of Umar

Umayyad Caliphate, 20, 22, 43, 49, 57, 69, 89, 94, 113, 115–16, 121, 141–2, 146–7, 151–3, 161
United States of America, 6, 24, 159
ushr, 60, 87, 94, 96
Uthman ibn Affan, 125, 136–7, 168, 171

Vajda, Georges, 34
van Ess, Josef, 73, 143, 147
Vaziri, Ahmad Ali Khan, 123
Vikings, 138, 141–5, 151–2, 165
violence, 4, 7, 14, 22, 78, 112, 117–18, 122, 126, 160, 164

Waardenburg, Jacques, 35
al-Wahidi, Abu l-Hasan Ali ibn Ahmad, 47–8
Wasif, 119
Williams, Alan, 21
wine, 62
Wink, André, 31
Wise Lord *see* Ahura Mazda
women *see* marriage

Yahya ibn Adam, 43, 59
Yahya ibn Sa'id, 64
al-Ya'qubi, Abu l-Abbas Ahmad, 143
Yarbrough, Luke, 23
Yasna, 2–3, 5
Yazd, 21, 25
Yazdagerd III, 20, 114
Yazidis, 14, 160–2
Yemen, 41–4, 46, 82, 93, 149

Zadeh, Travis, 71
Zakeri, Mohsen, 147
al-Zamakhshari, Abu l-Qasim Mahmud ibn Umar, 36
Zarathushtra *see* Zoroaster
Zia-Ebrahimi, Reza, 26
Ziyad ibn Abihi, 113
Zoroaster the Prophet, 5, 25, 33, 38–40, 60, 143
Zoroastrianism, 1–2, 4–5, 7, 13, 20–2, 25–8, 33–5, 37, 38–40, 44, 46, 50, 55, 57, 60, 63, 67, 69, 71–2, 79, 112, 115, 126–7, 130, 136–8, 141–3, 147, 151–3, 160, 162–5
  Zoroastrians, 1–5, 7, 9, 11–14, 20–8, 33–50, 55–72, 78–80, 88, 95, 97–8, 102, 112–17, 120–1, 123–4, 126, 129, 136–8, 140–5, 147–53, 159, 161–5
  see also Magians; Parsis
zunnar, 94–5, 170
Zurvan, 2–3

EU representative:
Easy Access System Europe
Mustamäe tee 50, 10621 Tallinn, Estonia
Gpsr.requests@easproject.com

www.ingramcontent.com/pod-product-compliance
Lightning Source LLC
Chambersburg PA
CBHW070355240426
43671CB00013BA/2513
* 9 7 8 1 4 7 4 4 8 9 5 3 9 *